The Critics' Choice

The Best of TV Sitcoms

BURNS AND ALLEN to THE COSBY SHOW, THE MUNSTERS to MARY TYLER MOORE

By JOHN JAVNA

Harmony Books, New York

Dedicated to Melissa
and to Andy
for making it through
a whole year.

Published by Harmony Books, a division of Crown Publishers, Inc. 225 Park Avenue South, New York, New York 10003,
and represented in Canada by the Canadian MANDA Group.

HARMONY and colophon are trademarks of Crown Publishers, Inc.

Manufactured in the United States of America

Design by Andrea Sohn

Library of Congress Cataloging-in-Publication Data
Javna, John.
The Best of TV Sitcoms
Bibliography: p.
1. Comedy programs—United States—History and criticism. 2. Television serials—United States—History and criticism.
I. Title. PN1992.8.C66J39 1988 791.45'09'0917 88-891
ISBN 0-517-56922-1 (pbk.)

10 9 8 7 6 5 4 3 2 1
First Edition

CONTENTS

THE CRITICS' CHOICE

THE '50s

The Best
1. "The Honeymooners"
2. "I Love Lucy"
3. "The George Burns and Gracie Allen Show"
4. "The Phil Silvers Show"
5. "Leave It to Beaver"

Runners-up
6. "The Jack Benny Show"
7. "The Many Loves of Dobie Gillis"
8. "Amos 'n' Andy"
9. "Father Knows Best"
10. "The Donna Reed Show"

The Worst
1. "Life with Luigi"
2. "Bonino"
3. "The Charlie Farrell Show"

Runners-up
4. "The Stu Erwin Show"
5. "Hey Mulligan"

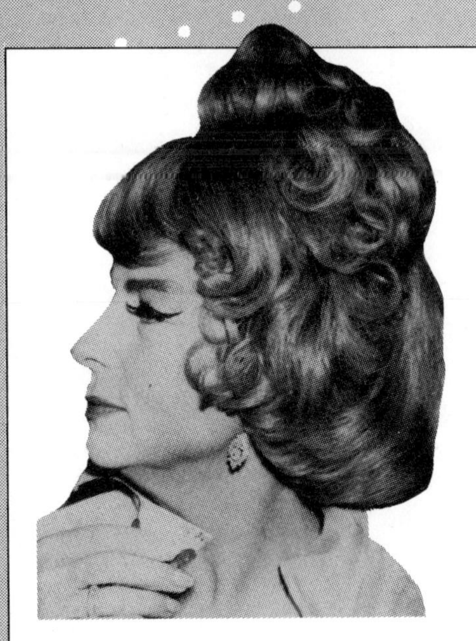

THE '60s

The Best
1. "The Dick Van Dyke Show"
2. "The Andy Griffith Show"
3. "Get Smart"
4. "The Addams Family"
5. "Bewitched"

Runners-up
6. "Green Acres"
7. "Car 54, Where Are You?"
8. "The Monkees"
9. "The Beverly Hillbillies"
10. "He and She"

The Worst
1. "My Mother the Car"
2. "Gilligan's Island"
3. "The Flying Nun"

Runners-up
4. "The Pruitts of Southhampton"
5. "Hogan's Heroes"

SCOREBOARD

THE '70s

The Best
1. "All in the Family"
2. "The Mary Tyler Moore Show"
3. "M*A*S*H"
4. "Barney Miller"
5. "Taxi"

Runners-up
6. "The Bob Newhart Show"
7. "Fawlty Towers"
8. "The Odd Couple"
9. "WKRP in Cincinnati"
10. "Maude"

The Worst
1. "Three's Company"
2. "Me and the Chimp"
3. "Rollergirls" / "Sugar Time!"

Runners-up
4. "Ball Four"
5. "Delta House"

THE '80s

The Best
1. "Cheers"
2. "Newhart"
3. "The Golden Girls"
4. "The Cosby Show"
5. "Family Ties"

Runners-up
6. "Buffalo Bill"
7. "Kate and Allie"
8. "Night Court"
9. "Police Squad"
10. "The Days and Nights of Molly Dodd"

The Worst
1. "We Got It Made"
2. "Mama's Family"
3. "Punky Brewster"

Runners-up
4. "Life with Lucy"
5. "Harper Valley P.T.A."

INTRODUCTION

The first TV sitcom was a live program called "Mary Kay and Johnny." It aired from 1947 to 1950 on the Dumont network. Four decades and hundreds of sitcoms later, the genre is still thriving—in fact, five of the top ten television shows of 1987 were situation comedies.

The main reason for this continued popularity, of course, is that sitcoms make their audiences laugh.

But it's not just laughter that makes sitcoms important to us. Sitcom characters have become America's faithful friends. They've kept us company when we were sick or lonely. They've shared their "secrets" with us. They've taught us lessons about ourselves. We've been with them as they've grown and struggled and tried to cope with new situations.

The somewhat bizarre result is that many Americans know sitcom characters better than we know the *real* human beings in our lives. This may be why we eagerly await their weekly visits... or rejoice in being reunited with them years after our first meeting, in reruns.

But although our relationships with sitcom characters might seem intensely personal, they're actually communal—shared with millions of other Americans who welcome the same good friends into their homes regularly.

Think about it; at exactly the same moment, fifteen or twenty million Americans have:

- Watched Lucy Ricardo inform her husband that they were going to have a baby.
- Cried along with Hawkeye, Radar, and their friends when they found out that Col. Henry Blake's plane had been shot down.
- Watched Diane break off her engagement with Dr. Frasier Crane.
- And so on.

Because they reach so many people with their larger-than-life versions of the American norm, sitcoms have become the definitive myths of contemporary culture. They project images that we—consciously or unconsciously—adopt as yardsticks to measure our own lives. Are we perfect mothers, like Donna Stone? Are we understanding fathers like Ward Cleaver? Are we as plucky as Mary Richards? Does our family get along as well as the Huxtables do?

Like all effective myths, sitcoms have supplied us with tools for dealing with the trials and frustrations of daily life. E.g., they've given us personal heroes to emulate, like Hawkeye Pierce and the Fonz; they've provided family role models like the Cleavers and the Nelsons; they've exposed us to new ideas and attitudes in "The Jeffersons" and "The Mary Tyler Moore Show"; they've allowed us to explore controversial issues with the characters in "All in the Family" and "Maude."

The best of these sitcom/myths express fundamental human values. They tell us something positive about the struggle that all human beings must endure to survive, and give us a glimpse of the rewards we might expect for trying ...usually love and a feeling of worthiness.

The worst of them highlight our least attractive sides. The heroes are silly caricatures or one-dimensional buffoons; the situations are sanitized; the dialogue is stilted. They do not respect humanity; they insult it.

How can we distinguish between the good sitcoms and the trash? In a way, we're all experts on sitcoms. After all, most of us have been watching them all our lives. But since we tend to develop emotional attachments to our favorite programs, we can't be objective about evaluating them.

So I decided to ask a group of newspaper TV critics and TV historians which sitcoms *they* consider the best and worst in the history of the genre. This book is based on their replies.

INTRODUCTION

Here is a complete list of individuals who contributed to the poll with their votes and/or comments; my sincere thanks to all of the participants:

TV CRITICS

•**Bill Anderson**, TV critic, *Canadian Press*
•**Yardena Arar**, TV critic, *Los Angeles Daily News*
•**Ed Bark**, TV critic, *Dallas Morning News*
•**Greg Bailey**, TV critic, *Nashville Banner*
•**Andee Beck**, TV critic, *Tacoma News Tribune*
•**Walt Belcher**, TV critic, *Tampa Tribune*
•**Erik Bergman,** correspondent, *TV Host*
•**Robert Bianco**, TV critic, *Pittsburgh Press*
•**David Bianculli,** TV critic, *New York Post*
•**Jeff Borden**, TV critic, *Charlotte Observer*
•**John Carman**, TV critic, *San Francisco Chronicle*
•**Bill Carter**, TV critic, *Baltimore Sun*
•**Art Chapman**, TV critic, *Fort Worth Star-Telegram*
•**Monica Collins**, TV critic, *USA Today*
•**Bob Curtwright**, TV columnist/movie critic, *Wichita Eagle-Beacon*
•**David Cuthbert**, TV editor, *New Orleans Times-Picayune*
•**Mark Dawidziak**, TV critic, *Akron Beacon Journal*
•**Michael Dougan**, TV critic, *San Francisco Examiner*
•**Rick Du Brow**, TV editor, *Los Angeles Herald Examiner*
•**Duane Dudek**, TV/film editor, *Milwaukee Sentinel*
•**Michael Duffy**, TV critic, *Detroit Free Press*

•**Douglas Durden**, TV critic, *Richmond Times Dispatch*
•**Peter Farrell**, TV columnist, *Oregonian*
•**Judy Flander**, TV critic, *United Features*
•**Bob Foster**, TV critic, *San Mateo Times*
•**Barry Garron**, TV/radio critic, *Kansas City Star*
•**Jim Gordon**, TV critic, *Gary Post-Tribune*
•**Marc Gunther**, TV critic, *Detroit News*
•**R. D. Heldenfels**, TV columnist, *Schenectady Gazette*
•**Michael Hill**, TV critic, *Baltimore Evening Sun*
•**Ken Hoffman**, TV critic, *Houston Post*
•**Barbara Holsopple**, TV critic, *Phoenix Gazette*
•**Tom Jicha**, TV editor, *Miami News*
•**David Jones**, TV critic, *Columbus Dispatch*
•**John Keisewetter**, TV critic, *Cincinnati Enquirer*
•**Phil Kloer**, TV critic, *Atlanta Constitution*
•**Eirik Knutzen**, syndicated TV columnist
•**Sandra Konte**, entertainment writer, *L.A. Times* syndicate
•**Robert P. Laurence,** TV writer, *San Diego Union*
•**John Marten**, TV critic, *Providence Journal-Bulletin*
•**Bill Musselwhite**, TV critic, *Calgary Herald*
•**Wally Patrick**, TV critic, *Asbury Park Press*
•**Joel Pisetzner**, TV critic, *Bergen Record*
•**Dusty Saunders**, TV critic, *Rocky Mountain News*
•**Mark Schwed**, TV critic, U.P.I.
•**Tom Shales**, TV critic, *Washington Post*
•**R. K. Shull**, TV critic, *Indianapolis News*
•**Ed Siegel**, TV critic, *Boston Globe*
•**Jim Slotek**, TV critic, *Toronto Sun*
•**Steve Sonsky**, TV critic, *Miami Herald*
•**Joseph Walker**, TV critic, *Salt Lake City Deseret News*
•**Tom Walter**, TV critic, *Memphis Commercial Appeal*
•**Dennis Washburn**, TV critic, *Birmingham News*

INTRODUCTION

GENERAL TV

•**Diane L. Albert**, editor, *TV Collector* magazine

•**Bart Andrews**, author of *The I Love Lucy Book, Holy Mackrel,* and *The Worst TV Shows Ever*

•**Peter Bieler**, president, Video Ticket Productions

•**Cheryl Blythe**, author of *Say Goodnight, Gracie*

•**Jim "Big Bucks" Burnett**, president, *The Mr. Ed Fan Club*
•**Harry Castleman**, coauthor of *Watching TV* and *The TV Schedule Book*
•**Jim Clark**, author of *The Andy Griffith Show Book*
•**Joel Eisner**, author of *The Batman Bat-Book* and *Sitcoms in Syndication*
•**Gary Gerani**, author of *Fantastic Television*
•**Gary H. Grossman**, author of *Superman: From Serial to Cereal* and *Saturday Morning T.V.*; producer of "Entertainment This Week"
•**John Javna**, author of *Cult TV, The TV Theme Song Sing-Along Songbooks* (Volumes I and II), coauthor of *60s!*, and others
•**Gordon Javna**, author of *Tough TV: The Television Guide to Your Mind,* and coauthor of *60s!*
•**Donna McCrohan**, TV historian, author of *The Honeymooners' Companion, The Second City: A Backstage History of Comedy's Hottest Troupe,* and coauthor of *The Honeymooners' Last Episodes*
•**Alex McNeil**, author of *Total Television: A Comprehensive Guide to Programming from 1948 to the Present*
•**Jack Mingo**, author of *The Official Couch Potato Handbook* and *The Couch Potato Guide to Life*
•**Rick Mitz**, author of *The Great Sitcom Book*
•**Danny Peary**, author of *Omni's Screen Flights/Screen Fantasies: The Future According to Science Fiction Cinema, Guide for the Film Fanatic,* and *Cult Movies 1, 2, & 3*
•**John Peel**, British author of more than eighty volumes of TV criticism; contributing editor to *TV Gold*
•**Walter J. Podrazik**, coauthor of seven books, including *Watching TV: Four Decades of American Television,* and *The TV Schedule Book* (a season-by-season schedule guide to the entire broadcast day)
•**Gene Sculatti**, author of *The Catalog of Cool*
•**Richard K. Tharp**, publisher, *RERUNS, the Magazine of Television History*
•**Vincent Waldron**, author of *Classic Sitcoms*
•**Ginny Weisman**, author of *The Dick Van Dyke Show Book*

Best of the '50s

TV's first great situation comedies were hybrids—a combination of the visual, physical humor that flourished on the vaudeville circuit in the '20s and '30s and the scripted domestic comedies popular on radio in the '40s.

In the early part of the twentieth century, vaudeville entertainers, performing live before large audiences (often with unsophisticated sound systems), developed a comedy style based on reaction and timing.

Some, like Phil Silvers, relied on physical antics to get laughs. They fell off ladders, got pies shoved in their faces, did lurching drunk routines. Others, like Burns and Allen and Jack Benny, developed characters who amused their audiences with corny jokes and personality quirks. And still others, like Jackie Gleason, developed their stage personalities as emcees, throwing in outrageous ad-libbed comic lines as part of the between-act patter.

But by the '40s, radio had practically wiped out vaudeville. It was cheaper, more accessible, and modern. And it required a different type of presentation; since it was purely verbal, much of radio's best comedy was story—not gag—oriented. Vaudeville routines like Burns and Allen's were adapted into weekly married-life adventures. But frequently, networks simply dreamed up situations and found stars whose personalities fit them. Thus, for example, a moderately successful film actress named Lucille Ball found herself a major star at last as a banker's wife on the radio sitcom "My Favorite Husband."

In the early '50s, television began to court radio sitcom stars in earnest. Ironically, most radio sitcoms failed when a visual element was added. But many individual stars became bigger than ever.

In fact, with the exception of "Leave It to Beaver," which was a classic well-written family comedy (and which could have done quite well on radio), the top five sitcoms of the '50s were each designed to showcase a specific star. In each case, the situation was tailor-made to allow Lucy to be Lucy, or Gracie to be Gracie, Silvers to be Silvers, etc.

In the latter part of the decade, when the sitcom was already established as a TV staple, television executives began experimenting by plugging faceless actors and actresses into assembly-line situations. But until then, a few comic geniuses were allowed to roam freely over the airwaves, and these shows are their legacy to us.

THE HONEYMOONERS

Alice and Ralph Kramden, the critics' favorite couple, returned in 1985 with 75 "lost" episodes that Gleason unearthed and released.

"The Honeymooners" is like a favorite song on a jukebox; the same thirty-nine episodes have been playing over and over again, but no one has ever seemed to get tired of them. In fact, the more familiar they get, the more valuable they seem to be. And more people are sighing, "They're playing our show" today than they did in 1956, when Jackie Gleason's masterpiece first aired as a regular series.

Why is it so popular? On the surface, it makes no sense at all as a comedy. Ralph Kramden, the hero of "The Honeymooners," is an overweight Brooklyn bus driver who hates his dead end, lower-class existence. He lives in a sparsely furnished tenement apartment with an icebox (no refrigerator), a beat-up table, and a couple of chairs. He doesn't even have a phone. And along with his best friend and neighbor, sewer worker Ed Norton, he keeps himself impoverished and humiliated by constantly investing his limited financial resources in "sure-thing" get-rich-quick schemes.

It sounds bleak, but there's an undercurrent of redemption running through the show: Alice Kramden clearly loves her blowhard husband. So do Ed and his wife, Trixie. And that solid core of caring and understanding gives the show heart. From the outside, the audience can see what Ralph does not—that he is already as rich as he deserves to be.

At the time it aired, "The Honeymooners" had some social significance. It was the first TV show to mirror the frustration of America's urban blue-collar workers, and to a lot of them, the comic scams of Kramden and Norton made their own situations easier to accept.

But today, viewers tune in to watch Gleason and Carney, both accomplished physical comedians, work together with the precision and timing of a vaudeville act. They tune in for sublime character comedy, to hear Gleason roar classic lines like "One of these days—Pow! Right in the kisser!" and "Bang! Zoom!" To hear Norton give his peculiar philosophy: "As we say in the sewer, if you're not prepared to go all the way, don't put your boots on in the first place." To hear Alice take the wind out of Ralph's sails. (Ralph: "This is the biggest thing I ever got into." Alice: "The biggest thing you ever got into is your pants.") And to witness what the show's writers came to call simply "Kissville," when Ralph embraces the forgiving Alice and tells her jubilantly, "Baby, you're the greatest!"

"The Honeymooners" was revived in 1966, but it wasn't the same. The Kramdens and Nortons went off to Europe together, and while Gleason and Carney were as much a joy to watch as ever, viewers found themselves missing those stark, confined surroundings at 328 Chauncey Street, where love and friendship could periodically cause a light to shine. When Gleason passed away in 1987, some newspapers awarded him the ultimate accolade with the headline "Ralph Kramden Dies"—a tribute to the strength of the character and his place in our culture. But as Ralph once said, "If you got some memories, some good memories, that's what keeps you young."

After thirty years of giving us marvelous memories, not even Alice would disagree.

Art Carney joined Gleason while he was still with the Dumont network, and "we clicked like we'd been doing an act together for years."

FLASHBACK

TRIXIE: "Do you want anything at the store besides milk, Alice?"
ALICE: "You'd better get a pound of margarine, too."
[Ralph enters, wearing his Raccoon Lodge outfit.]
ALICE: "Maybe you won't have to get the margarine. Four hundred pounds of lard just walked in."
RALPH: "You have just said the secret word, Alice. You have just won yourself a trip to the moon."

RALPH: "I'm ashamed, Alice! I'm embarrassed. Of all the guys down at the bus depot, I'm the only one that never has any money at the end of the week. Take tonight, for instance. Joe McCloskey had twenty bucks. Pete Crowley had thirty-five bucks. And Frank Willis had even more than that! Of all the bus drivers, I'm the only one that ain't got a dime!"
ALICE: "Well don't feel too bad, Ralph. You're the only bus driver that's got a uranium mine in Asbury Park."

VITAL STATS

POLL RESULTS:
First
PROGRAM INFO:
- Half-hour show. CBS
- First show: Oct. 1, 1955
- Last show: Sept. 22, 1956
- 39 episodes (plus 75 "lost" episodes)

TIME: The mid-'50s.

PLACE: A tenement apartment at 328 Chauncey Street in the Bensonhurst section of Brooklyn, the home of bus driver Ralph Kramden and his wife, Alice. It is a starkly furnished, drab flat that doesn't even have window shades. They lived there for fourteen years before they finally bought a new piece of furniture—which happened to be a TV set.

BACKGROUND: Ralph Kramden met Alice Gibson when she was handing out shovels at the WPA (Ralph is a former WPA snow shoveler). They have been married for fifteen years, have no children, and own almost nothing. Ralph has a regular job—he is a bus driver for the Gotham Bus Company, on Manhattan's Fifth Avenue line— but he barely earns enough to make ends meet. At one point he reveals that he and Alice have exactly $75 in their savings account. Yet his pride won't allow his wife to work, so he's stuck with his dreams of making it big. His partner in his bizarre plans is Ed Norton, who lives upstairs with his wife, Trixie, but seems to spend as much time in the Kramdens' apartment as in his own. Norton is a sewer worker with the New York City Department of Water Works. He makes $62 a week and seems to be slightly better off than Ralph.

MAIN CAST:
- **Ralph Kramden** (Jackie Gleason): A frustrated blue-collar worker. Likes to bowl and play pool. Belongs to the International Order of Friendly Raccoons. Loud, crude, childlike, and impractical.
- **Alice Kramden** (Audrey Meadows): Ralph's long-suffering spouse. An acid-tongued housewife in a frowsy housedress. Also played by Pert Kelton and Jane Kean.
- **Ed Norton** (Art Carney): "A sewer worker is like a brain surgeon—we're both specialists." Ralph's devoted best friend and co-conspirator. Not too bright. His slowness on the uptake and endless monologues about his job often blow Ralph's short fuse. Was once named Raccoon of the Year.
- **Trixie Norton** (Joyce Randolph): Ed's equally long-suffering spouse and a dear friend of Alice.

BELLY LAUGHS

Gleason never rehearsed, and generally didn't need to because he had a photographic memory—one look at the script and he had it down. Nonetheless, he occasionally forgot his lines. When he did, Gleason would pat his stomach—a sign for someone else to think of something...quick. Once Alice snapped, "If you get any bigger, Gasbag, you'll just float away." That wasn't in the script.

Another time, Gleason forgot to make an entrance. Art Carney, who was onstage at the time, calmly went to the ice box, pulled out an orange, and began peeling it until Gleason realized his mistake.

CODE WORDS

Besides *Kissville*, the "Honeymooners" scriptwriters had other codes.

• *Macaroni* meant that Ralph would flash one of his "I'm-an-idiot" looks.

• *Beached whale* meant that Ralph was supposed to faint.

• But Ralph's famous "Bang! Zoom!"s were never written into any script. Gleason just stuck them in whenever they seemed appropriate.

ORIGINS

The original "Honeymooners" skit aired on the now defunct DuMont Televison Network in 1950. The show: Gleason's "Cavalcade of Stars." The inspiration: Jackie's own boyhood in the Bushwick area of Brooklyn. Gleason, who grew up in poverty and quit school at sixteen to become a pool hustler, was surrounded by people like Ralph and Alice all his life."I knew a thousand couples like these in Brooklyn," he told a reporter. "My neighborhood was filled with them." But the concept was hard for his writers to grasp. They saw Ralph, with his threats of violence, as an animal—and they wanted to call the show "The Beast." Gleason disagreed; he wanted to stress that love lay underneath all that cacophony. So he insisted on "The Honeymooners."

The Kramdens and Nortons at home. Alice was pretty tough onscreen, and even tougher offscreen. Audrey (Alice) Meadows was the only one of the cast who asked for, and received, "royalties in perpetuity" for her work on "The Honeymooners." She went after the job in the first place mainly because Gleason told her she didn't look frumpy enough for the part. It was a challenge. Without telling the star, she redid her makeup and showed up for another audition. Gleason enthusiastically asked her name; she was so frumpy he didn't recognize her.

MISCELLANY

• The address of the Kramdens' flat (328 Chauncey Street) was actually Gleason's childhood home.

• A refrigerator company once offered to sponsor "The Honeymooners," on one condition: the Kramdens had to get a refrigerator to replace their icebox. Gleason, who was obsessed with the show's integrity, refused.

• Joyce Randolph's mother complained about Joyce's role on Gleason's show. Why? "She thought I could do better than marrying a sewer worker."

CRITICS' COMMENTS

ABOUT RALPH:

"Ralph is the best and the worst of us, all rolled up into one little person....Make that one *big* person. He's the guy who's got all the dreams, and he's always looking around the bend for the pot at the end of the rainbow. On the other hand, he's an egotistical blowhard. There's tremendous ego and tremendous humility all wrapped up in one package—he makes tremendous mistakes, and he's got a heart of gold. If you can't relate to that, I don't think your heart is beating."

—Mark Dawidziak,
Akron Beacon Journal

"Jackie Gleason had the perfect rage in the way that his eyes popped out when he talked. He was a master of the toe-to-toe stuff."

—John Carman,
San Francisco Chronicle

"The appeal of the show is that Kramden was everyman, a common guy. Most of us aren't going to be much more than bus drivers in the scheme of things. We're not going to be presidents, or generals, or anything important. Ralph was fighting to make the best of that situation. He wasn't railing against his fate, but he was trying to bend it just a little bit. There's a certain amount of common dignity in that, which set the show apart."

—Barry Garron,
Kansas City Star

ABOUT THE KRAMDENS:

"The interaction between Alice and Ralph is the strength of 'The Honeymooners'...because Audrey Meadows's deadpan humor offsets Gleason's physical humor perfectly. Just watch Gleason provoke the arms-crossed reaction from Alice. ...He storms around, raving, while Alice just stands there, looking at him....The longer he does it, the funnier it gets. And finally she lets loose with a great one-liner—you're seldom disappointed with her comebacks."

—Ed Bark,
Dallas Morning News

DISSENTING OPINION:

"'The Honeymooners' is the worst show of all time. Oh, I loved Art Carney...and I do get a kick out of Jackie Gleason, with his obvious physical humor. But it was basically the same show every week—i.e., Ralph makes a fool out of himself....It celebrated abuse. Even though he never hit her, he was always threatening to....and the thinking behind *that* was repulsive....

"For her part, Alice ran counter to just about every feminist principle you can think of—here she was in a loveless marriage, and instead of doing something about it, she would content herself with making fun of him all the time, being of no help to him when he was down and puncturing him when he was up. I'm not denying its appeal, or some of the comic value that it had. What I'm saying is that by every...social measure, it was a repulsive show."

—Ed Siegel,
Boston Globe

ABOUT ALICE:

"Audrey Meadows was really the very first feminist on TV, even though she was still a typical housewife. Ralph made all these blustery threats of physical violence, but she wasn't afraid of him. She'd tell him to go stuff it. And then he'd come crawling back. She was the one with power in that relationship."

—David Jones,
Columbus Dispatch

A rare shot of the '60s version of "The Honeymooners," with Jane Kean, Alice number three, in the background.

THE GEORGE BURNS AND GRACIE ALLEN SHOW

George Burns once said that he had no illusions about the secret of his success. "First of all, you've got to have talent," he explained. "And then you've got to marry her, like I did." Which, freely translated, meant he was lucky to have a co-star like Gracie Allen, his partner in vaudeville, radio, television, and life.

Burns and Allen, who were wed in 1926, were vaudeville headliners by the early '30s. But George decided that the future of entertainment lay in radio, and when Rudy Vallee quit his radio show, Burns grabbed the opportunity to take his place. The transition was successful. "The Burns and Allen Show" became one of the most popular radio programs in America, with 45 million people listening every week for twenty years.

But in 1950, George was ready to move again. He realized that *radio* was now a dying medium, and he made a deal to take his show to TV. The result: one of television's first successful sitcoms, a program that *People* describes as "still funny, because its stars are funny."

You notice they didn't say, "The situations are funny." They're not, particularly. For example, Gracie thinks a man she meets in a grocery store is romancing Blanche Morton and tries to "warn" the grocer's wife. Or Gracie misunderstands a doctor and believes she's dying. Or George's old flame announces she'll be visiting and Gracie gets paranoid.

But even the most inane situations are wonderful to watch on this show, because George and Gracie are wonderful to watch no matter *what* they're doing. "Burns and Allen" is character comedy at its finest.

The married performers play...George and Gracie, a pair of married performers. Gracie is the daffy one, the wide-eyed dispenser of the world's most convoluted logic. George: "Gracie believes everything she reads. She fried fish the other day, and I had to buy her a new dress. The recipe said, 'Roll in cracker crumbs.'"

George was the straight man and commentator. He'd talk to the audience about the plots as they were taking place. Sometimes, he'd tell us what was going to happen, and frequently he broke in on the action. Once, in fact, he introduced a new member of the cast to an old one—while the scene was in progress.

Often, he'd watch Gracie's antics on a closed-circuit TV set in the den, a plot within a plot that sponsors said was too surreal for the average viewer—but turned into one of the show's most fondly remembered devices.

At the end of each show, Burns and Allen forgot about the plot entirely, appearing onstage in front of the curtain to reprise one of their classic vaudeville routines. At the end, George would utter the classic line, "Say good night, Gracie," and our visit with the Burnses would be over for another week.

Although it was never in the annual Neilsen top ten, the show ran for eight seasons, ceasing only when an ailing Gracie announced her retirement in 1958. On the final show, George and Gracie fought back tears before their last closing routine. Afterward, the crew burst into applause and gave Gracie a standing ovation.

One of the secrets of the duo's enormous success was their very real love and devotion. "We made each other laugh," Burns recalled wistfully after Gracie's death in 1965. He added that throughout the show, fans would ask how he could possibly stay married to "that fruitcake." In 1955 he wrote a book with a title that summed up the answer nicely: *I Love Her, That's Why.*

His partner, in her goofy way, agreed:

GEORGE: "Would you ever think that such a beautiful mink coat would come from such an unattractive little thing that looks just like a weasel?"

GRACIE: "Oh, George, you're just fishing. You know I think you're handsome."

Say good night, Gracie.

George never made it on TV without Gracie, although he tried twice—in 1958 as a solo, and in 1964, with Connie Stevens in "Wendy and Me."

FLASHBACK

GRACIE: "Where are you going?"
GEORGE: "I'm going down to the store to get some cigars and stamps."
GRACIE: "Oh, who are you going to mail them to?"
GEORGE: "I'm going to smoke them myself."
[*Long pause*]
GEORGE: "Aren't you going to ask me why I'm going to smoke stamps?"
GRACIE: "Why should I? I've done one or two silly things in my life, too."

GEORGE: "Harry, what a coincidence. I was just thinking about you.
HARRY [flattered]: "Really, George?"
GEORGE: "Yeah. I was thinking that I haven't fired you in a long time. [pauses]... You're fired."

VITAL STATS

POLL RESULTS:
Second
PROGRAM INFO:
- Half-hour show. CBS
- First show: Oct. 12, 1950
- Last show: Sept. 22, 1958
- 239 episodes

TIME: The early '50s.

PLACE: Beverly Hills, California, home of the stars. Two of those stars, George Burns and Gracie Allen, live at 312 Maple Street. Most of the action takes place either there or next door at 314 Maple Street, home of the Burns's neighbors the Mortons.

BACKGROUND: George Burns and Gracie Allen aren't a typical American couple. They're a successful comedy team—although we hardly ever see them performing and *never* see them rehearsing. In fact, neither of them appears to work at all. Gracie spends all her time doing housework, like most '50s wives. However, her ability to create havoc out of the simplest situations constantly turns the Burns's love nest into a madhouse. Visitors begin wondering whether *they're* going crazy. Old friends are left waiting at the front door for hours. The mailman gets too confused to deliver the mail. Meanwhile, George watches the whole thing on a closed-circuit TV, with dry amusement, and frequently addresses the audience concerning each convoluted plot development.

MAIN CAST:
- **George Burns**: A master of the deadpan look, the omniscient observer who impishly delights in his wife's ability to screw everyone up.
- **Gracie Allen**: The Mrs. Malaprop of the twentieth century. Devoted wife and mother.
- **Ronnie Burns**: George and Gracie's hunky teenage son. The object of a loyal teenage following. Unpretentious, charming, and devoted to his mother, despite his puzzlement over her antics.
- **Harry Von Zell**: The announcer who plays George's announcer. Slightly dim-witted. Spends most of his time at the Burns's residence, acting as a good-natured foil for Gracie.
- **Blanche Morton** (Bea Benederet): Gracie's best friend. Caustic and sharp-tongued to her husband, but devoted to Gracie. More than anyone else on the show, she believes in the crazy conclusions Gracie arrives at every week.
- **Harry Morton** (Fred Clark/Larry Keating): Blanche's dour, accountant husband. Refers to Gracie as "that fruitcake."

HEADACHES

It's not easy being a scatter-brain. So intense was Gracie's concentration on her work that she frequently suffered from debilitating migraine headaches. She seldom had time to take to her bed, so she had their home decorated in subdued shades of green, pink, and brown in order to soothe herself.

WRITERS

"B&A" writers were sometimes prophets. Long before the AT&T divestiture, "B&A" talked about the practicality of owning one's own phone. In another episode, a friend of Harry Morton invented frozen yogurt (Blanche: "Harry, he couldn't have invented frozen yogurt when he was sober.") In another, Harry Von Zell tried to talk George into financing a device that fit on a car exhaust pipe to reduce smog. George thought it was a scam.

Ronnie Burns and his girlfriend at a soda shop. Ronnie had no plans to join the show until his father became disenchanted with the boy's inability to decide on a career. "Have you ever thought of acting?" George suggested. "No, Dad." "Well, think about it." And Ron became a television star, with an instant fan club of more than 5000 people.

CAMERA SHY

Despite her three decades in show business, Gracie suffered from severe stage fright—not to mention camera fright. Most of the time she managed to ignore the camera, but once she spotted it during a scene with George—and completely forgot her lines. Afterward, she took the producer aside and said, "What's that little red light on the camera?" He told her that it was taking the live picture she'd been playing in front of for a year and a half. She responded, "Turn it off! I never want to see it again! It scares me!"

LOST TREASURE

"The George Burns and Gracie Allen Show" was initially broadcast live from New York and filmed on poor-quality 16mm kinescope for West Coast viewing a week later. Unfortunately, because of this crude process, the first 50 shows have been lost. The programs we see in syndication date from 1952, when the show moved to Los Angeles. What sort of things did we miss? George says he once appeared with his fly open.

Left to right, Bea Benederet, Larry Keating, Gracie, George.

CRITICS' COMMENTS

ABOUT GRACIE:
"The real Gracie Allen was an artist, a writer....She wasn't at all like the Gracie Allen we saw on the show. *That* was something George wrote. Gracie was a consummate professional actress. She probably memorized dialogue six hours a night, because out of a fifty-page script, forty-three of those pages would be solid Gracie dialogue. And it was all non sequiturs. Trying to memorize that ... was no easy task. So she worked very hard to create the scatterbrained character we knew."

—Cheryl Blythe,
Say Good Night, Gracie

"Gracie Allen could turn any situation into a disaster. She was Charlie Chaplin or Buster Keaton, running through mine fields. Only in her case, they were *verbal* mine fields and everyone *else* would be blown to bits while she breezed through as if she were going for a walk in the country."

—Ed Siegel,
Boston Globe

"I love Gracie. If I have a little girl, I'd like to name her Gracie. I think she was the neatest woman ever in show business. She was feminine, and she was endearing without being a bimbo. Gracie had inimitable qualities. In fact, they were not only impossible to imitate, they're impossible to describe. You've just got to see her to appreciate her."

—Andee Beck,
Tacoma News Tribune

ABOUT GEORGE:
"George Burns always said he wasn't funny, that Gracie Allen was the funny one and he was just the straight man/business manager. It's not true. He *was* a great straight man. But at the same time, his delivery was flawless....It's the pause where he looks at the camera, the business with the cigar, the sort of droll look on his face, as if to say, 'God help me, Gracie's done it again—how do I get out of this mess?' He doesn't say that, but it all comes through anyway, without even a smile."

—Bill Musselwhite,
Calgary Herald

George and Harry Von Zell play cowboys. Harry is best known among the TV generation for his work on this show. But in previous years, he was known for one of the all-time great radio bloopers. He announced this on a national broadcast: "Ladies and gentlemen, the President of the United States, Mr. Hoobert Heever."

"It's a style that would be more at home in Malibu in the 1980s. He was an extremely laid-back comedian who let things happen and then registered the humor in very small and subtle ways. A take. A look at the camera. The way he took his cigar out of his mouth."

—Jim Gordon,
Gary Post-Tribune

"It's one of those shows that's often cited for being very avant garde, especially for breaking the fourth wall and talking to the camera."

—Michael Hill,
Baltimore Evening Sun

"The best part of 'Burns and Allen' was George's television set, which let him know what was going on in every room in the house. Like they'd be planning a surprise birthday for him, whispering, 'Don't tell George,' to each other. And then he'd come down and say, 'Where are my presents?'"

—Ken Hoffman,
Houston Post

ABOUT HARRY:
"I loved Harry Von Zell, the world's least attractive man. He was barely up from the primoridal soup, but he fancied himself as a ladies' man, and the show did nothing to dispel that. He was constantly supposedly going out on dates. Of course, his Neanderthal jaw would drop whenever he was fired, which was every three or four weeks. 'Harry, you're fired.' It would have been great if just once, Harry didn't come out for the announcement at the end of the show."

—Joel Pisetzner,
Bergen Record

I LOVE LUCY

With so many men in the service during World War II, there was a shortage of civilian laborers in America. So women stepped into "male" jobs. They took over as shipbuilders, welders, automobile workers, riveters, etc.

When the GIs returned, wives dutifully returned home and created the baby boom. But the seeds of change were sown—many women discovered that their traditional roles as cooks,housekeepers, and husband's helpmates were now unsatisfying. They dreamed of having their own identities, their own money, their own careers.

Just like Lucy.

Lucy Ricardo was the patron saint of the frustrated '50s housewife, the first female TV character to act out the secret fantasies of millions of American women. She was determined to make something of herself, to be more than a domestic drudge. So week after week, she risked everything—from her marriage to her dignity—to pursue independence.

But if Lucy embodied the fondest dreams of the average housewives, she also represented their worst fears—because no matter what Lucy tried to do, whether it was taking a job in TV or working on an assembly line, she failed. Miserably. Every effort became an embarrassing calamity and often she wound up bawling while her husband screamed at her.

It could have been a nightmare. But Lucille Ball's flair for physical comedy made it all funny instead. She was TV's first original genius, the Buster Keaton of the medium. Her ability to fall off ladders, to crawl on window ledges, to frantically stuff eggs down her dress made wildly improbable situations seem almost plausible—and hence, hilarious.

Once, for example, Lucy was trapped on the top floor of an apartment house and didn't want Ricky to know. Ethel [looking around]: "Lucy? Where are you?" Lucy: "Up here…I'm locked out on the balcony….Is Ricky there?" Ethel: "No-o-o." Lucy: "Good. I want you to help me down….I've figured a way to lower myself over the side, and I want you to pull me in when I go by." Right. We knew what was coming next, even if Lucy and Ethel didn't seem to. Mrs. Ricardo courted disaster with an innocence that bordered on imbecility. But she did it so well that audiences loved and looked forward to it.

Other factors in "I Love Lucy"'s success included witty and imaginative scripts and a sterling cast. Desi, a nonactor whose bug-eyed reactions to Lucy's antics made them even funnier, was utterly convincing as a frustrated husband . William Frawley and Vivian Vance, as the Ricardos' foils the Mertzes, were almost as popular as the stars. Frawley was always ready with a caustic comment and raised eyebrow. And Vance, for love of Lucy, was lured into one bizarre escapade after another.

In some ways, "I Love Lucy" hasn't aged well. Ricky Ricardo's determination to keep Lucy housebound now seems chauvinistic. Lucy's schemes, subterfuge, and the Ricardos' periodic desire to "teach each other a lesson" seem quaint and immature among today's complex sitcom relationships.

But what hasn't dated is the warmth and charm of Lucy and Ricky's obvious devotion to each other—despite their offscreen difficulties. (The real couple was in constant turmoil, and divorced in 1960.) The episode in which Lucy tells Ricky of her pregnancy during his nightclub act, for example, remains one of TV's most touching moments.

And the proof is that "Lucy" is still going strong. A whole new generation still revels in the ominous words "I have a brainstorm," "I've got it," and "Wait a minute!"—sure signs that Lucy is headed for trouble.

Maybe she's about to set a putty nose on fire. Maybe she's about to lock herself in a walk-in freezer. Whatever it is, it's a sure thin' she's doing it right this second, somewhere in the world, and will keep on doing it as long as people are watching TV.

Lucy with ardent anti-communist John Wayne. In 1952, Lucy's TV career was almost cut short when it was revealed she had joined a leftist organization in the '30s. But she was "cleared" of the charge. "The only red thing about Lucy," said Desi, "is her hair. And even that's not real."

FLASHBACK

RICKY: "Hey, Loooosy...I'm home."

LUCY: "Honestly, Ethel..."

RICKY: "Babalooooooo..."

RICKY: "These have been the best fifteen years of my life.... [sees Lucy is upset]...What's the matter?"
LUCY:"We've only been married thirteen years."
RICKY: "Oh, well I mean...it seems like fifteen."
LUCY: "What?"
RICKY: "No...uh...uh...what I mean is that it doesn...uh...seem possible...that all that fun could have been crammed into only thirteen years."
LUCY: Well, you certainly wormed out of that one."

LUCY: "Wah-h-h..."

VITAL STATS

POLL RESULTS:
Third
PROGRAM INFO:
•Half-hour show. CBS
•First show: Oct. 15, 1951
•Last show: June 24, 1957
•179 episodes

TIME: The early '50s.

PLACE: New York City, home of Ricky and Lucy Ricardo. The action takes place at their apartment at 623 East 68th Street and at the Tropicana, the nightclub where Ricky is an entertainer. Later, the Ricardos move to a farmhouse in Connecticut and Ricky gets his own nightclub, the Ricky Ricardo Babaloo Club.

BACKGROUND: Lucy Esmerelda McGillicuddy and Ricky Ricardo met aboard a Caribbean cruise ship, where he was an entertainer and she was a tourist. They fell in love and moved to New York. Ricky wants Lucy to be a contented housewife, but Lucy is desperate to break into show business—despite her utter lack of talent. She constantly schemes for her big break, usually driving Ricky crazy in the process. The Ricardos' best friends are their landlords, the Mertzes, who live in the next apartment. Ethel Mertz is also Lucy's accomplice in most of her ill-fated, harebrained schemes (although Ethel's husband, Fred, sometimes gets sucked into them, too). Invariably, when Ricky finds out about them, he is furious and breaks into an agitated stream of Spanish babble.

MAIN CAST:
•**Lucy Ricardo** (Lucille Ball): The frustrated housewife who wants to be a star.
•**Ricky Ricardo** (Desi Arnaz): Hot-blooded Cuban singer with his own band, "jus' makin' ends meet" when the show begins. By the end of the show, Ricky is a star, with his own TV show and enough money to buy the family a house. Struggles to keep Lucy at home, "where she belongs."
•**Fred Mertz** (William Frawley): The Ricardos' neighbor and landlord, a grumbling old codger.
•**Ethel Mertz** (Vivian Vance): Fred's wife, a frumpy houswife who's a little in awe of Lucy's daring, and a little in awe of her stupidity. Willingly joins Lucy's adventures.
•**Little Ricky**: The Ricardos' son, played, respectively, by a doll in a blanket, a pair of six-month-old twins (Richard and Ronald Simmons), three-year-old twins, and finally Richard Keith (real name: Richard Thibodeaux).

These happy couples weren't really so happy. Lucy tried to keep her marriage together by insisting that Desi play her TV husband. The show worked, but the marriage didn't. Vivian Vance and William Frawley never could stand each other.

BABY BOOM

Little Ricky, the Ricardos' newborn son, was America's first television baby:

•The birth of Little Ricky in 1953 was timed to coincide with the birth of the couple's real-life son, Desi Arnaz, Jr. Lucy had a Caesarian section that night.

•The episode in which Lucy gave birth ran opposite the inauguration of President Eisenhower. Lucy beat Ike in the ratings by 15 million viewers.

•Lucy was never allowed to say the word *pregnant* on TV.

•Desi and Lucy's *real* children, Luci Arnaz and Desi Arnaz, Jr., appeared just once—in the final epsiode, "The Ricardos Dedicate a Statue."

LUCY COLLECTIBLES

•Vol. 1, No. 1 of *TV Guide* (April 3, 1953), featuring Desi, Jr., and Lucy. The cover story read: "Lucy's $50 Million Baby." Current value: $200.

•Little Ricky doll, ca. 1953. Came dressed in a little outfit with the words, *Ricky, Jr.* embroidered on the blouse. Current value: $90.

•"I Love Lucy" comic books. Thirty-five of them were published by Dell Publications from 1954 to 1960. Current value: $5-10 each.

•"I Love Lucy" paper dolls from Whitman Publishing, 1953. They featured Lucy and Ricky cardboard cutouts and an entire wardrobe of paper clothes. Current value: $50-$75.

FOR THE RECORD

•According to a survey conducted by the We Love Lucy fan club in Los Angeles, the most popular episode of all time is "Lucy Does a TV Commercial," in which she hawks Vitameatavegemin and gradually gets smashed.

•The show's longest recorded audience laugh ever occurred in the episode "Lucy Does the Tango," when Lucy tried to conceal five dozen eggs she'd stuffed in her shirt.

CRITICS' COMMENTS

ABOUT ITS APPEAL:
"The best episodes were the ones where Lucy's slapstick was integrated into the domestic situation...and you almost believed it. One of the classics, Vitameatavegemin, is an example. She's essentially doing a 'drunk' act. But it's so beautifully integrated into the script, and what she does is so consistent with the character of Lucy that's been established, that it works out very well. It's just terribly funny."

—Tom Shales,
Washington Post

"Even though it represents an era of sexism that I don't think I'd want my kid watching—because I don't want him to believe that women should be that way—she was a riot. My mother [syndicated columnist Marilyn Beck] is a lot like Lucy Ricardo. She's a bright lady, but she's got a dingy side, and I like that."

—Andee Beck,
Tacoma News Tribune

ABOUT ITS HISTORICAL IMPORTANCE:
"The writers of 'I Love Lucy' are the fathers of the situation comedy as we know it. The guidelines they set up for themselves are still followed today. The rules were:

1. Put your character in a situation of jeopardy and have it resolved by the end of the episode.
2. Develop a camaraderie between the characters that is wholly believable and based on human impulse and behavior.
3. Have a simple, internal logic to the situation. Everything Lucy did, no matter how preposterous, was based on a series of logical, believable steps. When taken in toto, they were ridiculous. But step by step, the viewer could follow along with Lucy's plight. And every step was credible within her character. She came across as a human being—a strange, larger-than-life, *extreme* human being, but a human being nonetheless....Most of the fixes she found herself in were the results of her own human shortcomings."

—Vince Waldron,
Classic Sitcoms

ABOUT THE CAST:
"Lucille Ball has never been as funny as she was in 'I Love Lucy' because she's never had a supporting cast like Vivian Vance, William Frawley, and Desi Arnaz. Their... personalities *made* her funny. Lucy is a harsh comedienne; she needs someone who can stand up to her—someone like Desi Arnaz, who could bring her down and create sympathy for her character. When she plays against a weak character like Gale Gordon, she gets on your nerves because *he* doesn't serve as a counterbalance to the harder elements in her comedy style."

—Robert Bianco,
Pittsburgh Press

"Lucy is the female Charlie Chaplin!...There's nobody else that can do what she does with her face, with her walk, with her action....All the res' of us was jus' props—Bill, Vivian, me. Darn good props, but props. In a Lucy show, everythin' starts with Lucy."

—Desi Arnaz, *TV Guide*,
February 1, 1969

THE PHIL SILVERS SHOW

Phil Silvers and Paul Ford share a laugh on the set.

The year was 1955. It was only a decade since World War II had ended and a mere two years since American boys had been brought home from Korea. The veterans of those wars didn't necessarily have happy memories of their experiences in the military. But what the hell, they were patriotic citizens. They didn't want to say anything nasty about our army. Not out loud, anyway.

Ten...hut! Enter a fast-talking, quick-witted army sergeant named Ernie Bilko who said it all for them.

Bilko was a cynical wiseguy who understood that army bureaucracy was slow-moving, hypocritical, pompous, self-important...and *vulnerable.* It was the perfect mark for a hustler like him. So week after week he stuck to the military—as Hawkeye Pierce would two decades later.

Of course, unlike Hawkeye, Bilko had no "redeeming" qualities to offset his crass ones. He wasn't a brilliant surgeon; he wasn't a sensitive, warm human being. He was a con man, with a phony smile and a stainless-steel tongue. (To the colonel and his wife: "Oh, Colonel, I didn't know you had a *young girl* with you").

But viewers loved him anyway; the laugh track was even provided by a live audience of delighted GIs. After all,you had to hand it to a guy who could talk his commanding officer into lending him the money for a high-stakes poker game. Or who managed to turn a Pentagon training film into a showcase for his theatrical talents.

Every once in a while he'd get caught (like the time he started an on-base sports-car factory). But with his white-toothed smile and a hasty explanation ("Where would Al Capone be today if he wasn't willing to take chances?") he'd be off the hook once more and ready for another scam. Nothing could stop Bilko.

Indeed, his indestructibility was part of his charm. As Silvers once told the *New York Times,* "I can do some things that they'd stone everybody else for doing. The audience somehow forgives me. People like to root against the system."

To his credit, this shady Robin Hood was protective of the Merry Men in the motor pool, dimwits like "Slob of the Century" Pvt. Duane Doberman and the unworldly Rocco Barbella. He cared about them, that is, as long as he was lining his own pockets in the process. But the brass—that was another matter. Col. John T. Hall was such a putz that he really deserved the constant indignities Bilko heaped on him. Have you ever noticed that he never had a car? It was always in the motor pool being "fixed" by Bilko, who drove it himself. As Bilko frequently asked, "Who's in charge here, me or the colonel?" We knew.

"The Phil Silvers Show" is still extremely popular for two reasons: First, Phil Silvers, a comic genius, was *born* to play Ernie Bilko. And second, the little-guy-against-the-system theme is always appealing—especially to those of us under various bureaucratic thumbs. Maybe someday we'll have the chutzpah to convince the jerks in charge that we need a "second Sunday in February party" or a "Favorite Girl of the Month Club." But until then,we'll just enjoy watching Bilko do it for us.

Bilko relaxes with a "nice, friendly little game of poker." Joe E. Ross (middle) went on to star in two more sitcoms—"Car 54, Where Are You?" and "It's About Time."

FLASHBACK

BILKO [trying to drum up business for one of his pool games]: "Fifty cents a ball, boys?"

ZIMMERMAN: "Imagine, Bilko's doing something without making a profit."
PAPARELLI: " Even the chaplain is stunned. He's using it for the subject of next Sunday's sermon."

BILKO: "How do you like my luck? Every time opportunity knocks, I ain't got enough money to open the door."

VITAL STATS

POLL RESULTS:
Fourth
PROGRAM INFO:
- Half-hour show. CBS
- First show: Sept. 20, 1955
- Last show: Sept. 11, 1959
- 138 episodes

TIME: The 1950s.

PLACE: Camp Fremont Army Base, Fort Baxter, Roseville, Kansas. Home of Company B, 24th Division, US Army.

BACKGROUND: The Korean War is over and America has a scaled-down peacetime army. What do the soldiers do while they're waiting for freedom's call? Play poker, run meaningless drills, cater to the whims of pompous and overblown officers. Sgt. Ernest Bilko, con artist supreme, heads the motor pool in one peacetime army unit, and he's going to make the situation work for him. He's constantly looking for creative ways of separating the soldiers from their paychecks—poker, pool, raffles—and to separate the officers from their perks. Although most of the brass is taken in by Bilko's sleezy charm and believe he's a good soldier, he's actually "borrowing" their jeeps, misappropriating their funds, and turning target practice into a crapshoot. Although Col. John T. Hall has Bilko's number, but he's outwitted by the grinning sergeant again and again.

MAIN CAST:
- **Sgt. Ernie Bilko** (Phil Silvers): Charming, ingratiating, and totally insincere con artist. Heads the motor pool, but you rarely see his men working on cars. Perennially interested in making a buck. His only sensitive spot is the top of his head—he's embarrassed about being bald.
- **Pvt. Duane Doberman** (Maurice Gosfield): The ugliest GI in the Northern Hemisphere. Also called "Slob of the Century." Dumb but devoted.
- **Col. John T. Hall** (Paul Ford): The unit's incompetent, blustery, by–the–book commanding officer. Bilko drives him crazy, but the colonel's not smart enough to catch him.

AND:
- **Sgt. Francis Grover** (Jimmy Little)
- **Pvt. Dino Paparelli** (Billy Sands)
- **Cpl. Henshaw** (Allen Melvin)
- **Pvt. Zimmerman** (Mickey Freeman)
- **Pvt. Fender** (Herbie Faye)
- **Sgt. Rupert Ritzik** (Joe E. Ross)
- **Cpl. Rocco Barbella** (Harvey Lembeck)

After "Bilko" was canceled, Silvers starred as "small-time swindler" Harry Grafton in "the New Phil Silvers Show." It lasted for only one season.

SILVERS SPEAKS

We don't often think of "Bilko" in political terms, but in the Vietnam years, Phil Silvers wasn't crazy about what his show had wrought: "The Pentagon loved the show, and enlistments tripled. Those young guys thought that that's what army life was *really* like. I feel guilty about that, about the waste."

NAME GAME

•The name Bilko came from a minor-league baseball sensation named Steve Bilko, who hit fifty-six home runs the year that Phil Silvers and Nat Hiken created the show.
•The name Rocco Barbella was the real name of casting director Rocky Graziano, an ex-boxer.
•Maurice Gosfield, nicknamed "Five-by-Five" by the cast and crew, inspired his stage name, Doberman, because Nat Hiken thought he looked like a dog.

BUT NOT FORGOTTEN

After his show was canceled, Phil Silvers's career went into decline. Nonetheless, in the '70s he sued the *National Enquirer* for $10 million for referring to him as a "lonely has-been."

ORIGINS

At the behest of CBS program manager Hubbell Robinson, Silvers and producer Nat Hiken tried to come up with a sitcom format that would be a good vehicle for Silvers's talents. They considered making him a Little League manager, the operator of a Turkish bath, a stock swindler, and an army sergeant. Hiken liked the army sergeant. Silvers didn't: "I could see nothing in it but phony drills and flimsy facetiousness. But in the end, we made a kinescope Bilko pilot, and when Bill Paley, the head of CBS saw it, he put it away so nobody else could see it. 'This,' he said, 'is money in the bank,' "

Paley liked the show so much that he put it opposite Milton Berle, who was then known as the invincible "Mr. Television." Within two months, Bilko accomplished what no one had been able to do since the beginning of network TV—he outdrew Milton Berle.

BLACK HUMOR

"The Phil Silvers Show" was the first to use black actors as a matter of course. Besides pioneering equality on TV, this breakthrough was important in another way: Once Phil Silvers was mugged by a black man in New York...until the man realized who he was attacking. "You're okay," he told Silvers—and let him go.

PEOPLE-WATCHING

Among the people who were associated with the show:
•One of the staff writers was future playwright Neil Simon.
•The clapper holder (who yelled "Take one!") was Bill "Jose Jimenez" Dana.
•Joe E. Ross, later of "Car 54, Where Are You?" got his start on "Bilko." So did his future partner, Fred Gwynne, also known as Herman Munster.
•Other bit players included Dick Van Dyke, Dick Cavett, and a twenty-two-year-old named Alan Alda.

CRITICS' COMMENTS

ABOUT SGT. BILKO:
"Bilko was very much in the mold of Ralph Kramden and Archie Bunker—he was a guy on the bottom who was trying to get to the top...and never did. But if he ever had, that would have been the end of the series. It's sort of like 'Three's Company.' If Jack Tripper had ever slept with Suzanne Somers... *that's the end.* But 'Bilko,' like all of these shows, was about unrequited longing, so nothing like that ever quite happened."

—Rick Mitz,
The Great Sitcom Book

"Bilko knew the system better than his superiors did and employed it for his own welfare. He never bucked the rules—he only bent them. That was his appeal. Ultimately, he was a good soldier and a leader of men—but he always had a little action on the side."

—Michael Dougan,
San Francisco Examiner

"Bilko is...a guy who beats the system—a wise ass who, on one hand, is a figure of authority because he's a sergeant, and on the other hand is always *undermining* authority.

It's a timeless theme, and Silvers is a timeless comic. He's the perfect reactor, the master of the punch line, a master of double take."

—Steve Sonsky,
Miami Herald

ABOUT PHIL SILVERS:
"Silvers was an old vaudevillian. He knew how to get a laugh, even if he was only in front of a camera crew. And believe me, the camera crew *did* laugh. In fact, on the back handle of the camera, they had a big rubber sponge wrapped around one of the controls. When the guys started to laugh, they would bite this thing so they wouldn't shake the camera. That's the only way they were able to keep it still."

—Bob Foster,
San Mateo Times

"He had complete command over his voice; when he got angry, he used to be able to get angry in octaves—he could take his voice right up the ladder. A real bellwhether for a comedian is: How funny is he when he's playing angry? It's the easiest thing to do, and therefore the hardest thing to do *well.* Silvers really did good angry."

—Jim Gordon,
Gary Post Tribune

ABOUT ARMY LIFE:
"My father and I would watch 'Bilko' together. He'd been in the army and loved the show because that anti-establishment feeling was a very real part of being in the service. Bilko was just doing what *everyone* dreamed of doing. He lived out a lot of people's fantasies in that show."

—Michael Duffy,
Detroit Free Press

Left: Col. John T. Hall and his wife, Nell. Paul Ford felt the greatest compliment he ever got was from GIs who told him, "We've seen plenty of colonels who are just like you."

LEAVE IT TO BEAVER

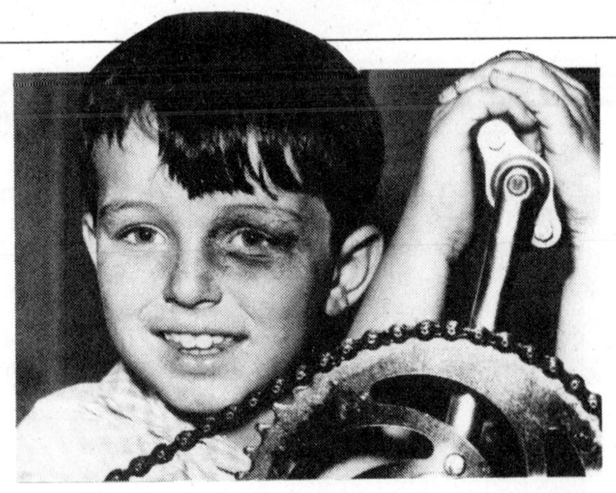

Parents weren't ready for it, but by the mid-'50s there was no escaping the truth: Baby boom kids were growing up. Suddenly they weren't just symbols of a happy middle-class life anymore; they were (oh, my God) independent beings, with their own personalities, habits, and opinions.

"Leave It to Beaver" was the first show to recognize this and incorporate it into a family sitcom format. Its creators, Bob Mosher and Joe Connelly, were sick of the annoyingly precocious, ridiculously perfect offspring who kept popping up on programs like "Father Knows Best." They wanted to do a show about *real* kids. So they created characters based on their own childhoods and on the concerns and adventures of their children (Connelly had six , Mosher had two). "[And] if we hire a writer," Connelly explained in the '50s, "we tell him not to make up situations but to look into his own background."

All of this made "Beaver" the first sitcom in history to show us life from a kid's-eye view. Beaver and Wally weren't just part of their parents' world—they had one of their own. We followed them to school, where Beaver was accused of being a teacher's pet, to a party where the panicky Beaver was cornered by a bunch of girls who want to play "post office," to the playground where Beaver accidentally ripped the pants of his best suit, to the boys' bedroom, where they pondered the meaning of life. "Wally," mused Beaver, "the rules are a lot easier on grown-ups than they are for little boys." "Well sure they are," Wally answered, "the grown-ups are the ones that *make* the rules."

Their conversations were just like ours. Once, Beaver decided to find out how his brother felt about him. Beaver: "Do you really like me, Wally?" Wally: "I guess so." Beaver: "Do you like me a whole lot?" Wally: "Look, don't get sloppy on me. I might slug you one."

Of course, the producers didn't mean to make the show so realistic that they sacrificed the warm family relationships that sitcom audiences demanded. So in casting the show, they picked a TV family that could communicate affection honestly. And the Cleavers really *did* behave like a family offscreen. Hugh Beaumont, a Methodist minister in real life, dispensed advice. Barbara Billingsley looked after her two "sons." Jerry Mathers looked up to Tony Dow as if he were a big brother. Maybe that's one of the reasons "Beaver" is still so convincing.

Another is the appeal of the supporting characters' personalities. True, Ward got a bit sanctimonious at times, but he was still the only sitcom parent who'd occasionally admit he was wrong. And June was goodness itself. Both were always there with advice, a hug, and a plateful of cookies and milk.

Then there were the boys' buddies, as motley a crew as ever infested a sitcom. There was Lumpy, that manipulative, dopey tub of lard; Gilbert, the brains behind most of Beaver's misadventures; the cowering Whitey; Larry, who was always whining or eating; and of course, Eddie Haskell, "that creepy wise-guy rat," the Uriah Heep of the '50s. "Good morning Mrs. Cleaver," he'd ooze, "what a pretty dress you have on today." But to Beaver, it was, "You gnaw down any trees today? Heh, heh, heh." Eddie was vicious and dishonest, but he was familiar. All of us knew a real-life Eddie.

Above all, "Leave It to Beaver" was one of the most beautifully written sitcoms ever, with dialogue that compares with the best of Thornton Wilder.

"You know something, Wally?" Beaver says. "The fun of catching polliwogs isn't really catching polliwogs. It's lyin' there with the other guys and talkin'. Like the time we were at the lake and we were pretendin' the lake was an ocean, and the polliwogs were whales. And we were on a whaling ship. Remember, Wally? Well, we didn't catch one polliwog that day. But that was the best day I ever spent at the lake."

"Beaver" was entertaining because its believable situations and characters struck a chord in all of us. More than any show of its time, it was just like home—or the way we wished home could be.

Jerry Mathers's first acting role was in Alfred Hitchcock's *The Trouble with Harry*, in 1955. Not a bad start.

FLASHBACK

BEAVER: "Wouldn't it be neat if a guy could stay a kid all his life?"
WALLY: "Aw, you'd never get away with that. But you know, when you get real old, you have what they call a second childhood."
BEAVER: "No foolin'? Boy, at least I got somethin' to look forward to."

WARD: "When did Miss Landers first ask you to do this?"
BEAVER: "Hmmm-m-m...just about three weeks ago."
WARD: "Three weeks ago? Then why are you coming to me about it tonight?"
BEAVER: "'Cause it's due tomorrow."

WARD: "What kind of girl would you have Wally marry?"
JUNE: "Oh, some very sensible girl from a nice family....One with both feet on the ground, who's a good cook and can keep a nice house and see that he's happy."
WARD: "Dear, I got the last one of those."

VITAL STATS

POLL RESULTS:
Fifth
PROGRAM INFO:
- Half-hour . CBS/ABC
- First show: Oct. 4, 1957
- Last show: Sept. 12, 1963
- 234 episodes

TIME: The late '50s.

PLACE: Mayfield, USA, a typical American suburb. The center of the action is the Cleaver house, located at 485 Maple Drive during the series' first two years and 211 Pine Street thereafter (they moved between the second and third seasons). There are side trips to places like Mayfield High School, which Wally attends, Grant Avenue Grammar School, which all the kids attend; Metzger's Field, where they play ball; and various other spots where the boys like to "mess around."

BACKGROUND: The Cleavers are the '50s American dream family. Dad is an accountant; Mom is the perfectly groomed housewife totally devoted to her family; their two sons aren't wimps, but they're close to both their parents *and* to each other—they even share a bedroom peacefully. The boys have the privilege of growing up in relative affluence, so they're free to experience childhood without major sacrifices. Each week they have an innocent "kid" problem at school, with their buddies, or even within the family circle. It's usually resolved with some help from Dad, who offers a weekly Lesson in Life.

MAIN CAST:
- **Theodore "Beaver" Cleaver** (Jerry Mathers): A lovable little kid with a big heart. "You know something, Wally, I'd rather do nothin' with you than somethin' with anybody else." Well-intentioned but willing to break the rules. Also willing to pay the price if he's caught.
- **Wally Cleaver** (Tony Dow): Good son, understanding brother. An all-American high school student— athletic, good-looking, popular. Fortunately, he's not conceited and is generally unimpressed with his accomplishments.
- **Ward Cleaver** (Hugh Beaumont): Their father. A suburban philosopher who has plenty of time for man-to-man talks and seems to know something about everything. Beaver: "What makes it rust, Dad?" Ward: "Oxidation. It eats into metal."
- **June Cleaver** (Barbara Billingsley): Their mother. Always impeccably dressed ; always ready with cookies and milk or a sandwich.
- **Eddie Haskell** (Ken Osmond): A "bad influence," Wally's nasty, manipulative, wise-ass pal, the most insincere kid ever on TV.

GROAN-UPS

"Leave It to Beaver " was the only sitcom ever to be resurrected with virtually the entire original main cast. First, in 1984, came "Still the Beaver," which floundered on the Disney Channel for two years. Then came "The New Leave It to Beaver," which made its debut on WTBS in 1986. Each featured Wally as a lawyer, June as a widow (Hugh Beaumont had passed away), Beaver as a floundering businessman and a divorced father of two, and Eddie Haskell as a construction worker. In 1987, Jerry Mathers—who had ballooned to 215 pounds—lost weight and announced that the show's writers had finally decided to portray Beaver as a happy, successful adult.

BAD RAP

Believe it or not, Eddie Haskell was capable of a good deed or two on the show:

- He once faked a sore throat so Wally could take a girl they both liked to a dance, since he knew that Wally, a loyal friend, would never ask the girl on his own.
- He suggested that Wally and he wear sport coats to a party when he discovered that Beaver had accidentally gotten a spot on Wally's new suit.
- He even once admitted to Beaver that he knew nobody liked him and was sometimes scared when he was alone. (Don't panic, fans. Later in the episode he rubbed candy in Beaver's hair.)

Wally and Eddie crowd around a...a...girl!

LEAVE IT TO JERRY

Eight-year-old Jerry Mathers was extremely nervous when he went to audition for the part of Beaver—but not because he was worried he wouldn't get the part. Frankly, that was secondary to him. Producers Bob Mosher and Joseph Connelly watched little Jerry squirm distractedly until they finally had to ask what the matter was.

Mathers recalls that he blurted out, "I gotta go to my Cub Scout meeting."

Jerry's mom was aghast, but the producers agreed that Jerry had his priorities straight. They sent him away—and then hired him. Why? Because he was perfect for the part.

"They told me," says Mathers, "that was the exact quality of real little boyishness that they hoped to see in every episode of their television series."

NAME GAME

The creators, Mosher and Connelly, initially called the show "Wally and the Beaver," perceiving Beaver as a friendly, gap-toothed kid, much like "Little Beaver" in the *Red Ryder* serials. But the show's sponsors thought the title sounded too much like a nature show. So Wally was dropped from the title at the last minute. The inspiration for the show's new name probably came from a short-lived 1952 sitcom starring Eddie Albert. Its title: "Leave It to Larry."

CRITICS' COMMENTS

ABOUT EDDIE:
"Eddie Haskell was, I think, the first nasty character in a sitcom. Certainly he was the first authentically nasty *kid*. In one episode, Eddie's sitting in the bedroom with his feet on Wally's pillow. Wally walks in and tells him to take his feet off. Eddie just swings around and puts his feet on *Beaver's* pillow. That's just what a kid like Eddie would really do."

—Alex McNeil,
Total Television

"Thirty years later, I sort of feel like Ward. I was Eddie Haskell when I was in college, but I grew up to be Ward. I've got two kids, a wife, a dog. We look like the Cleavers—everybody says it."

—Duane Dudek,
Milwaukee Sentinel

ABOUT WARD AND JUNE:
"I liked the fact that Ward would get sarcastic with June every now and then. That was something you didn't see on a lot of sitcoms at the time, and it added an edginess to their relationship that made it more plausible."

—R. D. Heldenfels,
Schenectady Gazette

ABOUT THE KIDS:
"Kids were respected on 'Beaver' without being 'cherished.' It wasn't an *earnest* show; it could make friends with kids without patronizing them. Look, in real life kids know much more than parents think they do. They're aware that their parents have the responsiblity of teaching them right and wrong and all that. But kids also know that they don't have to worry about what life is about until they grow up. And who wants to think about that stuff when you can avoid it? It's much more fun to see how much you can get away with 'Beaver' was the first show to capture that side of being a kid."

—David Jones,
Columbus Dispatch

"Beaver was a kind of cool character—in fact, that's why I hated the revival on WTBS. It bothers me to think that Beaver grew up to be this overweight nerd.

—Jeff Borden,
Charlotte Observer

ABOUT ITS APPEAL
"This year there's a lot of talk about half-hour programs that walk the line between comedy and drama. But 'Beaver' did that same thing thirty years ago. The scenes don't always end with a little boffo laugh; they're very serious, poignant moments, done with a real gentle touch. I hope my kid will be able to watch it. I have a warm spot in my heart for this show."

—Michael Hill,
Baltimore Evening Sun

50s

AMOS 'N' ANDY (1951-53)
"Amos 'n' Andy" is probably the most controversial TV show in the medium's history. Fans also consider it one of the funniest. As a popular radio program, it featured white actors playing ethnic black parts. When it moved to TV, however, blacks were hired. It ran from 1951 to 1953 and was syndicated by CBS after that. But in the '60s, it was pulled off the air as a result of protests from black groups. For a while, videotapes of the show were available, but CBS cracked down on them. Today it is literally a buried program.

"Most people don't know anything about 'Amos 'n' Andy.' And the problem with addressing people who don't know anything about it is that usually they know *something* about it. They know that it stunk, or was racist, etc. Even very young people, especially blacks, will have heard something negative about 'Amos 'n' Andy,' all of which, I think, is unfortunate bad press.

"Go back and look at an episode.... There's some crudity there, but ... it's not any more distasteful—if it was at *all* distasteful—than an episode of 'Good Times,' or 'What's Happening?' To me they had a lot more negative statements to make, or negative feelings to portray, about black people, than 'Amos 'n' Andy' ever had.

'Amos 'n' Andy' worked as a television show because of the actors. The writing was not very strong.

"Once I did an excercise with a script. I took one of the scenes and removed all of the ethnic sounds. It wasn't funny. Without the 'ain't's and the 'Whoa's and the 'dis' and the 'dat,' it was nothing. It sat there on the page. So it was the brilliance of the four or five main characters that made the pedestrian lines in the show come alive. ...

"Unfortunately, it will never again air on TV."

—Bart Andrews,
Holy Mack'rel: The Story of "Amos 'n' Andy"

LOVE THAT BOB (1955-59)
"Bob Cummings was great as a rakish fashion photographer. He was way ahead of his time, chasing women on TV in the mid-'50s while Dwayne Hickman, who played his nephew, rooted for him and his sister 'tsk-tsk'ed. I was always fascinated by the way the 'glamorous' pinup models of the '50s looked. And Bob's baggy, pleated pants always cracked me up—now they're in style. But the best character was Schultzy the secretary, played by Ann B. Davis, who turned up later as a maid on 'The Brady Bunch.' Her line was 'Right, boss.' Good show. Sure like to see it again."

—Gordon Javna,
The TV Guide to Your Mind

WILLY (1954-55)
"A little-known show that Desilu produced, starring June Havoc. The show went through two different story lines. First she was a woman attorney; then they gave her a vaudeville-type family. But it was charming, and Havoc is a wonderful actress, very underrated, always in the shadow of her sister, Gypsy Rose Lee. It was well done, the writing was good, it had a flavorful background. Plus you never saw characters like that in the early '50s—a woman attorney was very unusual."

—David Cuthbert,
New Orleans Times-Picayune

Worst of the '50s

A great many of TV's earliest sitcom failures can be attributed to the fact that the '50s were still a period of experimentation; the sitcom genre—and the medium of TV itself, for that matter—was not yet established; producers were still learning by trial and error.

According to critics, some of their "errors" were virtually unwatchable, even at the time they were introduced. They're so bad, in fact, that it's hard to imagine what they would look like today if they were available for viewing.

Because of this, it's difficult to select a "worst" list for the '50s. By what standards do we evaluate the old shows? Ours? Or theirs? "Beulah," for example, a popular and fairly well-acted program by '50s standards, received a substantial number of "worst" votes in an '80s poll because it was racially offensive. (Beulah was an Aunt Jemima-style black maid.) Some critics, however, pointedly refused to name "Beulah" to the list, claiming that it is improper to judge a program based on another era's values.

In any case, there aren't any run-of-the-mill bad shows about goofy teenagers and secretaries on this list. Instead, there is an opera singer who disciplines his eight kids while singing arias around the house; an aging no-talent silent movie-star who was promoting his real-life tennis club; and an exaggerated Italian immigrant who implicitly maligned all Italian-Americans.

These shows are bad bad. There's nothing funny about them now, and there never was. They don't even qualify as "camp." They're genetic failures, the shortest of dead-end roads in television's early efforts to find its future.

LIFE WITH LUIGI

It's only when you look at something like "Life with Luigi," a monument to the bad old days when venal ethnic attacks were acceptable on TV, that you begin to understand just how much progress America has made in the last three decades. This so-called sitcom was nothing more than a half-hour insult to Italian immigrants. It made fun of every stereotype ever associated with Italians and degraded the whole "melting-pot" concept.

Luigi Basco, played by Irish-American actor J. Carroll Naish, was a recently arrived Italian immigrant who rolled his eyes, gesticulated a lot, and moaned unintelligibly in a thick Italian accent. He tried valiantly to understand the culture and idioms of his new homeland, but he was clearly overmatched. His childlike mind couldn't grasp the complexities of our way of life. When he sold a bust of George Washington for $50, for example, a scheming compatriot informed him that he'd broken a law. Luigi moaned and wrung his hands (he looked like he'd peed in his pants) until finally his blonde-haired, blue-eyed English teacher set him straight. Mama mia! Oh, whatta gratefulla guy he was! Godda bless America!

Two surprises here: J. Carroll Naish was really a distinguished actor who had been nominated for two Academy Awards before he slapped on a black mustache. Also, "Luigi" started as a big hit on radio. In fact, most of its performers, including Naish, came directly from the radio cast....Except for supporting actor Sig Ruman, who had spent his previous career playing offensive German stereotypes. He played one here named Schultz.

J. Carroll Naish tried and failed with three different TV series. "Life with Luigi" was the shortest-lived of the three; it ran from September 22, 1952, to December 22, 1952.

Actually, it wasn't the TV audience that bumped Luigi outta da lineup. The show did quite well in the ratings. But well-deserved criticism from Italian-American groups led to sponsor problems. So poor "Luigi" was canceled after three months.

Attsa good news, boss.

BACKGROUND

Luigi Basco is an Italian immigrant who now lives in Chicago. His home at 231 North Holstead Street also houses his new antiques store. When he isn't trying to understand his new country (he officially became an American citizen in the show's first episode) and run his business, Luigi is taking night classes to improve his garbled English and is trying to escape marriage with Rosa, the daughter of his best friend, fellow Italian Pasquale.

MAIN CAST

- **Luigi Basco** (J. Carroll Naish): Brand-new American citizen, naive bordering on moronic. Wins everyone over with his sweet nature.
- **Pasquale** (Alan Reed): Luigi's walrus-mustachioed friend, owner of Luigi's Pizza Palace. Brought Luigi from Italy to marry his daughter and is now furious to discover that Luigi won't oblige him.
- **Rosa** (Jody Gilbert): The hopeful bride, 260 pounds of giggling Italian pulchritude.

Luigi's classmates:

- **Schultz** (Sig Ruman): German.
- **Olson** (Ken Peters): Swedish.
- **Horwitz** (Joe Forte): Jewish.

FLASHBACK

LUIGI: "Oh, howa my gonna thanka you, Pasquale, for-a bringin' me to-a thissa wond'aful America?"
PASQUALE: "Hey—I do you a little-a fave-a; now you-a gonna do me a littla fave-a."
LUIGI: "Wella sure, Pasquale, whatta littla fave-a you want I'ma gonna do f'you?'
PASQUALE: "Marrya Rosa. Well, whatta you say, my son? "
LUIGI: "Goo-bye, Pop....No, Pasquale, eetsa no usa talkin'. I'ma don' lika you daughter Rosa. She's...she's-a too fat."
PASQUALE: "Rosa's a-no fat. She's...uh...bubbly."
LUIGI: "She's-a too mucha bub. No use-a talkin' as-a long as she-a weighs-a two hundred-a-fifity pounds.
PASQUALE [defensive]: Two hundred a-forty. She's-a no hadda din-na yet."

Naish's last shot at a TV series came in 1960, on a show called "Guestward Ho." It was a sitcom about a dude ranch, and Naish played an American Indian named Hawkeye, who dressed in full red-skin regalia and read *the Wall Street Journal*. The show lasted one season and thirty-eight episodes.

CRITICS' COMMENTS

"The attempt at ethnic humor was more insulting than it was funny."
—Walt Belcher, *Tampa Tribune*

"It was a stupid ethnic joke. It probably couldn't get on the air now. But in those days, you were allowed to shit all over groups that weren't in favor. Even though I was only about six years old, I remember thinking, 'I'm not watching that anymore,' because it was so insulting."
—Tom Jicha, *Miami News*

"It was a wonderful radio show, during the time when ethnic comedy was big on radio. There was 'Abie's Irish Rose,' 'The Goldbergs.'...It wasn't considered offensive to do ethnic humor then. And you know, the country was much more traditional in its orientation toward the 'melting pot.' ... But 'Life with Luigi' arrived on television at a bad time. The world was changing, away from ethnic humor, and there was great sensitivity about it. Italian groups would protest about Italian stereotypes, Jewish groups would protest about Jewish stereotypes....Network people got scared and they took it off the air. Of course, it wasn't the greatest show to put on television to begin with because you could imagine characters and settings on radio that didn't translate very well to TV."
—Rick Du Brow, *Los Angeles Herald Examiner*

"I interviewed Naish once; we sat and talked in his dressing room, and he was a very serious guy. He wasn't anything like that Italian comedy stuff. I don't think he even particularly cared for 'Luigi,' but it was money. He was a pro, so he did what they told him to."
—Bob Foster, *San Mateo Times*

J. Carroll Naish displays some more ethnic variety.

BONINO

Ezio Pinza was better known for his roles in musicals than for his brief attempt at TV sitcoms. "Bonino," one of television's happily forgotten half hours, littered the airwaves from September 19, 1953, to December 26, 1953.

It's a fact of life on television that successful shows get ripped off. Come out with an original concept that works in a series, and the next season you'll see three more like it. TV was only six years old when it reached one of its first milestones in this practice.

In 1953, NBC came up with the dumbest ripoff of the decade. That year, Danny Thomas was making a splash playing a nightclub entertainer who had a hard time balancing his professional and family life in "Make Room for Daddy." In one of countless inexplicable programming decisions, someone thought it would be neat to transpose this theme to the wacky world of opera. The result: that well-known sitcom "Bonino."

Try this out for size: A world-famous opera singer abandons his touring career when his wife dies. He decides to be just another dad—while singing arias around the house, accompanied by a full orchestra. Then he wonders why his kids can't relate to him.

Honest, this was the plot of "Bonino," which was designed to showcase the talents of former Metropolitan Opera basso Ezio Pinza. Pinza had become a big star after his success in *South Pacific.* Unfortunately, while he had a magnificent singing voice, he couldn't speak English all that well, and didn't exactly sparkle on the comic lines. Sometimes the show's humor was based on his garbled dialogue—shades of "Luigi."

Most of the success of "Make Room for Daddy" was due to the charm and personality of its star. But Pinza also wasn't particularly charismatic ("wooden" is a more apt description). And when he wasn't singing, Pinza looked like he had a sincere desire to be somewhere else. Apparently, so did the audience. The show lasted a mere three months before it was mercifully canceled.

Pinza went back to Broadway, where he belonged.

BACKGROUND

Opera singer Babbo (yes, Babbo) Bonino spent most of his life on the road, touring with a major opera company. As a result, he never really spent much time at home and never got to know his eight children. Now his wife has suddenly died, and on the spur of the moment, Babbo decides to give up his opera life and return to New York City to raise the kids himself. When he gets there, he discovers they're practically strangers to him. He not only has to play the part of their parent, he's got to get to know them all over again.

MAIN CAST*:*

- **Babbo Bonino** (Ezio Pinza): The opera star who gives up fame and fortune to be a real dad to his kids.
- **Edward Bonino** (Conrad Janis): The eldest son.
- **Doris Bonino** (Lenka Patterson): The eldest daughter.
- **Jerry Bonino** (Chet Allen, Donald Harris): Another son.
- **Carlo Bonino** (Oliver Andes): Yet another son.
- **Francesca Bonino** (Gaye Huston): Yet another daughter.
- **Andrew Bonino** (Van Dyke Parks): The youngest (and last) son.
- **Martha** (Mary Wickes): The wisecracking, hatchet-faced maid.
- **Walter Rogers** (David Opatoshu): Bonino's harried manager.

FLASHBACK

"If you can accept the unlikely premise on which the entire show is based, you'll like Ezio Pinza's new TV series....

Ever since Pinza's smash success in the Broadway production of *South Pacific*, the movies and TV have been trying to convert him into the Frank Sinatra of the housewife set. To date, this has resulted only in a couple of uninspired Technicolor opuses and some undignified clowning by the former Metropolitan Opera basso whenhe headed his own TV variety show....

'Bonino' gives him another chance to star in his own series, and if the situation comedy writing matches his ability, then he's in."

—*TV Guide*, original review, October 1953

"Bonino" didn't do well, but two of the supporting actors had very successful careers. Conrad Janis (above) went on to star in "Quark," "Mork and Mindy," and other TV shows. Van Dyke Parks was hailed as a musical genius in the '60s, when his *Song Cycle* album was released. More recently, he worked with the Beach Boys.

CRITICS' COMMENTS

"The thing that made 'Bonino' bad was the simple fact that they didn't know what they were doing. The people didn't seem to have an idea of how to plot for television, how to direct for television, or how to get laughs. Ezio Pinza wasn't a comedian. And the dialogue seems to have been written by throwing monkeys at typewriters until they came up with a script. There were a lot of shows like that. The '50s were supposed to be the Golden Age of Television, but they featured some of the worst programs ever conceived."

—Bill Musselwhite, *Calgary Herald*

"'Bonino?' Are you sure that's not a cheap wine? Ezio...he was really a wooden Indian."

—Tom Shales, *Washington Post*

"There wasn't that much warmth to the fellow. I think he was more or less faking it on TV. When you saw him on TV, you could immediately tell that there wasn't the personal warmth and dynamism that an actor needs to come through the screen—especially as the leading character of a series. So often there are people like him who might be great in a supporting role, but can't sustain a show. They don't have the...magnetism that it takes to make it on TV. And that was the problem with this show."

—R. K. Shull, *Indianapolis News*

Ezio relaxes by his swimming pool, Hollywood movie-star style.

THE CHARLIE FARRELL SHOW

Charlie Farrell (second from left), movie star and future real-life mayor of Palm Springs, in the '30s. His TV show aired for three months, from July 2 to September 24, 1956.

TV producers have always loved star vehicles. They guarantee a built-in audience of devoted fans and offer writers the opportunity to build stories and situations around a performer's surefire schtick (e.g., Jackie Gleason's bombastic roar, Lucille Ball's pratfalls).

Unfortunately, in TV's early days most big stars had more important things to do than star in sitcoms. So star vehicles were built around lesser-known celebrities with fewer distinguishing characteristics, and frequently, lesser talents.

Take poor Charles Farrell. He caused women to swoon as a silent-film matinee idol (*Seventh Heaven*, *Street Angel*). But except for his three-year stint as the idiot father, Vern, on "My Little Margie," most '50s audiences couldn't tell him from Charles Chaplin. Nevertheless, producers decided to use his somewhat obscure name as the title for "I Love Lucy"'s summer replacement show in 1955. To make stiff Charles more accessible to the masses, it was called "The Charlie Farrell Show."

In real life, Farrell didn't exactly *do* anything, except play a lot of tennis in his spare time at the Palm Springs resort he owned and managed. So it was decided not to even try to hamper him with a character to play. In a fit of creative inspiration, Charles Farrell played...Charles Farrell...who played a lot of tennis at the Palm Springs resort he owned.

But although a pleasant fellow, Farrell didn't really do anything on camera, either. He merely looked mildly harried by the wacky goings-on in Palm Springs. Only problem was—how many wacky things actually go on in Palm Springs? And how many of them would amuse the kind of audience who'd been getting its bellylaughs from the lowbrow antics performed on the show Charlie was replacing?

Wacky Charlie's program lasted only for two summer months. Farrell went back to work in Palm Springs and eventually was elected the city's mayor. Presumably, no one ever called him "Charlie" again.

BACKGROUND

Charlie Farrell, who is hypnotically attractive to a surprising number of women, is a retired silent-film star. He is also owner/manager of the Palm Springs Racquet Club and Vacation Resort, home away from home for the athletic and the affluent. Charlie, more of a tennis ace than a management ace, has all sorts of problems with his staff, including his assistant manager, his chef, and his housekeeper. On the home front, he is constantly at odds with his bumbling father and his sniveling nephew. He also finds time for love off the court, in the guise of a rich matron named Doris Mayfield.

MAIN CAST

- **Charlie Farrell** (Charles Farrell): Ingenuous rich person and friend of rich people.
- **Dad Farrell** (Charles Winninger): His father.
- **Sherman Hull** (Richard Deacon): The resort's assistant manager, a humorless, pedantic snob.
- **Mrs. Papernow** (Kathryn Card): The housekeeper, with something nasty to say about everyone.
- **Pierre** (Leon Askin): The French chef.
- **Rodney** (Jeff Silver): Charlie's perennially broke nephew.
- **Doris Mayfield** (Anna Lee): Charlie's girlfriend.

FLASHBACK

[*Three beautiful models spot Charlie at the Racquet Club, where they're participating in a fashion show.*]

MODEL 1: "Oh, look! It's Charlie Farrell!"
MODEL 2: "How nice to meet you! I've heard so much about you."
MODEL 3: "May I have your autograph?"
CHARLIE: "Oh, my goodness. Don certainly knows how to pick pretty models. You're a wonderful addition to Palm Springs. [Gazing appreciatively] Lovely, *lovely*.
MODEL 1: "Oh, this is so exciting, meeting a great movie star."
CHARLIE: "Oh ...[laughs self-deprecatingly]...I've just been lucky. I hope you won't let my fame interfere with our...friendship."

Richard Deacon, best known as Mel Cooley in "The Dick Van Dyke Show," played another prissy manager here. He was the practical assistant who ran around bothering Farrell with details about running the club.

CRITICS' COMMENTS

"It was the kind of show you watched because it was on the air, because it was opposite Gorgeous George doing wrestling—although Gorgeous George was a lot funnier than Charlie Farrell."

—Bill Musselwhite, *Calgary Herald*

"It was desperately unfunny but not as wildly stupid and amphetamine-driven as [his other show] 'My Little Margie.'"

—Tom Shales, *Washington Post*

"The problem was that there was really no compelling reason to like this character—which is important, obviously, if you're going to be a lead character in a series."

—R. K. Shull, *Indianapolis News*

"The guy was playing off the fact that he was supposed to be rich, charming, attractive, etc. But he wasn't. He came off as pompous, in a goofy way, and as a guy so full of himself that you could barely stand to be in the same room with him, let alone watch him on TV for a half hour. Honestly, I think someone must have owed him a favor."

—Jack Mingo,
The Official Couch Potato Handbook

Charlie Farrell's most famous (or infamous) TV role was as Vern Albright on "My Little Margie." Here he's posing with his co-stars from the show—in Palm Springs, where he was the perennial mayor.

50s

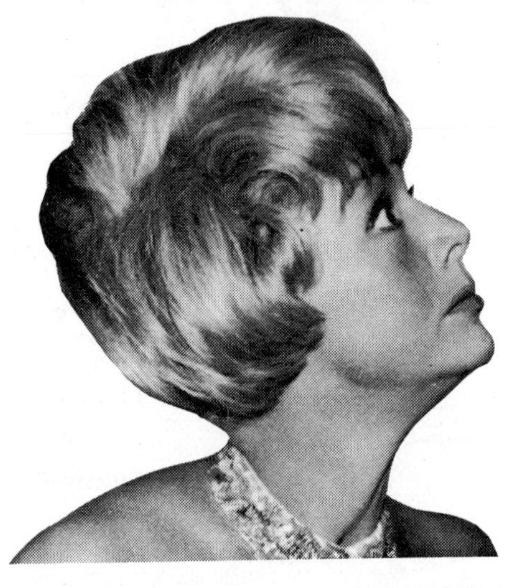

Betty Hutton wasn't able to transfer her movie popularity to television.

THE EGG AND I (1951-52)

Old MacDonald had a farm—a chicken farm—and she turned it into a sitcom. Don't ask how. Bob and Betty MacDonald's real-life misadventures on their broken-down chicken farm were the basis for this short-lived CBS series.

THE DUKE (1954)

So here's whut happinz in dis show. A boxer name 'a Duke London loins how ta paint when he ain't fightin', see? An' den he meets up wid a highbrow-type Harvard guy name'a Rudy, who likes his woik an' wants tuh help 'im loin stuff about da finah t'ings in life. See? But w'uncha know it, da bum's trainuh and manageuh keep tryin' to trick him into goin' back to da ring. Dat's pretty funny awready, huh? An' ya know sumpin' else? He's got a real dish, a blonde society chick name' a Gloria, hangin' on his arm mosta da time. Whutta guy! Whutta show! Too bad it only wuz on TV fuh two months. I bet th' Duke didn't loin much in only two months, huh?

THE GREAT GILDERSLEEVE (1955-56)

The misadventures of a lovable water commissioner and his two nieces? Hmmm. Would you believe a rusty pipe and two faucets? How about a drip and two bubbles? This was popular on radio, but really, what was the chance of it surviving more than fifteen minutes on the tube?

LOVE AND MARRIAGE (1959-60)

Rock and roll is here to stay. But a crochety old-time music publisher refuses to publish any rock music, so he's going broke. Meanwhile, his daughter is trying to save the business by signing up some "hep" composers. And for some reason, Stubby Kaye sits around singing and talking about "the good old days in the music-publishing business." This is definitely one of the lamest ideas for a sitcom in the entire decade. Presumably, the target audience was old codgers who wanted to pretend rock and roll didn't exist. Great marketing concept. After only three months, it was this show that didn't exist.

DICK AND THE DUCHESS (1957-58)

A humorous peek at the wacky world of insurance. Dick Starrett, an insurance claims investigator, is stationed in London. He meets a beautiful gal who turns out to be...a duchess! Wow—English royalty, an American's dream. Her snooty family thinks ol' Dick isn't good enough for her, but the Duchess is pretty down-to-earth; she marries him. Well, as you can imagine, the common American has a *really* rough time with his aristocratic in-laws. And the wacky, well-intentioned bride insists on getting involved in Dick's investigations, which she invariably screws up. Sounds like a real gut buster.

THE BETTY HUTTON SHOW (1959-60)

A manicurist's rich customer dies and leaves her $60 million— plus his kids. And all she's been doing is his nails, honest. The rest of the show deals with the "humorous situations" that arise when a low-class broad tries to fit into upper-crust society.

THE SITCOM ZOO

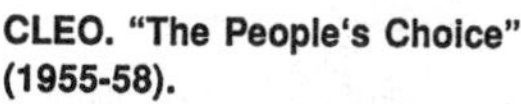

ARNOLD. "Green Acres" (1965-71).
Arnold Ziffel might be the weirdest sitcom character in the history of television. Nobody in Hooterville (except Oliver Wendell Douglas) seemed to notice that he was a pig. His "parents," pig farmers Fred and Doris Ziffel, regarded him as their son; the school board thought it was perfectly normal that he should attend school with the "other kids." Arnold became so popular that Arnold fan clubs sprang up in colleges all over America, and his costars complained that he was getting all the attention. "I'm not Eddie Albert," said one. "I'm that fellow on television with the pig."

MR. ED. "Mr. Ed" (1960-1965).
TV's first real-life talking animal; a sarcastic palomino whose opinion of the human race was so low that he thought architect Wilbur Post, his owner and "buddy-boy," was a fascinating specimen.

Ed didn't talk to anyone except Wilbur. And when he did talk, he was snide ("Time and Ed wait for no man"); he was opinionated ("If that filly doesn't come to me of her own free will, then I say bring her in on a rope!"); he was cynical (to Wilbur: "You hold still and I'll sit on your back"). In other words, he was a perfect modern conversationalist.

He was also a classic animal folk hero, reminiscent of Uncle Remus's wisecracking Br'er Rabbit. His character is much better than the show he appeared on and will live on in American lore long after people stop watching "Mr. Ed" reruns.

CLEO. "The People's Choice" (1955-58).
In the history of TV, Cleo is the undisputed queen of canine wisecracks. In critical moments, Cleo the basset hound would turn to the audience and comment on the action by "thinking out loud." She didn't move her mouth, as Mr. Ed did, but she was just as sarcastic.

THE "CRITTERS." "The Beverly Hillbillies" (1962-71).
Elly May had a way with animals. So she brought home a few dozen pets. In addition to the family bloodhound, Duke, some of them were: Fairchild the bear, Homer the pigeon, Smelly the skunk, Earl the rooster, Skippy the dog, Rusty the swimming cat, and a hippopotamus that Granny called "the biggest hog I've ever seen."

TRAMP, the family dog in "My Three Sons."

BEST FRIENDS

DOBIE GILLIS (Dwayne Hickman) and MAYNARD G. KREBS (Bob Denver), "Dobie Gillis" (1959-63)
"You rang, good buddy?" An ambitious teenager, who loves girls more than anything, and his backward beatnik buddy, who probably hasn't figured out the difference between the sexes yet. Maynard is the most loyal friend in TV history, outclassed only by Lassie and Rin Tin Tin.

SGT. MORGAN O'ROURKE (Forrest Tucker) and CPL. RUDOLPH AGARN (Larry Storch), "F Troop" (1965-67).
The Sgt. Bilko of the U.S. Cavalry, Sgt. Morgan O'Rourke, is busy negotiating souvenir concessions with the Indians while Cpl. Agarn runs around Fort Courage making sure their schemes are unfolding as planned. They never are, but what the hell.

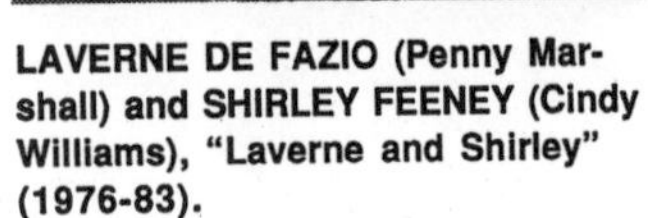

LAVERNE DE FAZIO (Penny Marshall) and SHIRLEY FEENEY (Cindy Williams), "Laverne and Shirley" (1976-83).
Best friends, blue collar roommates in a Milwaukee basement apartment. Laverne is brassy, cynical, militantly defensive. Shirley is sickeningly romantic, naive, gullible—a dreamer.

RICHIE CUNNINGHAM (Ron Howard) and ARTHUR FONZARELLI (Henry Winkler), "Happy Days" (1974-84).
"Ayyyhh." "The Fonz" is perhaps the coolest character ever to emerge from a sitcom. He's a superman in a black leather jacket, sensitive, strong, a stud. Richie is a "gee whiz" straight-arrow suburban kid, an earnest piece of white bread dying for a piece of the action. The Fonz saves Richie, Richie redeems Fonzie.

KATE McARDLE (Susan St. James) and ALLIE LOWELL (Jane Curtin), "Kate and Allie" (1984-currently in production). Two divorcees, high school chums, move in together to save cash. TV's best portrayal of female friendship.

Best of the '60s

Historically, the '60s were divided into two distinctly different periods by the Kennedy assassination.

In attitudes and taste, the first four years resembled the Eisenhower era. There was little of the experimental frenzy we associate with the decade. Family life was stable; there was no question that men were breadwinners and women homemakers.

In that atmosphere, traditional domestic comedies continued to flourish. The two best sitcoms of the period, "Dick Van Dyke" (1961) and "Andy Griffith" (1960) represented the next developmental stage in the genre. Home life was essential in each, but a good part of the action took place elsewhere as well. They were ensemble comedies (although few people would have called them that at the time) with plots built around characters, not wacky antics. And the players were imbued with a sense of individuality—in contrast to shows of the '50s, when they were happy conformists.

Networks still didn't allow controversial stories onto the air in the early '60s, but these two programs did represent opposite sides of the social/political spectrum. "Andy Griffith" glorified country life, traditional values, and the South. "Dick Van Dyke" celebrated the modern urban (or suburban) lifestyle of young northerners. This dichotomy would continue to surface in sitcoms throughout the decade.

Both "Van Dyke" and "Griffith" survived the cataclysm of Kennedy's assassination. But in general, the family sitcom did not. In the national nuclear family, the president was the father figure. And he was dead. "Father Knows Best" couldn't provide a sense of security anymore—it was a reminder that the real world was full of sadness and insecurity. We looked to television for something to *relieve* the pain, so sitcoms took a detour from relevance and became escapist suburban fantasies featuring witches and ghouls and genies in bottles.

The other three sitcoms selected as the '60s' best fall into this category. Two debuted a year after the assassination, the other a year later. All owe their success to the fact that they were better written, better acted, and for the most part, better executed fantasies than their peers. So now, as "The Addams Family"'s Lurch would say, "Fol-l-l-o-o-o-o-ow mee-e-e-e-e...."

THE DICK VAN DYKE SHOW

As "I Love Lucy" defined the sitcom for the '50s, "The Dick Van Dyke Show" defined it for the post-Eisenhower era. Rob and Laura Petrie were TV's first modern couple; they were vanguards of the New Frontier—intelligent, liberal, upwardly mobile, with their feet planted firmly in the future.

Of course, the program was still a family sitcom, with all the traditional trappings of the genre. There was the house in the suburbs, the nice-looking wife, the adorable kid, the goofy neighbors.

But "Dick Van Dyke" gave these symbols a new meaning. Rob's home in New Rochelle wasn't his castle—it was just a nice place to live. Richie Petrie was neither precious nor precocious, and he wasn't merely an excuse for Rob to dispense fatherly wisdom. In fact, he frequently pinned his old man down with embarrassing questions. "Daddy," he once insisted, "where did I come from?" Rob hemmed and hawed, but finally confronted the issue. "New York," he said.

And Laura was *not* the "little woman." She was Rob's partner, half of the most equal male-female relationship that sitcoms had ever seen. Although she was still a housewife (the show wasn't *that* radical), she was hip and witty. And sexy.

There was another entirely new element in "The Dick Van Dyke Show," too. Unlike the vague sources of income hinted at in '50s sitcoms, Rob actually supported his family with a job that was as important to him (and the plot) as his domestic life. It was a creative, interesting, *modern* (there's that word again) one, too. Rob Petrie worked in the television industry, as head writer for "The Alan Brady Show."

And when he went to work, we went along with him. We watched him and his co-workers plot comedy sketches, act goofy, even occasionally worry about getting fired. ("Alan won't fire me," Rob told Buddy once after a major screw-up. "It'll look bad in the papers." "Yeah," Buddy replied, "It looks bad to fire a guy the same day you kill him.")

All this gave Rob's world more dimension than any sitcom character's had ever had. It also gave the show's writers the best opportunity to create realistic situations and characters that *they'd* ever had. And they took advantage of it.

The result: With "Dick Van Dyke," for the first time a sitcom's humor was based on behavior, not antics. And the situations were funny because...well...*life* is funny. Episodes were based on Rob's sudden paranoia that he and Laura brought the wrong baby home from the hospital, on Laura accidentally dropping a hideous brooch given to her by her in-laws down the garbage disposal, on Richie's curiosity about his middle name. The plots were familiar, they were plausible, and they were hilarious.

The talent on this show was awesome—from Rob Reiner, who created it, to Jerry Paris, the next-door neighbor who became one of TV's most successful producers. But it never felt overwhelming. It felt as though any member of the cast was exactly the kind of person you'd like to invite over to your house to share a few laughs and then sit down and watch your favorite TV program—"The Dick Van Dyke Show."

When the series began, Mary Tyler Moore confided to producer Sheldon Leonard that she hoped the show would last long enough so she could "buy herself a new set of drapes."

FLASHBACK

[*Sally introduces her boyfriend to Laura*]
SALLY: "Laura, I don't think you've ever met Herman Glimcher."
LAURA: "No, but I've heard you speak of him."
SALLY: "Well, forget what I told you. This is what he really looks like."

MEL: "You can't be replaced."
BUDDY: "Why?"
MEL: "Because I don't know what you are."

[*Laura refuses to go to a party because Richie is sick, she says*]
ROB: "Is he in pain?"
LAURA: "Well, no...."
ROB: Then how do you know that he's sick?"
LAURA: "There are symptoms...."
ROB: "What symptoms?"
LAURA: "Well..."
ROB: "Come on, tell me, I'm the boy's father."
LAURA: "He turned down his cupcake!"

VITAL STATS

POLL RESULTS:
First
PROGRAM INFO:
- Half-hour show. CBS
- First show: Oct. 3, 1961
- Last show: Sept. 7, 1966
- 158 episodes

TIME: The early '60s.

PLACE: At home: 448 Bonnie Meadow Road in New Rochelle, New York. At work: Manhattan, in the offices of "The Alan Brady Show."

BACKGROUND: Rob Petrie met Laura Meehan at Camp Crowder in Joplin, Missouri. She was a USO dancer; he was an army sergeant. He accidentally broke her foot on their first date, but that didn't prevent them from falling in love and getting married. They moved to Ohio where they struggled to make ends meet, until finally Rob was hired to head the writing staff of TV's "Alan Brady Show." Despite initial hostility from co-workers Sally Rogers and Buddy Sorrell, who resented him being hired above them, they became a bright, creative team and close personal friends. Rob commutes every day from New Rochelle.

MAIN CAST:
- **Rob Petrie** (Dick Van Dyke): A former disc jockey. Clever, funny television writer.
- **Laura Petrie** (Mary Tyler Moore): Impulsive, slightly daffy, slightly insecure suburban housewife.
- **Richie Rosebud Petrie** (Larry Mazzeo): A normal kid, nice but not exceptional.
- **Buddy Sorrell** (Morey Amsterdam): Rob's fellow writer, a diminutive wisecracker. Endlessly spins yarns about his wife, Pickles, and harrasses the show's pedantic producer, Mel Cooley.
- **Sally Rogers** (Rose Marie): Rob's other co-worker. Although a successful career woman, she 's desperate for a husband. Many plots revolve around bittersweet romances with men like Herman Glimcher and Ric Vallone. In one episode, as a gag, she advertises for a mate on TV.

Listening for spooks in "The Ghost of A. Chantz."

- **Mel Cooley** (Richard Deacon): "Yech!" The humorless producer of "The Alan Brady Show." Alan's brother-in-law.
- **Dr. Jerry Helper** (Jerry Paris): The Petries' brash neighbor and friend. A successful dentist.
- **Millie Helper** (Ann Morgan Guilbert): His ditzy wife, Laura's best friend.
- **Alan Brady** (Carl Reiner): The egomaniacal star of "The Alan Brady Show."

Morey Amsterdam

ACTING LESSONS

Dick Van Dyke credits producer Sheldon Leonard with giving him his "first and only acting lesson." "Dick," Leonard told him early in the show's run, "you're talking in a monotone. Make your voice go up and down more." "I did," says Van Dyke, "and have never had any trouble since."

S.O.S.

During rehearsals, the cast of comics came up with such good lines on their own that an "SOS File" was created. If the lines couldn't be fit into one episode, they were saved for "some other show."

SAY IT AIN'T SO

Comedy writer Alan Zweibel was a devoted fan of "The Dick Van Dyke Show." So he was thrilled when, one day, he found himself sharing an elevator with Van Dyke. Eagerly, he told Van Dyke how he had patterned his life after Rob Petrie's: He had become a writer for a TV variety show ("Saturday Night Live"), he had married a beautiful brunette, and he'd bought a home in New Rochelle. Van Dyke gently told Zweibel, "But my show was canceled after five years, and I became an alcoholic." According to *Saturday Night Live: A Backstage History*, Zweibel was so shattered by the truth that he began screaming, "No, no, no!" and banged his head against the elevator while Van Dyke tried to comfort him.

MISCELLANY

•The search for an actor to play Rob Petrie ended with a choice between two relative unknowns—Van Dyke and a TV game-show host named Johnny Carson.
•"The Dick Van Dyke Show"'s connection to JFK and the New Frontier was more than figurative. Kennedy's father financed the program's original pilot.
•Rob's home at 448 Bonnie Meadow Road was extremely close to Carl Reiner's actual address. Reiner just eliminated a digit.
•Jerry Paris, who played neighbor Jerry Helper, was so captivated by the planet Twylo in the classic "Van Dyke" episode "It May Look Like a Nut" that he was inspired to help create an alien named Mork and a show called "Mork and Mindy" over a decade later.

THE BRADY BUNCH

Carl Reiner's Alan Brady didn't emerge as a bona fide character until the third season. Before that, viewers saw the back of his head, saw him wrapped in a barber-shop towel, or, on a Christmas show, in a concealing Santa Claus suit. But Reiner frequently popped up as a guest star. Most memorably, he was the goofy painter Serge Carpetna in "October Eve" and society snob Yale Simpson in "I'm No Henry Walden."

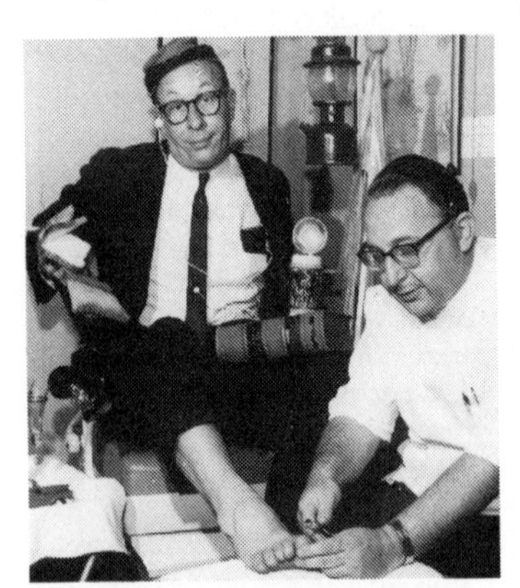

Richard Deacon was irritated by Morey Amsterdam's constant ribbing, even though he knew it wasn't personal. One day he mentioned to Carl Reiner that he ought to have a comeback to Buddy. Reiner asked, "Well, what would you say?" and Deacon went, "Yeccchhh." So that became Mel's standard reply.

CRITICS' COMMENTS

ABOUT THE OPENING:
"For many years, in the opening of the show, Van Dyke tripped over the ottoman as he came into the house. And then at some point the writers changed the bit so he'd dance around it. That showed the awareness of the show, the way they kept it fresh. They didn't keep doing the same thing over and over again. They put a little twist on it to keep it interesting."

—John Keisewetter,
Cincinnati Enquirer

ABOUT ITS STYLE:
"The hallmark of 'The Dick Van Dyke Show' is its timelessness. Part of that is the quality of its dialogue and situations. But a bigger part comes from the fact that Carl Reiner specifically directed the show's writers not to use colloquialisms of the time or to refer to topical issues in the script. He knew that people would be watching the show in the future, and he didn't want to date it. Today, for example, a lot of sitcoms make references to Vanna White. But twenty years from now, what is a joke about Vanna White going to mean to someone? Next time you watch a 'Dick Van Dyke' rerun, look for it. It's quite interesting. You'll see that they never, ever refer to a particular time."

—Ginny Weisman,
The Dick Van Dyke Show Book

ABOUT THE CHARACTERS:
"Laura was more of a whole human being than Margaret Anderson or June Cleaver. She wasn't just there to react, to support her husband. She had her problems, and they were dealt with in the context of the show."

—Michael Hill,
Baltimore Evening Sun

"Earlier sitcoms had all been set in the home, and often they had focused on an ineffectual father. In 'Dick Van Dyke,' we had a competent father who worked for an ineffectual boss. So the concept of the ineffectual authority figure was moved out of the living room and into the office."

—Michael Dougan,
San Francisco Examiner

"I wanted to establish [Laura] as a woman who had her own point of view and who would fight with her husband—a good fight, if necessary. She wasn't a 'yes' wife, nor did she focus everything on him. But that's about as liberated as Laura Petrie was. I think she truly believed that her only choice was to be a wife and mother and couldn't combine that with a career."

—Mary Tyler Moore

"'The Dick Van Dyke Show' was the happiest five years of my life."

—Rose Marie

Rose Marie and Vic Damone, a.k.a. Ric Vallone.

THE ANDY GRIFFITH SHOW

The TV industry called them "rural sitcoms," but shows like "The Beverly Hillbillies" and "Petticoat Junction"—TV staples in the '60s— weren't really about country living. They were about one-dimensional rural stereotypes: the sexy innocent in tight jeans; the dumb, uneducated bruiser; the lazy con man; the struggling widow.

"The Andy Griffith Show," on the other hand, is the genuine article. It's a picture postcard of a small southern Main Street, a slice of steaming apple pie, a little bit of Brett Harte come to life.

It is TV's nostalgic salute to a part of America that has disappeared into the space age—the simple, unhurried life of a rural community where everyone belongs and where a little common sense is all you need to get through life.

Widower Andy Taylor, sheriff of Mayberry, is an even-tempered, practical man who lives with his son, Opie, and his Aunt Bee, in a home so cozy you can smell the baked beans bubbling for Sunday dinner. His job isn't very exciting; the biggest crimes in town generally consist of Otis the drunk's periodic binges—after which he obligingly locks himself into one of Mayberry's two "maximum-security" cells.

But Andy is more than a sheriff. He's the town's emotional center. He's the voice of sanity in a sea of small-town eccentricities. As critic Michael Dougan said, "He's a bright humanist with a badge who enforces the law by bringing out the best in everybody."

And that's not too easy, considering some of the zany characters roaming around the streets of Mayberry. There are Goober and Gomer, the dimwitted Pyles; county agent Howard Sprague, the mama's boy with the swinging bachelor pad; dingy Floyd, the barber ("Oh, what *did* Calvin Coolidge say, anyway?"); Emmet, the handyman. And so on. They're all pretty weird, but the show never laughs at them. It has respect for their childish innocence and the fact that they're not trying to impress anyone. All except Deputy Barney Fife, that is. Barney, Andy's cousin, eventually decides to hit the big time and moves to Raleigh. But until then,

Andy and Opie at the "fishin' hole."

he virtually carries the show on his bony shoulders.

Barney is basically an idiot, really believing his job as peacekeeper in crime-free Mayberry is meaningful. He calls his gun his "baby," but he doesn't have any bullets in it (though he is allowed to keep one in his shirt pocket). He makes posturing references to his sophistication ("I sent my compliments to the chef. They appreciate them things"), but he spends his vacations in the YMCA in Charlotte. Invariably, he gets himself into trouble (like his legendary habit of locking himself in the jail cells), and the benevolent sheriff always has to bail him out.

But everybody in Mayberry loves him, and so do we. He's a nice guy who has no idea of what he's up against in the real world, and you kinda hate to see him get hurt. So when the church choir tries to drown out his off-key singing rather than hurt his feelings, we too are drawn into the conspiracy.

Andy does what he can to keep Barney going. But his strongest relationship is with Opie, his "young'un." Andy is tender and wise with Opie and tries to pass on the awareness of life that makes him a unique and admirable character.

The plots aren't much; nothing ever seems to happen in the country. Ernest T. might wander in from the mountains; or Aunt Bee might find a new recipe; ol' Barn and Andy might sit on the porch and discuss the weather. But that's exactly right for this show. Before the world went crazy, we used to take our time and enjoy the little things in life. And that's what "Andy Griffith" is all about.

"Shazam!" Gomer Pyle was perhaps the most successful spinoff character in the '60s. His show was in the top ten every year it aired.

FLASHBACK

BARNEY [*discussing youthful vandals*]: "Well, just don't mollycoddle them."
ANDY: "I won't."
BARNEY: "Nip it in the bud! You go read any book you want on the subject of child discipline, and you'll find every one of them is in favor of bud-nipping."
ANDY: "I'll take care of it."
BARNEY: "There's only one way to take care of it."
ANDY: "Nip it..."
BARNEY: "In the bud."

[*Opie shoots a bird with a slingshot, and Andy confronts him about it.*]

ANDY: "I'm not going to give you a whipping. [opens a window] Do you hear that? That's them young birds chirping for their mama that's not coming back. You just listen to that awhile."

VITAL STATS

POLL RESULTS:
Second
PROGRAM INFO:
- Half-hour show. CBS
- First show: Oct. 3, 1960
- Last show: Sept. 16, 1968
- 249 episodes

TIME: The early '60s.

PLACE: Mayberry, North Carolina.

BACKGROUND: Mayberry is a typical small southern town, where the same families have lived for generations and change is imperceptible. Says Sheriff Andy Taylor: "There's not much to tell. It's just a little town. We hang around, get up in the morning and go to work and come home. For entertainment, we have television and movies, and we take rides in the car out of town on Sunday. We have our local baseball team, and we fish, and we have creeks we swim in. Evenings we sit around on the porch and visit, watch the children playing under the streetlights."

MAIN CAST:
- **Andy Taylor** (Andy Griffith): A widower, father of one son. Sheriff of Mayberry for at least a dozen years, known locally as "the sheriff without a gun" because he doesn't believe in earning respect with a weapon. World War II veteran (briefly stationed in France). A gifted storyteller. Lives by the Golden Rule. Favorite foods: leg of lamb, fried chicken with a crust, pumpkin pie a la mode.
- **Opie Taylor** (Ronny Howard): Andy's "young'un," curious and sensitive. Close to his dad and proud of his father's position in Mayberry.
- **Barney Fife** (Don Knotts): Andy's cousin, Opie's godfather. The wiry, excitable deputy. Constantly in hot water due to a persistent illusion that he's an ingenious urban crimefighter. Likes to knit and crochet.
- **Beatrice "Aunt Bee" Taylor** (Frances Bavier): Andy's buxom, motherly aunt. She raised Andy and moved into the Taylor home in 1959 when their housekeeper left. Serious and oversensitive. Makes the best pies in Mayberry. Her specialty: strawberry ice cream.
- **Gomer Pyle** (Jim Nabors): The dim-witted gas station attendant.
- **Goober Pyle** (George Lindsey): Gomer's beanie-clad cousin.
- **Floyd Lawson** (Howard McNear): The distracted town barber.
- **Howard Sprague** (Jack Dodson): The town clerk.
- **Helen Crump** (Anita Corsaut): Town schoolteacher, Andy's longtime girlfriend, and the future Mrs. Andy Taylor.

Gomer's cousin, Goober.

INSIDE BARNEY

Don Knotts described his interpretation of Barney Fife this way: "I thought of Barney as a childlike man who was funny mainly because he was never able to hide anything in his face. If he was sad, he really looked sad. If he was angry, he acted angry. Children do that—pout, get overjoyed, or whatever. Barney never hid anything. He wasn't able to. In my mind that was really the key to Barney's character."

According to Richard Kelly in his book, *The Andy Griffith Show*, producer Aaron Ruben believed that "there was a great deal of Don Knotts in Barney Fife." When someone told Knotts about it, Don's "eyes grew round and he exclaimed, 'Gee, I hope not *too* much!'"

OPIE DOKEY

•The cast is practically unanimous in describing Ronny Howard as a pleasant, professional coworker, even at age six. People went out of their way to make things easier for him; they let him bring his roller skates onto the set and always kept ice cream in the refrigerator for him.

MISCELLANY

•George Lindsey originally wanted the part of Gomer Pyle and thought he had it sewed up—until Jim Nabors showed up to audition. When Nabors left, Lindsey was called back and offered the chance to replace Nabors as Goober.

•Originally, the town of Mayberry had no specific location. But Griffith felt it was important for the audience to know where it was—so they placed it in North Carolina, Griffith's home state. In fact, Mayberry is loosely based on Griffith's hometown, Mount Airy, North Carolina.

HAIR TODAY

•Howard McNear, who played Floyd, the barber, had a stroke in 1963. He was paralyzed on his left side and had to retire from the show. But after almost two years without him, the "Griffith" crew called to see if he could return. "It would be a godsend," said his wife. So he was written back into the show. For the next two years, Floyd made appearances on the program, usually sitting down, and never walking. He also could only use one hand. When he stood behind the barber chair, he was supported by a structure specially built for the scenes. He died in 1967.

The country bumpkins—Deputy Barney Fife, the avenging angel of Mayberry, North Carolina, and Gomer Pyle, a country boy so dumb he could barely figure out how to pump gas.

CRITICS' COMMENTS

A quiet night at home in Mayberry with Aunt Bee's scrumptious cookin' and the Taylor family's favorite television show.

ABOUT ITS APPEAL

"Not too many people found it hilariously funny....It's more of a warm show—maybe the first 'warm-edy'— just a pleasant half hour to watch. I didn't roll over laughing over 'Andy Griffith,' but I always felt good after watching an episode of it. It's a kind of small-town America that will never find its way back into prime time, but you can tell from the ratings of the 'Return to Mayberry' TV movie that people still feel affection for that place."

—Ed Bark,
Dallas Morning News

"I grew up in North Carolina, and was proud that the show captured the basic integrity of the people of the state....I think it's great to have a law enforcement official like Andy on TV, someone who can be a role model—someone who kept his word, someone you could count on. We see that too rarely on TV."

—Dennis Washburn,
Birmingham News

"One of the attractions was that Andy was so nice all the time. So understanding. And he could solve problems without being too intrusive. He controlled everything but never imposed himself on a situation. He never made the characters *feel* that he was controlling everything. His relationship with Mayberry was like a fantasy of what a perfect father should be."

—Doulgas Durden,
Richmond Times Dispatch

ABOUT THE CHARACTERS:

"Griffith was a man who was less concerned with the law per se than he was with keeping the gears greased and his community running smoothly. He was a rural sheriff without being a cowboy. Barney Fife, on the other hand, was a man with a dramatic overview of life. Incidents that Griffith would see in proper perspective became an inspiration for adventure to Barney. He kept praying for a major crime, and Mayberry just never had any. Barney was a comical Chester, to Griffith's Dillon."

—Michael Dougan,
San Francisco Examiner

"Don Knotts was a physically funny guy to look at. He was just the opposite of Jackie Gleason but had many of the same qualities—good timing and the ability to bring a laugh out of material that wouldn't seem funny on the page. I guess people identified with him as a little guy, although he kind of walked a fine line between being a pathetic figure and being an endearing figure. I felt both ways about him."

—Jack Mingo,
The Official Couch Potato Handbook

Don Knotts, Andy Griffith, and Jim Nabors on the set of their hit TV series in 1965.

GET SMART

In 1963, the unsolved mystery of John Kennedy's assassination focused the public's attention on the netherworld of politics—the intrigue behind the headlines. Spies. Hired assassins. Secret organizations. We knew they were there, and we wanted them on our side—if not in real life, at least in the movies.

So James Bond, Our Man Flint, Matt Helm, and Napoleon Solo became America's favorite fantasies. Three consecutive Bond films hit number one at the box office; and when "The Man from UNCLE" entered TV's top ten in 1964, television producer Dan Melnick decided the subject was ripe for a spoof.

Interestingly enough, no parody had *ever* succeeded on television. But Melnick proposed it to Mel Brooks and Buck Henry anyway, and they agreed to give it a shot.

"I wanted to do a crazy, unreal, comic-strip kind of thing about something besides a family," Brooks explains. "No one had ever done a show about an idiot before. I wanted to be the first."

The result: Maxwell Smart, Agent 86, TV's first sitcom spy. Sitcoms have had dumb leading characters before (some even intentional), but as his partner/lady love, Agent 99, would gasp, "There's no one like you, Max."

Smart was the top agent for CONTROL, a sort of mom-and-pop super spy network fighting to save the free world from KAOS ("that international organization of evil"). Unfortunately, CONTROL didn't have much to work with. Its state-of-the-art equipment included devices like the Cone of Silence, a clear, soundproof dome that covered people's heads like a cheap plastic umbrella. It was supposed to prevent the enemy from eavesdropping on secret meetings but was so impervious to sound that people *under* it couldn't hear, either.

When Max was on assignment, he kept in touch with his superiors via a shoe phone ("Hi, Chief, this is Max!" "Max? Where are you?"). In addition to being inconvenient to use, it also rang at inappropriate times—when Max was undercover at the opera, for example. And the calls frequently turned out to be wrong numbers. ("Sorry, I can't talk right now. I'm being shot at.")

But the free world survived, because the villains from KAOS were just as stupid as Max was. God forbid that he might have encountered Dr. No or a member of UNCLE's enemy, THRUSH. Max could barely handle Mr. Big, the evil dwarf; Harry Hoo, the Oriental detective-turned-murderer ("Who done it?" "Not who, Hoo!"); or the Claw, an Oriental bad guy with a magnetized prosthesis. (The Claw: "Do you know what they call me?" Max: "Er...Lefty?")

On the good guys' side, "Get Smart" had wonderful characters like Hymie the robot, who took every command literally (i.e., "Kill the lights"). And Charlie Watkins, the male agent disguised as a beautiful woman (played by a starlet with a dubbed male voice). Or Agent 13, who hid in things like cello cases, grandfather clocks, and mailboxes.

And there are those great lines, still imitated today as though they came from last week's "Saturday Night Live": "Sorry about that, Chief." "Missed me by that much." "That"s the second biggest _____ I ever saw." And of course, the inevitable, "Would you believe..."

"Get Smart" probably wouldn't work today; the spy fad has long since faded. But it's a great example of striking while the cigarette-lighter-that's-really-a-gun is hot. It remains an affectionate icon of an American fad, which we can still enjoy because it's still genuinely amusing.

Besides his work on "Get Smart" as the chief, Edward Platt's best-known role was in the film *Rebel Without a Cause*. He played the cop who befriended James Dean.

FLASHBACK

[*Max is trapped by Rex Savage, an agent for KAOS who's been blowing up government buildings.*]

MAX: "You'll never get away with this, Savage."
SAVAGE: "Oh? Why not, Mr. Smart?"
MAX: "Because at this very moment, twenty-five CONTROL agents are converging on this building. Would you believe it? Twenty-five CONTROL agents."
SAVAGE: I find that hard to believe."
MAX: "Would you believe two squad cars and a motorcycle cop?"
SAVAGE: "I don"t think so."
MAX: "How about a vicious street-cleaner and a toothless police dog?"

MAX: "If only he had used his genius for niceness."

MAX: "It's the old bulletproof cummerbund-in-the-tuxedo trick."

VITAL STATS

POLL RESULTS:
Third
PROGRAM INFO:
- Half-hour show. NBC/CBS
- First show: Sept. 18, 1965
- Last show: Sept. 11, 1970
- 138 episodes

TIME: The mid '60s.

PLACE: The headquarters of CONTROL, a supersecret spy organization located at 123 Main Street, Washington, D.C. It is ten stories below street level, but agents can gain access by entering a phone booth, dialing the correct phone number, and then plummeting through the floor. Action also takes place at Max's residence, in apartment #86.

BACKGROUND: Most people don't realize it, but a desperate struggle is taking place at this very moment—a struggle between the forces of good (CONTROL) and evil (KAOS). The weapons they're using include the electro-retrogressor gun, which temporarily turns adults into eight-year-olds; Dante's inthermo, a heat ray that melts everything it hits; Dr. Haskell's invisible-ray gun; and absorbo pills, which soak up forty times their weight in alcohol and prevent people from getting drunk. On the good guys' side, there's Maxwell Smart and Agent 99. On the bad guys' side, there's an endless parade of clever crackpots that includes Rembrandt von Bronzefinger; Melnik, "the smiling killer"; Octavia the seductive robot; and Harvey Satan. So far, it's a draw.

Would you believe...Max on disc?

MAIN CAST:
- **Maxwell Smart** (Don Adams): Inexplicably, CONTROL's top agent. Inept but enthusiastic. He poses as a salesman for the Pontiac Greeting Card Company. Manages to defeat his enemies without even knowing who they are.
- **Agent 99** (Barbara Feldon): Max's partner and future wife. Poses as his secretary. Did she have a real name? In one episode she was called "Susan Hilton," but that was later revealed to be a cover name. The truth: according to the show's writers, she was never named.
- **The Chief** (Edward Platt): Max's long-suffering boss. His real name is Thaddeus, but he uses the cover name "Howard Clark."
- **Hymie the robot** (Dick Gautier): CONTROL's robot. Loyal to Max because Max saved his "life." Superstrong, superintelligent—but incredibly dense. Takes all commands literally.
- **Conrad Siegfried** (Bernie Koppell): The top KAOS agent.
- **Starker** (King Moody): His assistant.
- **Agent 13** (Dave Ketchum): The spy who showed up everywhere.
- **Larrabee** (Robert Karvelas): An agent even dumber than Max.

Hymie and friends.

MISCELLANEOUS MEL

- Mel Brooks was cocreator of "Get Smart." Today he's world famous as an actor/director. But back then, he was still fairly obscure. How obscure? An article about his wife, actress Anne Bancroft, referred to him as Mel *Blanc*.
- "Get Smart" was Brooks's first TV show. What inspired him to give it a shot? "I was sick of looking at all those sensible situation comedies....If a maid like Hazel ever took over my house, I'd set her hair on fire."
- Ten years later, Brooks created another satire, called "When Things Were Rotten." Its star was Dick Gautier, who had played Hymie in "Get Smart."

PILOT TO BRIDGE

The original "Get Smart" pilot was commissioned by ABC. However, when they read the script they withdrew from the project.

Why?

Because it was about a plot to blow up the Statue of Liberty, and ABC execs considered that sort of story "UnAmerican."

So the other networks got a crack at it. NBC thought it was funny; they bought the script, the pilot, and the series.

The result: The pilot was nominated for an Emmy award; the subsequent series was the most successful new program of the 1965-66, and NBC's second most popular show overall.

ABC came in last in the Nielsens that season.

Max goes undercover.

BRAINS AND BEAUTY

- In 1957, Barbara Feldon won top prize in the quiz show "The $64,000 Question." Her specialty: Shakespeare. "I had just gotten out of Carnegie Tech Drama School, where I'd reread all of Shakespeare, and I was still reading *King Lear*. You won't believe this, but the test they gave me was on *King Lear*."
- In the early '60s, she became famous for an ad in which she purred to the men in the audience, "Sic 'em, Tiger." She looked so sexy that she got the audition for "Get Smart." At first, she wasn't hired as a regular character—she was only scheduled for the pilot and three other episodes. But her character worked so well that Feldon became a permanent cast member.
- Although she never matched her success on "Get Smart," Barbara was not forgotten. The rock group Toto's 1979 hit "99" is reportedly a tribute to Max's beautiful partner.

INSPIRATIONS

- Max was called Agent 86 because that's the bartender's code for cutting a drinker off, as in "Eighty-six that guy." Ninety-nine, the number chosen for his partner, was reputed to have been a second choice to the number sixty-nine.
- Smart's voice came from Adams's days as an impressionist, when he mimicked actor William Powell. Adams just exaggerated it in "Get Smart" for comic effect.
- Much of Maxwell Smart was developed on the old "Bill Dana Show." Adams played a house detective named Byron Glick, who said things like "Would you believe..."

Max and 99 take on KAOS.

CRITICS' COMMENTS

ABOUT MAX'S APPEAL:
"Max's flawed character was the secret of his success. On one hand, he's a total screwup, but on the other, he always comes out smelling like a rose. People can identify with that; we all screw up. But we like to think that no matter what we do, eventually things will work out for the best.

It's like Sam in "Cheers" in a funny way—he's two sides of us. The screwup side and the side that we'd like to believe exists, the side that not only survives, but always winds up winning."

—Joseph Walker,
Salt Lake City Deseret News

ABOUT 99:
"99 was a liberated woman on TV back before we figured out what a liberated woman on TV was supposed to be. Among other things, she was a woman who carried a gun and was in a position of responsibilty. Look back at what women did in comedies—they were school teachers and secretaries. The idea that a woman could be trusted to have the fate of the world in her hands was a real departure. And she was the brains of the outfit. She did more with the role than you would have expected. But she wasn't Emma Peel to Max's John Steed. She was more like Moneypenny to James Bond."

—Donna McCrohan,
TV historian

"We had this bimbo guy, for a change, and somehow he had this incredible glamorous woman who not only put up with his incompetence but *loved* him. It made no sense whatsoever, in retrospect, but it was important because it made Max seem a little less ridiculous. It got him away from the total lunatic fringe."

—Yardena Arar,
Los Angeles Daily News

ABOUT THE SHOW'S SUCCESS:
"I was working on a newspaper while the show was on, and when we wanted to tell a secret we went to an outer room where no one could hear us. We used to call it the Cone of Silence. I don't know if it was because what it was parodying was so rich, but 'Get Smart' managed to find all sorts of parallels in the real world and create its own bizarre subtext."

—Duane Dudek,
Milwaukee Sentinel

Neither Barbara Feldon nor Don Adams have managed to duplicate their success with "Get Smart," although each has tried other TV shows.

THE ADDAMS FAMILY

By the mid-'60s, the domestic sitcom format had been squeezed dry, and producers were looking for new...blood. One day, TV executive Dave Levy put down his *Hollywood Reporter*, picked up *The New Yorker*, and took a hard look at those ghoulish cartoons Charles Addams had been drawing for twenty years. The result: "The Addams Family," one of the first monster sitcoms.

Most fans think it should have been the *only* monster sitcom, but CBS also jumped on the genre; "The Munsters" made its debut the same week as "The Addams Family." To many people the shows are interchangeable. In fact, they're not. "The Munsters" was little more than "Leave It to Beaver" in Halloween masks (it was actually created by "Beaver"'s Joe Connelly and Bob Mosher). "The Addams Family" was far more.

For one thing, it was inspired by the eclectic sensibilites of the Addams cartoons. The Addams mansion, for example, was filled with the most outrageous furnishings any sitcom abode ever had. Like the wolverine cukoo clock, the bear rug that growled when you walked on it, the suit of armor that coughed when you flicked ashes into it, the stuffed fish with the human leg sticking out of it. As Morticia Addams, queen of the castle, purred when nervous guests commented on her interior decoration, "We like it. It's so nice and gloomy."

Furthermore, in an age where nonconformity was beginning to be regarded as an asset, not a liability, the Addamses were almost countercultural role models. They were bizarre, they were outlandish, they were different, and they were happy. They were oblivious to the screams and stares of their infrequent vistors, except to murmur things like "Poor man, he must be working too hard."

The Addams family "did its own thing," and if that thing involved blowing up toy trains or decapitating Marie Antoinette dolls, who cared?

But the Addamses were also one hell of a nice family. Gomez Addams lusted joyfully after his wife, kissing his way up her arm and going crazy when she spoke French to him. Morticia was a doting mother to Wednesday and Pugsley. Uncle Fester, who enjoyed lighting light bulbs by placing them in his mouth, was appreciated for his unique talents. Even Lurch, the seven-foot-tall butler who groaned, "You rang?" whenever Morticia pulled her hangman's noose, was regared more as a member of the family than a servant.

This all-American, albeit spooky, family, and the creatures who lived with them, were created by a group of writers who obviously gave full vent to their imaginations. Audiences still remember Thing, the disembodied hand that traveled from box to box, performing household chores like delivering the mail, and Cousin Itt, the tiny ball of fur that lived upside down in the chimney and mumbled high-pitched, garbled nonsense.

Unfortunately, "The Addams Family" was largely perceived as a gimmick show. And because it went head to disembodied head with "The Munsters," it wore out its welcome after only two seasons.

But it's still revered by horror and fantasy fans, and by people with an offbeat, dark sense of humor, who can appreciate the genius of John Astin's and Carolyn Jones's characterizations. Oh, well. *"C'est la vie."*

"Tish! That's French!"

Jackie Coogan was one of the original child-stars of film; in the '20s, he starred with Charlie Chaplin. But by the '60s, he was a has-been. When he showed up to audition for the role of Fester, he had a big walrus mustache and was told that Fester was supposed to be hairless. So he want home and shaved off every hair on his body. The next day, he got the job.

FLASHBACK

LURCH: "Uhhhhhgh."
COUSIN ITT: "What did you mean by that, Lurch?"
LURCH: "Just uhhhhhgh."

[*A princess arrives to stay at the Addams home.*]
MORTICIA: "You'll love your chamber, your highness. It has such a *lovely* view. On a clear day, you can see all the way to the swamp."
GOMEZ [grinning]: "But of course, who'd want a clear day?"

[*Fester is trying to convince a stockbroker to give him a job.*]
FESTER: "Let's face it, J.D., you need a man like me. I'm magnetic! [*He holds out his hand, palm down, and a metal paperweight flies up off of J.D.'s desk .*] See?"

VITAL STATS

POLL RESULTS:
Fourth
PROGRAM INFO:
- Half-hour show. ABC
- First show: Sept. 18, 1964
- Last show: Sept. 2, 1966
- 64 episodes

TIME: The '60s.

PLACE: 000 North Cemetery Ridge. A Victorian mansion overlooking a cemetary, the home of the Addams family.

BACKGROUND: "They're creepy and they're kooky, mysterious and spooky." The ghoulish—but very sweet—Addams family lives in a world all its own, primarily because no one will come near them. They happily pass their days tending gardens of deadly nightshade, playing with their pets (a lion and a black widow spider) and stretching out on the rack in the torture chamber downstairs. The only sour note comes when the outside world intrudes; it never seems to appreciate the Addamses. For some reason, guests invariably flee, screaming wildly.

MAIN CAST:
- **Gomez Addams** (John Astin): Head of the family, a lawyer with maniacally glowing eyes. Independently wealthy. Probably of Spanish ancestry. Always wears the same double-breasted, pinstriped gangster suit and smokes long cigars. For fun, he swallows swords, fences with his wife, and blows up model trains.
- **Morticia Addams** (Carolyn Jones): The lady of the house, a loving wife and understanding mother. She wears her black wedding gown at all times. Unfailingly polite, gracious, and considerate. The spiritual center of the family.
- **Uncle Fester** (Jackie Coogan): Morticia's uncle, hairless, moon-faced, with a high, squeaky voice. Really a kid at heart, he loves playing with his explosives and riding around inside the house on his motorcycle.
- **Lurch** (Ted Cassidy): "You raaaaang?" The hulking, zombie-like butler who leads guests through the house with a menacing "Follow meeeee." Relaxes by playing the harpsichord.
- **Pugsley Addams** (Ken Weatherwax): The pudgy son.
- **Wednesday Addams** (Lisa Loring): The solemn daughter.
- **Grandmama** (Blossom Rock): Scraggly-haired Addams matriarch.
- **Cousin Itt** (Felix Silla): A walking ball of fur with a hat.
- **Thing** (Ted Cassidy's hand): A helpful hand in a box.

Carolyn Jones in an episode of "Wagon Train." It took two hours to put on her Addams makeup.

LITTLE JACKIE

Ted Cassidy had no acting experience when he auditioned for the role of Lurch. But the producers wanted him badly. As Dave Levy recalled, "When Ted walked into the office and said 'Hello' in that voice of his, I looked up—and up—at him, and just said 'You're Lurch.'"

This was a disappointing development to John Astin, who had wanted the role for himself. But as Astin left the audition, Levy spotted him. He ran over and offeed John the part of Gomez. instead—provided he would grow a mustache.

LURCH

The Addams family weren't as monstrous as they seemed, and authorities occasionally saluted them for it. After its premiere episode, in which the family lectured a school truant officer on nonviolence, the show received a letter of commendation from a Washington, D.C., foreign-policy committee, signed by dozens of politicians, dignitaries, and celebrities, including Dr. Henry Kissinger.

Said producer Nat Perrin: "A newspaper psychology columnist—it may even have been Dr. Joyce Brothers—once did a column recommending that all American families watch 'The Addams Family' as a form of therapy, because they were such a loving and together unit, they never bickered.... We were always proud of things like that."

In the midst of dance crazes like the Frug and the Chicken, Ted Cassidy introduced "The Lurch."

PEACE AND LOVE

When David Levy decided to try to develop Charles Addams' *New Yorker* cartoons into a TV series, he called Addams and set up an appointment. Here is his account of that meeting, as told to writer Michael Shore: "We spent two hours over drinks at the oak room in the Plaza Hotel. Addams was tall, younglooking for his age, with a twinkle in his eye. He was modest, laid-back, spoke laconically, and had a very dry wit....But for two hours...we spoke of nothing but the novelist John O'Hara. Seems Addams and O'Hara had been drinking buddies since Prohibition. I knew O'Hara from trying to do some of his stories on TV. I gathered that Addams had been approached about TV shows before but had been diffident and that the O'Hara connection is what endeared me to him. Addams said, 'Let's meet again tomorrow to discuss this. At my place.' So, next day I went to his place—a little fifth-floor walkup atop a small Manhattan apartment building. It was a pretty Addamsy place, with suits of armor in the living room, a huge collection of antique crossbows, and so on. I told him that since he'd never named the characters in the cartoons, I would need names and character sketches. A few days later, we met again and he had it all down on paper. Except for the husband's name. He had Gomez, but he also had 'Repelli,' for 'repellent.' I liked Gomez, because it was one of the few nongimmicky names there. So I asked him about Gomez, and he just said, 'I think he has some sort of Spanish blood in him.' That was it....Addams never had any further input or [gave us any] feedback after those first meetings."

Wednesday buries her dolls.

CRITICS' COMMENTS

ABOUT ITS APPEAL:
"'The Addams Family' needed more understatement. It would have been a brilliant show if it had no laugh track. All it had to do was keep people from howling madly when Fester popped a light bulb in his mouth and it would have been wonderful dark humor. Incidentally, *Uncle Fester* is the greatest character name in history, I looked up *fester* in the dictionary after watching that show and appreciated what a disgusting concept it was. Cousin Itt was pretty good, too. Itt is the only sitcom character ever named for a pronoun."

—Joel Pisetzner,
Bergen Record

"It appealed to people with a kind of weird sense of humor, like the *New Yorker* cartoons—which is why it was never really as roaring a success as it might have been. But it had a lot of imagination. And speaking of imagination, half the males in North America were lusting after Carolyn Jones."

—Bill Musselwhite,
Calgary Herald

ABOUT THE CHARACTERS:
"The person I liked best on that show was John Astin. As the head of the household, he was like Groucho Marx, with manic energy, puffing away wildly on the cigar, eyes rolling around. He was like the keeper of the asylum."

—Mark Dawidziak,
Akron Beacon Journal

"The props are first-rate, but the people are even better. Beautiful Carolyn Jones plays Morticia with a chilling verve that should make any dead-blooded man want to share a bier with her."

—Time,
original review,
December 3, 1964

"My role model, inspiration, and heroine is Morticia Addams."

—Punk rocker
Siouxsie Sioux of
Siouxsie and the Banshees

ABOUT THE TRAINS:
"I was a Lionel train freak as a kid, and it just pained me to watch them wreck the trains. In fact, I asked John Astin about it during an interview, and he said, 'Yeah, after the first season it got expensive, so they'd just set it up and then stop the trains and insert file footage.' So they only blew up the trains once or twice, it cost so much money in the '60s."

—John Keisewetter,
Cincinnati Enquirer

"I loved the theme song. I knew all the words then, I know all the words now—something to be proud of."

—Jeff Borden,
Charlotte Observer

Welcome to the Addams mansion.

BEWITCHED

For all practical purposes, the traditional family sitcom of the '50s was dead by 1963. A few limped along until the end of the decade, but the world they portrayed was out of date. It no longer represented the ideals of a generation.

This was the space age, after all, the era of color TV.

The only problem was that TV is not a revolutionary medium. The industry could not keep up with the rapid changes in the culture; they'd just perfected the family sitcom and had nothing to run in its place. So they made a few alterations instead. The lead characters became a little younger, and family life was jazzed up with gimmicks.

Producer Harry Ackerman, who'd been an integral part of another domestic sitcom called "I Love Lucy," came up with the most successful of these. He added a dose of magic to suburbia, and presto! Samantha Stephens, the sexy witch on "Bewitched" appeared. She was a suburban housewife, but by wriggling her nose, she could break up her day by having parties with Napoleon Bonaparte or visiting the court of Henry VIII. Instead of receiving daily phone calls from her mother, she received messages attached to a flaming spear. And she read tomorrow's newspapers, which probably beat watching soap operas.

"Bewitched"'s format was one the traditional audience was comfortable with—a housebound wife was trying to expand her limited role, to the consternation of her husband. But instead of shaking this format by doing something *really* strange, like getting a job, Samantha broke through her boundaries with her mastery of magic. Audiences didn't find that fairy-tale situation threatening at all. In fact, it enchanted them for eight years.

"Bewitched"'s success depended on two elements that worked together like a magic charm. For one thing, scriptwriters were given the luxury of letting their imaginations run wild. For another, it had a supporting cast playing Sam's family that was comprised of some of the best character actors in the business, headed, of course, by four-time Oscar nominee Agnes Moorhead.

As the interfering mother-in-law, Endora, Moorhead got her kicks by changing her daughter's husband into a billy goat, a toad, or a child. And the relatives conjured up houseguests ranging from Paul Revere to a *Playboy* bunny. Even the cute kids had magic powers, much to the distress of their straight-arrow father.

And then there was Elizabeth Montgomery, a skilled and demurely sexy performer who somehow made the whole premise believable.

In fact, the witchery was *not* the most unbelievable part of the show—it was the fact that Darrin (both of them) wouldn't take advantage of Sam's powers. We knew he was dumb, but come on. If you found out your spouse could supply anything you needed just by wiggling her nose, would you spend your life slaving at an advertising job in New York City? And what self-respecting witch would put up with the chauvinistic nonsense about a "wife's place" that Darrin spouted?

"We-e-ell"...maybe that was all part of the charm of the show. In any case, while certain parts of the series seem dated, its imagination, wit, and cleverness clearly do not. It's still fun to flip on the TV in the middle of the day and catch a few magic moments at the Stephens residence.

Agnes Moorhead was invited by NASA to witness the 1969 moon shot, because as Endora, she'd "visited the moon many times."

FLASHBACK

SAM [in her kitchen, speaking to thin air]: "Mother, come here this *instant*!...[sternly] Mo-ther! [more softly] Mom?"

DARRIN: "My wife's a witch. What'll I do?"
BARTENDER: "You oughta see *my* wife."

ENDORA [casting a spell on Darrin]: "Durwood, I do not like the way you gloat, so I'm turning you into a billy goat."

GLADYS KRAVITZ [*the nosy neighbor, after seeing Samantha transform into an animal*]: "I bet she has some strange disease and we can catch it. You want to wake up with something strange?"
ABNER KRAVITZ [her husband]: "I've been doing that for twenty years. Why change now?"

SAM: "We-e-e-ell..."

VITAL STATS

POLL RESULTS:
Fifth
PROGRAM INFO:
- Half-hour show. ABC.
- First show: Sept. 17, 1964
- Last show: July 1, 1972
- 254 episodes

TIME: The mid-'60s.

PLACE: 1164 Morning Glory Circle, Westport, Connecticut (an archetypical upper-middle-class suburb), home of the Stephens family. Darrin, an advertising executive, commutes to New York City, where he works for the firm of McMann and Tate.

BACKGROUND: Darrin Stephens met and fell in love with a pretty blonde named Samantha. There was just one thing he didn't know when he proposed to her: She's a witch. For him it's a shock; for her it's a scandal—She's the first witch in her family ever to fall in love with a mortal, and her mother absolutely does *not* approve. How can she even think of marrying Durbin, or Durwood, or Dumbo, or whatever his name is? The rest of Sam's family seems to find it amusing. Sam reveals the truth on her wedding night, and Darrin is floored. He concludes that the only way to deal with it is to pretend it never happened. He instructs his witchy spouse never to use her powers, and she implausibly agrees. Now they're ensconced in a suburban conformist lifestyle, keeping their horrible (Darrin thinks) secret from the rest of the world.

Darrin makes the mistake of insisting to his mother-in-law that he's "all ears."

MAIN CAST:
- **Samantha Stephens** (Elizabeth Montgomery): A witch posing as a suburbanite. Clever and vivacious, witty and creative. It's too bad Darrin doesn't encourage her to use her powers. With a twitch of her nose, she could end nuclear war.
- **Darrin Stephens** (Dick York/Dick Sargent): Her manic, straight-arrow husband. Loves Sam, but pathologically objects to her powers, constantly lectures her on their misuse. The butt of his mother-in-law's whims, as she turns him into an ass, or a hog, or makes his ears huge.
- **Endora** (Agnes Morehead): Samantha's glamorous mother, clearly enjoys being a witch and can't understand why Sam won't join in the fun. Vindictive, opinionated, vain. A real terror.
- **Larry Tate** (David White): Darrin's boss at the McMann and Tate Advertising agency. A caricature of an ad man, phony and uncreative.
- **Gladys Kravitz** (Alice Pearce): The nosy neighbor .
- **Abner Kravitz** (George Tobias): Gladys's long-suffering husband.

LUCKY BREAK

•The original star of "Bewitched" was to be Tammy Grimes, an English stage actress who'd just signed a deal with ScreenGems TV.
•But she didn't like the script. She turned it down in favor of a concept that became "The Tammy Grimes Show."
•"The Tammy Grimes Show" was among the shortest-lived sitcoms in history. It lasted exactly a month in 1965.
•"Bewitched," on the other hand, became one of the most successful in history and made Elizabeth Montgomery—who sold her share of the series to Screen Gems—fabulously wealthy.

MISCELLANY

•Richard Dreyfuss appears in one "Bewitched" episode as a neurotic warlock who changes into a dog.
•On another, unknown starlet Raquel Welch had a bit part as an astronaut.
•Due to Sam's wacky powers, Darrin was fired in nineteen shows, threatened with firing in seven shows, quit in two shows, and retired in one show.
•Dick York had to leave the series when an old back injury practically paralyzed him. He was replaced, inronically, by Dick Sargent, who had just come from "The Tammy Grimes Show."

AWARD BY ANY OTHER NAME

•Agnes Moorhead, who played Endora, was nominated for five Oscars. She never won.
• Moorhead was also nominated for six Emmys for her portrayal of Endora —and lost every time there, too. So did Elizabeth Montgomery, who was nominated five times.
•The only "Bewitched" winners were Alice Pearce (Gladys Kravitz) and Marion Lorne (Aunt Clara), for Best Supporting Actress in a Comedy.
•Neither of them was particularly pleased with the awards—the Emmys were bestowed on both comediennes posthumously.

NOSE FLUTE

•Elizabeth Montgomery's weird ability to wiggle her nose—the way some people wiggle their ears—inspired the show's writers to turn make it Sam's conjuring trick.
•Notice that you never see anyone else on the show doing it—that's because no one else on the show *could* do it. Try it—it's next to impossible.

CHILD STAR

Out of all the babies born to sitcom moms while a show was running, only one has gotten a show of her own. It was Tabitha the witch, born on January 13, 1966. Somehow, eleven years later, she was already a young adult working in the TV industry, at station KXLA in Los Angeles. Tabitha, who was originally played by twins Erin and Diane Murphy, was now played by Lisa Hartman in the regular series (called simply "Tabitha"). It lasted only a year, from 1977 to 1978.

CRITICS' COMMENTS

ABOUT THE SHOW'S APPEAL:

"First of all, I liked the supernatural aspect of it. I loved watching strange things happen when she twitched her nose. Good special effects. The only thing I could never understand was why her husband was so down on it. The guy had it made—he could wish for anything, and he never really put it to good use."

—Joel Pisetzner,
Bergen Record

"Bewitched" brings up an interesting question: What were these light fantasy shows really about? Is it possible that programs like "Bewitched" and "I Dream of Jeannie" were a reaction to the earliest feminists? After all, they gave us a comforting, traditional world into which both men and women could escape, as opposed to the frightening prospect that men and women would have to reinvent their roles."

—Marc Gunther,
Detroit Free Press

"Elizabeth Montgomery exudes so much warmth that I can't help but like her no matter what she's doing. And every woman can identify with the idea of being able to just twich her nose and having the house magically cleaned up in seconds.

Also, the relationship between Sam and Darrin was about as adult as they got in family shows of that era. Darrin was often presented as a buffoon, but you always felt that there was a balance—an equality—to their relationship. Samantha was probably one of the most positive female role models on '60s TV."

—Diane Albert,
TV Collector

"It was somewhat adventurous to put a witch on television, because fanatics could've protested that it advocated cults or had "religious overtones."...Today people probably would. But they carried it off so lightly, no one could be offended except the people who think *The Wizard of Oz* is a cult, and that Halloween is a cult holiday."

—Bob Curtwright,
Wichita Eagle-Beacon

ABOUT THE CHARACTERS:

"I was crazy about Agnes Moorhead. She was totally believable as Darrin's mother-in-law. In fact, she's the kind of mother in law I would've liked to have had. My mother-in-law is a woman I dearly love, but Endora was mean as a snake, someone you could cheerfully hate."

—Dennis Washburn,
Birmingham News

"The witches and warlocks are the only interesting people in the whole show. In fact, almost all the supernaturals are really fascinating, while all the humans are extremely boring. And when you think of the husbands, you wonder: 'Why on earth would she have married either of them?' You inevitably come to the conclusion that her family was right—she shouldn't have married a human at all."

—Harry Castleman,
Watching TV

60s

GREEN ACRES (1965-71)
A successful New York lawyer named Oliver Wendell Douglas dreams of moving "back to the land" and becoming a farmer. So he buys a spread in Hooterville, sight unseen, from a country con man named Mr. Haney. He moves there, accompanied (reluctantly) by his glamorous wife, Lisa, and discovers that his "estate" is a ramshackle hut and his "farm" is acres of nothing. He also discovers that the entire population of Hooterville is wacko.

"'Green Acres' is probably the most misunderstood TV program of the last thirty years. Most critics originally regarded it as one of the insipid rural comedies that littered the airwaves in the '60s. And most of the audience probably did, too—which is why it was so popular. But there is a surreal sensibility hidden in the show that's absolutely hilarious. Eddie Albert plays the bewildered straight man perfectly, and Eva Gabor, who's blithely gliding around the countryside in designer gowns is the perfect dingbat. Arnold the pig, the Ziffles, Zeb the handyman, Mr. Drucker, and of course Pat Buttram, play as weird a bunch of characters as you'll ever see on TV. "

—Jack Mingo,
The Official Couch Potato Handbook

"'Green Acres' was almost like a Kafkaesque nightmare. You can watch it on a lot of different levels. I mean, here's this one sane man in a world of lunatics. And they were *such* lunatics—it was almost like *Alice in Wonderland.* It was like an *acid* trip."

—Steve Sonsky,
Miami Herald

HE & SHE (1967-68)
Dick Hollister (Richard Benjmin) is a successsful New York cartoonist who's hit the jackpot—his "Jetman" cartoon has been turned into a TV series. Unfortunately, the show stars a haughty actor named Oscar (Jack Cassady), who thinks he understands the character better than Dick does. And Dick's wife (Paula Prentiss), a scatter-brained lovely who works for Traveler's Aid, is always getting them both into complicated situations with the people she helps.

"For the time, it was a very sophisticated show. I thought the 'Jetman' character, Jack Cassady, was an inspired screwball invention. He played a comic-book character come to life, running around jumping up and going, 'Jet ma-a-an.' It was sort of an MTM-type of show, ahead of its time. It was a more sophisticated kind of humor than anything that was on the air at that time. The characters had more wit and intelligence than the rest of the fall schedule combined."

—Michael Duffy,
Detroit Free Press

"When Mike Dann, president of CBS, presented the show with an Emmy Award in 1968, he said, 'This is the best show I ever canceled.' Richard Benjamin was so upset with the whole situation—having a great show that was universally acclaimed by critics but ignored by the audience—that he stopped doing TV and went into the movies."

—Donna McCrohan,
TV Historian

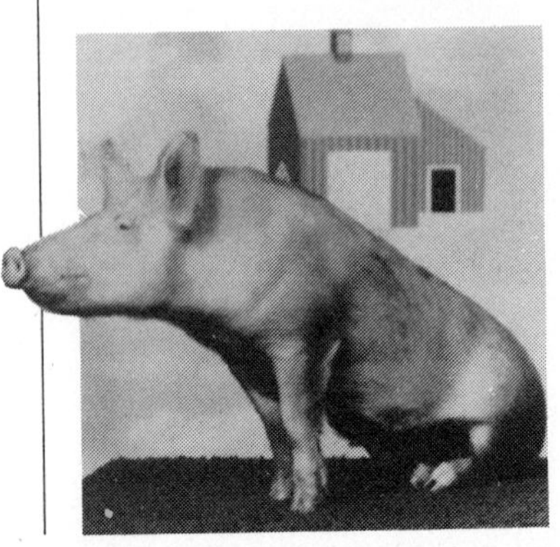

Worst of the '60s

To be fair, we should note that there were more sitcoms on television in the '60s than ever before. That may be the reason that there were also more *bad* situation comedies than ever before—or since. As one critic put it, these shows make you wonder, "Why is there TV?"

In fact, there was so much sitcom junk on television during the decade that critics frequently reiterated that it's impossible to pick the worst.

So instead of torturing themselves by wading through lists of unwatchable shows, they have selected the ones that embarrassed the medium most conspicuously as the worst three of the decade. "These are the ones that really did some damage," explained a voter.

MY MOTHER THE CAR

The critics named shows starring Van Dykes as both the best and the worst of the '60s. "My Mother the Car" ran for a full season, from September 14, 1965, to September 6, 1966, before it ran out of gas.

"My Mother the Car" was a nightmare answer to the question "How stupid can TV get?" Many questionable sitcom premises have come and gone, but this one still causes eyes to cross more than two decades after its brief run. How could they have come up with a show like this? You picture the program's creators pondering sitcom ideas in 1963. "Let's see, what do Americans like? Mom, family, cars, cute dogs, blondes, California, Jerry Van Dyke, life after death? How to choose...how to choose....Hey, let's create a sitcom using *every one of them.*"

The result—a California lawyer with two kids, a pretty blonde wife and an adorable dog discovers that his antique car is the reincarnartion of his mother. Although this may be hard to believe, at least part of this preposterous plot may seem a trifle familiar. When he gets behind the wheel, the car talks to him (shades of "Mr. Ed"). He's the only one she talks to (shades of "Mr. Ed"). Everyone thinks he's crazy (shades of—well, you get the point).

At any rate, the lawyer lavishes care and attention on the car, not wanting his mother to depreciate further. But his family gives him no support; this all-American bunch wants him to junk Ma and buy a station wagon. Well, that's what makes this country great.

"My Mother, the Car" was one of the "gimmick" sitcoms that began popping up when the conventional domestic format appeared to have been exhausted. In some cases ("Bewitched," "The Addams Family"), the skewed situations worked. But in this case, Mom was a lemon. She was also, it must be added, a party to the worst pun ever perpetrated on TV: rein*car*nation.

Too bad for Ann Sothern, the voice of Ma, who had a distinguished sitcom career ("Private Secretary," "The Ann Sothern Show"). After this role, she attempted no further afterlives. Jerry Van Dyke moved on to other sitcom embarrassments like "Accidental Family" and "13 Queens Blvd." Avery Schreiber now does potato chip commercials.

BACKGROUND

While searching for a used car, Dave Crabtree of Los Angeles comes across a battered 1928 Porter. He's about to pass it by when he discovers that the voice he hears on the car radio belongs to his dead mother, Abigail Crabtree, who has been rein*car*nated as a mode of transportaton. Needless to say, he decides to keep the car. He restores the vintage touring automobile (license number PZR 317) and lives happily ever after. Except for the constant complaints of his nagging family, who desire a cool '60s car, and the evil Captain Manzini, who longs to add Mom to his personal collection.

MAIN CAST

- **Dave Crabtree** (Jerry Van Dyke): A small-time lawyer of modest means but a devoted son to his beloved Porter.
- **Mother's voice** (Ann Sothern): Aka Abigail Crabtree, ex-human.
- **Barbara Crabtree** (Maggie Pierce): Dave's wife, who can't understand her husband's love for the old car.
- **Cindy Crabtree** (Cindy Eilbacher): Dave's daughter.
- **Randy Crabtree** (Randy Whipple): Dave's son.
- **Captain Manzini** (Avery Schreiber): The villainous car collector.

FLASHBACK

CAR: "Did you find my registration slip yet?"
DAVE: "Not yet, but I'm looking."
CAR: "Then I'm leaving. Out of my way."
DAVE: "C'mon, Mom, give me another chance."
CAR: "I'll give you exactly three minutes to find that registration slip."
DAVE: "Thanks, Mom."
CAR: "Three minutes, David, remember.... Get set, go—one...two...three...four..."
DAVE: [As he sprints into his house frantically]: "C'mon, Mom, count slower."

BARBARA'S MOTHER: "We're trading in that freeway fossil for a brand-new station wagon."
BARBARA: "Oh, mother! That's wonderful!...But it's Dave's car."
MOTHER: "Oh, honey, you leave Dave to me. Even Dave can't turn down a brand-new station wagon."

Jerry Van Dyke was offered the role of Gilligan in "Gilligan's Island," but his agent turned it down...in favor of this.

CRITICS' COMMENTS

"I often wonder what Ann Sothern thought when she watched. It had to be humiliating to hear her voice coming from that car.... The whole show was just a one-joke...umm...vehicle."

—Joseph Walker, *Salt Lake City Deseret News*

"'My Mother the Car' is the TV equivalent of *Plan Nine from Outer Space*, which seems to be universally recognized as the worst movie ever made. 'My Mother the Car' holds that honor in TV mythology—deservedly so."

—Steve Sonsky, *Miami Herald*

"'My Mother the Car,' by all standards, was the worst show of the decade. The whole concept of a woman being brought back to Earth as a car is ridiculous—especially when you stop and realize how cars are actually made."

—Bob Foster, *San Mateo Times*

"'My Mother the Car' was *good*. You know, I was always making 'My Mother the Car' jokes, but when I did the sitcom book, I said, 'All right, I'll watch a couple of "My Mother the Car"s.' Now, it is not the *best* show in the world. But it *is* created by the 'Mary Tyler Moore' people. And it's certainly better than a lot of the stuff that's on TV today; it's just got a silly premise. But then 'Mork and Mindy' had a silly premise, and 'Bewitched' had a silly premise."

—Rick Mitz, *The Great Sitcom Book*

"The reason 'My Mother the Car' was bad was not the car—it was Jerry Van Dyke. He was a terrible actor and a terrible comedian.... You might say that 'My Mother the Car' is the Edsel of sitcoms. It's beyond a lousy show—it's a transcendent symbol of bad TV."

—Joel Pisetzner, *Bergen Record*

GILLIGAN'S ISLAND

Ship ahoy. Bob Denver looks in vain for an escape from "Gilligan's Island." The show ran from September 26, 1964, to September 4, 1967.

"Gilligan's Island" is an anomaly. On one hand, it isn't all that bad: It's occasionally funny, even to people who find it offensive; it's well produced; and it features some talented TV actors, including Bob (Maynard G. Krebs) Denver and Jim Backus.

On the other hand, it represents the worst and most destructive power that television wields—the power to paralyze bodies and minds, to induce human beings to squander productive potential and sacrifice their time. What do they get in exchange? Numbness of the brain and a TV dependency.

"Gilligan's Island" was the story of seven dimwits who were stranded on an "uncharted desert isle." For the entire run of the series, they tried to get off. That's it. Obviously, this offered limited opportunities to the writers. But they sank to the challenge. If things got dull Gilligan would engage in a tug-of-war while he was fishing and get drenched. Or a pile of coconuts would fall on his head. And when all else failed (which was at least once per episode), the Skipper would hit Gilligan with his hat.

The truly amazing—no, make that reprehensible—thing about "Gilligan's Island" is that it was created by a talented, educated man. Sherwood Schwartz, the "brains" behind the show, was an award-winning comedy writer with master's degrees in both zoology and psychology.

And according to him, he was even motivated by intellectual idealism in presenting the show. The island, he has explained, was meant to be a microcosm, a miniature version of Our World. He hoped it would promote the cause of peace to demonstrate that cooperation between disparate elements of society is possible. Right.

What Schwartz wound up with was TV junk food—insidiously palatable but utterly devoid of substance—and apparently that was ok, too. As long as the sponsors kept paying their bills.

This attitude is too prevalent in TV. At some point, TV executives—especially talented ones—have to take responsibility for what they dump on a nation of consumers. And there is simply no excuse for expending creative energy producing gourmet junk food like "Gilligan's Island."

BACKGROUND

Skipper Jonas Grumby and his first mate, Gilligan, run a tour boat in some unnamed resort. While taking a remarkably unprofitable boatload of five passengers on a three-hour tour, the S.S. *Minnow* gets caught in a bad storm. The boat crash-lands on an island in the middle of nowhere. Despite the presence of a brilliant professor and two experienced seamen, as well as a perfectly working radio, no one seems to have a clue as to how to get rescued. The passengers must learn to deal with the primitive conditions and their disparate personalities as they struggle to be saved.

MAIN CAST

- **Gilligan** (Bob Denver): The simple-minded first mate.
- **The Skipper** (Alan Hale, Jr.): The beefy, marginally intelligent capt.
- **Thurston Howell III** (Jim Backus): A dim-witted millionaire.
- **Lovey Howell III** (Natalie Schafer): His wife, a silly snob.
- **The Professor** (Russell Johnson): The brains of the outfit, the only passenger with no extra clothes.
- **Mary Ann Summers** (Dawn Wells): A naive farm girl, not even mentioned in the theme song until the third season.
- **Ginger Grant** (Tina Louise): A dumb movie star.

FLASHBACK

[*Two Russian cosmonauts land on the island and decide the castaways are part of a secret American space program*].

COSMONAUT: "Especially that Gilligan. He acts too stupid to be stupid. He must be the cleverest one of all."

[*The wealthy Erika Tiffany-Smith lands on the island. The Professor thinks she's interested in his mind.*]

PROFESSOR: "Together, we'll burst through the walls of ignorance and discover one of the most important things in life."
GILLIGAN: "What's that?"
PROFESSOR: "The mating cycle of the angleworm."

The castaways pose on "Gilligan's Island." Actually, the island was manmade, located in the middle of a lake in CBS Studio Center in Hollywood. It was surrounded with painted scenery, fake palm trees, and wind machines.

CRITICS' COMMENTS

"The fact that 'Gilligan' was a hit is the single greatest argument I can think of against the value of democracy."

—Michael Dougan, *San Francisco Examiner*

"Some things are just so bad that they won't go away, and 'Gilligan' is one of them."

—Duane Dudek, *Milwaukee Sentinel*

"I want you to know that I have seen every episode. I was a child, watching this show, and I knew it was atrocious, and I still watched every single episode. There was something wrong with that, and I knew it at the time. But it was almost an incurable disease. I couldn't shake it. I'd call it the worst show of all time. It was cheesy. There was nothing credible about the island, the props, the characters, the dialogue, the makeup, or the wardrobe. Beyond that, it was believable beyond help.

—Andee Beck, *Tacoma News Tribune*

"On Halloween, my younger brother, who is a lawyer, wound up in Miami with a bunch of his yuppie friends, dressing up as the Howells, going around saying, 'Lovey, Lovey.' And when yuppies do that, there's got to be some sort of sickness involved. Maybe there was a subliminal message in there that made people watch that show. It certainly was one of the worst shows ever on television, and I loved it."

—Mark Schwed, UPI

Bob Denver says Gilligan had no first name. But the creator, Sherwood Schwartz, says he did. It was Willie.

"You don't really expect comedy to be realistic, yet the fact is that they had so many chances to get off that goddamn island, and didn't... bothered me. It also bothers me that apparently nobody had sex on that island except the Howells—and I suspect that they didn't have a whole lot. I mean, if I was there with Ginger and Mary Ann for an unknown period of time, I don't think I 'd be quite so interested in erecting a telescope out of coconuts. And where'd they get all those clothes? Why was Ginger going on that boat with all those formal gowns ? And why was Mary Ann so implacably perky?"

—Jim Gordon,
Gary Times Register

THE FLYING NUN

Idiotic sitcoms become even more insufferable when they begin to take themselves seriously. "The Flying Nun" had one of the most unbelievable premises ever, but the show was praised by some religious orders for "humanizing nuns and their work," and one of its producers, with a straight face, expressed pleasure at "bringing God one step closer to America."

Yeah. "The Flying Nun." Religion's finest hour.

A tiny novice at a convent in Puerto Rico discovers that the huge winged coronet the nuns wear, cobined with her minimal weight and the strong local winds, gives her the ability to fly. When she's not on her knees, Elsie Ethington, a.k.a. Sister Bertrille, spends her time soaring around the island, mostly meddling in the business and private affairs of a local casino owner named Carlos Ramirez.

Sally Field was such a likable performer that she almost pulled this travesty off. But in a show without romance (except a chaste spark between Sister and Carlos), the plots had to become more and more outlandish. Once, a pelican fell in love with Sister Bertrille. Another time, she was almost shot down by enemy (what enemy?) aircraft. A couple of times, she almost crash-landed in the ocean.

Based on a book called *The Fifteenth Pelican*, by Terry Rios, "The Flying Nun" took off when nuns seemed as though they were becoming a national habit. *The Sound of Music* was the most popular movie to date. "The Singing Nun" was a popular recording star, and the film about her life (starring Debbie Reynolds) was a success. It was perfectly understandable that Sister Bertrille would get swept up in the fad.

Sally Field's confidence was mortally shaken when her first sitcom, "Gidget," was canceled; she couldn't believe that anyone would ever want her to star in a TV show again. So she was delighted to get the opportunity to perform as a nun. The show drifted along for three years, from September 7, 1967, to September 18, 1970—then the ill wind finally died down. Above, she and Alejandro Rey have it out.

But pretensions at spirituality? Giveth us a break. The show's producers were so desperate for plots at the end that they had Sister Bertrille show home movies of her past life to liven things up. Several of the bikini-clad surfing scenes were from "Gidget."

"The Flying Nun" was grounded after three seasons. Field has gone on to win two Academy Awards. When someone mentions this show, she winces.

BACKGROUND

Sister Bertrille (Elsie Ethington) is a novice at the Convent San Tanco, located on a hilltop in Puerto Rico. When "lift plus thrust is greater than load plus drag," anything flies, especially Sister, who weighs only ninety pounds. So, she flies...and learns to steer, land, and when things get dull, go into orbit. Her fellow sisters make her wear some extra-heavy rosary beads to keep her out of mischief, but it's no use. Sister Bertrille continues to poke her coronet into just about everybody's business.

MAIN CAST

- **Sister Bertrille** (Sally Field): The fun-loving young nun who inexplicably left a surfing colony in Malibu to join a religious order.
- **Sister Jacqueline** (Marge Redmond): Her appreciative mentor and friend. Thinks Bertrille's talents certainly beat bingo games.
- **Mother Superior** (Madeleine Sherwood): Conservative head of the convent, who is embarrassed and humiliated by the whole thing.
- **Carlos Ramirez** (Alejandro Rey): The local playboy and patron of the convent who becomes Sister Bertrille's mission of mercy—to his perpetual annoyance. Well, actually, he's impressed with the flying nun, but he doesn't let on.
- **Sister Sixto** (Shelley Morrison): A Puerto Rican, English-garbling nun. Ethnic relief.

Sister Jacqueline and Sister Bertrille, in the episode, "This Convent Is Condemned." The plot: Captain Fomento, head of the San Tanco police force, thinks of resigning because there's no crime. So the sisters tell him about customers who are stealing ashtrays from the casino.

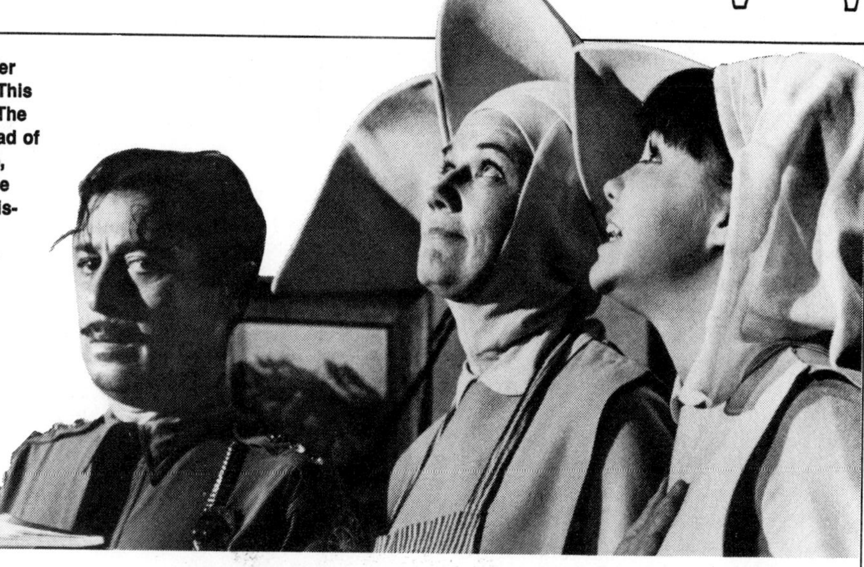

FLASHBACK

SISTER BERTRILLE: "When I was little, I was clumsy, but I always wished I was a bird. They seem so free and graceful."

SISTER JACQUELINE: "I can't bear to think of her flying out there without instruments."

SISTER SIXTO: "The plumbing, she's on the blank."

SISTER BERTRILLE: "It all has to do with my coronet. It's when the lift plus thrust is greater than the load plus drag."

Sister Sally and Brother Rich Little in the episode, "Breakaway Monk."

CRITICS' COMMENTS

"'The Flying Nun' is really, lethally bad. The acting is so inept—everybody acts like they know they're in a sitcom. And there's nothing behind the characters. I couldn't watch it. It was meant for an audience who didn't want to go beyond one dimension."

—**Mark Dawidziak, *Akron Beacon Journal***

"Anybody over fifteen years of age who watched this show should probably seek medical attention."

—**Alex McNeil, *Total Television***

"'The Flying Nun' is one of those shows, like 'Hogan's Heroes,' where when you scratch the surface, you find a clearly objectionable premise."

—**Steven Sonsky, *Miami Herald***

"I was amazed by it—just the whole concept of having a nun as the main character of a sitcom took me a back at first as much as 'Hogan's Heroes' did. The subject matter is something you'd expect the networks to avoid, just because there's so much room to be offensive there. I could see Catholics objecting to it the way Jews objected to 'Hogan's Heroes.' I mean, a nun with supernatural powers? It was one of those shows that I would watch like a zombie for about five minutes and then say, 'Why am I watching this?' and flip the dial."

—**Ed Siegel, *Boston Globe***

"In the most profound way, 'The Flying Nun' is a stupid show. Here's this little nun in a big hat, zooming around in the air—I mean, nuns at the parochial school in *my* neighborhood very rarely flew, except into rages."

—**Jim Gordon, *Gary Post-Tribune***

60s

Grandpa Luke Carpenter, freshly unfrozen in "The Second Hundred Years," visits a disco with his grandson and valiently rescues a go-go dancer from her cage.

MY LIVING DOLL (1964-65)
An Army psychiatrist who lives with his sister brings home a gorgeous woman one day, explaining that she's got severe mental problems and needs constant care. He neglects to explain that she's not really a person at all—she's a robot who's so lifelike and sexy that men lust after her. She calls the psychiatrist "Master," and she'll do anyting (*anything*) he tells her to. So what does he do? What would *you* do? Well, all *he* wants is to teach her good manners. That's enough to qualify this show as preposterous right there.

HOGAN'S HEROES (1965-71)
Supposedly, this show was inspired by William Holden's film *Stalag 17*. But the relationship is obscure; the only similarity is the setting—a Nazi POW camp. *Stalag 17* is a poignant study of desperate men and their will to survive; "Hogan's Heroes" is a laff-riot about outsmarting those nutty, nasty Nazis. Boy, oh boy, it's a wonder those silly strudel eaters ever thought they could win the war, huh? Granted, this show was often funny and well acted. But there's simply no excuse for turning the grim reality of Nazi atrocities into fodder for yet another brainless joke. As one critic asked at the time, "What's next? A family sitcom set in Auschwitz? "

RUN BUDDY RUN (1966-67)
A couple of goofy assassins try to catch and kill a guy who accidentally overheard their secret plans in a Turkish bath. Some fun.

THE SECOND HUNDRED YEARS (1967-68)
The cryogenics sitcom. A 33-year-old prospector is frozen alive in an avalanche in 1900. Sixty-eight years later he thaws out. Surprise! He's still 33 and full of pep. He goes to live with his son, who's now older than he is, and his grandson, who's the same age. In fact, he and his grandson look exactly alike. What a conincidence!

MONA McCLUSKEY (1965-66)
A Hollywood star makes forty times as much money as her husband, an Air Force sergeant (he gets $500 a month, she gets $5000 a week). But the guy won't let her spend any of her dough—they live on his salary or nothing. Well, she's so in love that she agrees; she moves into a two-bedroom apartment and then spends all her time trying to figure out ways to secretly use her own money. The show lasted longer than the marriage would have—seven months.

THE PRUITTS OF SOUTHHAMPTON (1966-67)
A rich Long Island family is allowed by the authorities to maintain a facade of wealth, despite the fact that they're $10 million in debt. They keep their mansion, a car, and even a butler. Well, which "authorities" would be so generous? The police? Nope. Their bank? Nope. Ok. Would you believe the IRS? Neither did the audience. The matriarch of the family, by the way, was played by Phyllis Diller. Enough said.

MANY HAPPY RETURNS (1964-65)
Listening to people bitch about defective merchandise isn't a likely gimmick for a sitcom. CBS couldn't find many people who, after a hard day's work, wanted to tune in this sitcom about the complaint department at Krockmeyer's Department Store.

IT'S ABOUT TIME (1966-67)
Two astronauts accidentally break through the time barrier and wind up in a prehistoric era. There they coexist with a bunch of Neanderthals until they fix their space capsule—and then they head for L.A. But whoops! A couple of cavemen hitch a lift into the present. Hmm—what to do? Intelligently, the astronauts hide the Neanderthals in an apartment and try to teach them about modern life. This inanity could only come from the fertile mind that also gave us "Gilligan" and "The Brady Bunch."

THE PERFECT MOM

MARTA HANSON (Peggy Wood), "I Remember Mama" (1949-57).
TV's first all-American sitcom mom was a Norwegian immigrant. Mama held her family together through hard times with love, compassion, and common sense.

SHIRLEY PARTRIDGE (Shirley Jones), "The Partridge Family" (1970-74).
The post-Monkees preadolescent American fantasy was to go on tour with a rock band and bring your mother along.

HARRIET NELSON (Harriet Nelson). "Ozzie and Harriet." (1952-66).
TV's first true Queen of Suburbia and a real-life rock star's mom. As smart as her husband, for a change.

JULIA BAKER (Diahann Carroll), "Julia" (1968-71).
You've come a long way, baby. TV finally admitted in 1968 that a black woman could be an All-American mom.

JUNE CLEAVER (Barbara Billingsley), "Leave It to Beaver" (1957-63).
The mom who cleaned her house every day wearing high heels, pearls, and a party dress. Offered milk and cookies as a solution to every problem.

DONNA STONE (Donna Reed), "The Donna Reed Show" (1958-66).
Last of the '50s sitcom moms. No one ever had a mother as sympathetic, understanding, kind, and good-looking.

MARGARET ANDERSON (Jane Wyman), "Father Knows Best" (1954-62).
Typical "little woman" of the '50s. Devoted homemaker, hapless with mechanical things and real-world issues. Born to be a housewife.

PRECOCIOUS KIDS

They're cute! They're cuddly! And every sitcom family should own at least one. Here are some of your favorite oh-so-adorable offspring.

Rusty Williams (Rusty Hamer)
"The Danny Thomas Show," 1953-65

Dennis Mitchell (Jay North)
"Dennis the Menace," 1959-63

Corey Baker (Marc Copage)
"Julia," 1968-71

Jeff Stone (Paul Petersen)
"The Donna Reed Show," 1958-66

Ernie Douglas (Barry Livingston)
"My Three Sons," 1960-72

Buffy (Anissa Jones)
"Family Affair," 1966-71

Trisha Stone (Patty Petersen)
"The Donna Reed Show," 1958-66

Robbie Douglas (Don Grady)
"My Three Sons," 1960-72

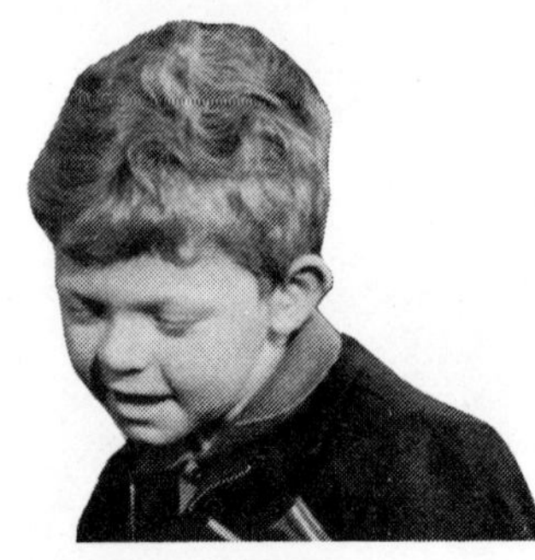

Jody (Johnny Whitaker)
"Family Affair," 1966-71

THE SITCOM HALL OF FAME

Marcia Brady (Maureen McCormick)
"The Brady Bunch," 1969-74

Greg Brady (Barry Williams)
"The Brady Bunch," 1969-74

Luke McCoy (Micahel Winkelman)
"The Real McCoys," 1957-63

Jan Brady (Eve Plumb)
"The Brady Bunch," 1969-74

Peter Brady (Christopher Knight)
"The Brady Bunch," 1969-74.

Eddie Corbett (Brandon Cruz)
"The Courtship of Eddie's Father,"
1969-72

Cindy Brady (Susan Olsen)
"The Brady Bunch," 1969-74

Bobby Brady (Michael Lookinland)
"The Brady Bunch," 1969-74

Arnold Jackson (Gary Coleman)
"Diff'rent Strokes," 1978-85

Tracy Partridge (Suzanne Crough)
"The Partridge Family," 1970-74

Ricky Stevens (Ricky Segall)
"The Partridge Family," 1970-74.

Webster Long (Emmanuel Lewis)
"Webster," 1983-present

ALL-AMERICAN DADS

DR. HEATHCLIFF HUXTABLE (Bill Cosby), "The Cosby Show" (1984-currently in production).
This obstetrician is what Ozzie Nelson would have been like if he'd been the author of the best-selling book on the subject of being a dad, *Fatherhood.*

OZZIE NELSON (Ozzie Nelson), "The Adventures of Ozzie and Harriet" (1952-1966).
Good-natured, bumbling, earnest. We still wonder what—if anything—he did for a living. Famous for his sweaters.

JIM ANDERSON (Robert Young), "Father Knows Best" (1954-62).
An insurance man, the sitcom pillar of middle-class values and conventional wisdom.

TOM CORBETT (Bill Bixby), "The Courtship of Eddie's Father" (1969-72).
A hipper dad, a widower and '70s professional trying to fit his relationship with his son between business commitments.

STEVE DOUGLAS (Fred MacMurray), "My Three Sons" (1960-72).
TV's most popular widower. Understanding, softspoken, thoughtful.

HOWARD CUNNINGHAM (Tom Bosley), "Happy Days"(1974-83).
A nostalgic recreation who was actually born over two decades after Jim and Ozzie.

WARD CLEAVER (Hugh Beaumont), "Leave It to Beaver" (1957-62).
A loving father who expects the best—but not the impossible—from his kids. The first sitcom dad to regularly admit he makes mistakes.

DR. ALEX STONE (Carl Betz), "The Donna Reed Show" (1958-66).
A clean-cut pediatrician who tries real hard to spend "quality time" with his kids.

Best of the '70s

The '70s were the golden age of sitcoms. Not only were there more genuinely funny comedies than ever before, but for the first time sitcoms also commented intelligently on important issues in American society. Episodes of "M*A*S*H," for example, were written with Vietnam in mind. "All in the Family" featured a running battle between liberal and conservative ideology. "Barney Miller" gave us cops we could respect as human beings. This was so different from anything that had ever appeared on the small screen before that one has to wonder what brought it about. It may have been that the shows' creators were influenced by the political activism of the '60s and wanted to make their own statements. Or perhaps, inspired by the debates of the '60s, they realized that sitcoms didn't all have to be like "Gilligan's Island," catering to the lowest common denominator. Maybe they gave the American public credit for having intelligence. Or maybe they realized that communicating with millions of people every week gave them a responsibility to fulfill—to produce the best, most thoughtful, most creative work they could and hope that the public would appreciate it. In any case, a handful of dedicated sitcom producers and writers revolutionized the most important medium in modern society by taking it—and us—seriously.

The qualitative changes weren't all in the area of social relevance, though. The jokes got better, for one thing. Brilliant one-liners flew across the airwaves with regularity. And writers took the time to develop more facets of their characters' personalities. In the '70s, for the first time, a nice guy could have a dark side, a sexy woman could be smart. Characters could relate to each other as real human beings did. They did real things—got drunk, divorced, frustrated, depressed. And then (miracle of miracles) at the end, they didn't necessarily solve their problems. The best sitcoms weren't twenty-two minutes to a happy ending anymore—they offered twenty-two minutes of intelligent humor and poignant character exposition. They gave us personalities and stories we would never forget.

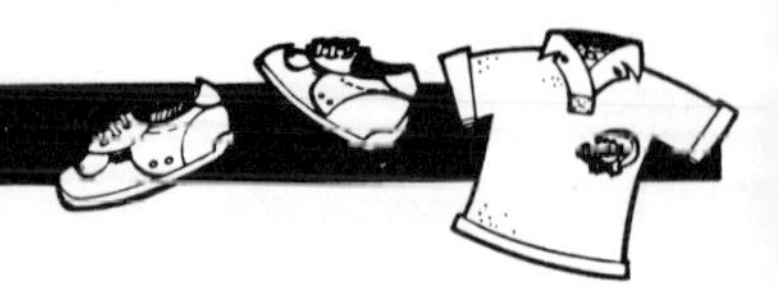

ALL IN THE FAMILY

"All in the Family" is the single most influential program in the history of television.

•It destroyed TV's taboos about dealing with controversial subjects like death, menopause, homosexuality, and even rape.

•It helped close the gap between sharply divided factions of American society by providing a forum in which to dramatize it. For the first time, sitcom characters had political views; Archie Bunker, the main character, was a chauvinistic reactionary who hated pinkos, hippies, and peaceniks. His son-in-law, Mike, was a hot-headed, self-righteous liberal whose pie-in-the-sky rhetoric could be insufferable. Intellectuals could laugh at Archie, conservatives could laugh at Mike—and we could all laugh at each other.

•It brought racial and ethnic prejudices out in the open, making it easier for society to recognize and deal with them. And laugh at them. Archie's prejudiced statements about Hebes, Spics, and jungle bunnies were so outrageous that viewers gasped—and then cracked up. "Look," Archie once told his neighbor, "Archie Bunker ain't no bigot. I'm the first to say—it ain't your fault you're colored!"

•It demonstrated that American TV audiences will respond to topical issues and sophisticated humor. Its phenomenal ratings (it was the highest-ranked show in America for five years) heralded a new era of sitcoms with believable situations and good writing.

Perhaps the most phenomenal aspect of its accomplishment is that "All in the Family" was written and performed in a standard family sitcom format—the same one that gave us "Ozzie and Harriet." "Their secret," explains a critic, "was simple: They had fantastic acting, fantastic writing, and a producer with more guts than any executive in TV history." Indeed, anyone who cares about the quality of television programming owes Norman Lear a debt of gratitude. In the face of network pressure, he refused to water down his creation, and as a result, he revolutionized the medium.

The Bunkers/Stivics of Queens, New York, consisted of four unexceptional individuals. Archie was the head of the house. His wife, Edith, was a well-intentioned, slightly dingy homemaker. His "little goil," Gloria, was a moderately bright woman in Shirley Temple curls and miniskirts. And then there was Mike, the "meathead."

In the real world, this quartet would be regarded as a normal blue-collar family. But on television, they were a revolution, because they spoke and related to each other in realistic, down-to-earth terms. When Edith asked, "Do you love me?" Archie's reply wasn't sitcom saccharine. "Edith," he said, "where the *hell* are you getting these questions from?" And when he finally, grudgingly, had to admit that he cared about her, there was no romance in it. "I answer that question every day," he grunted, "by the fact that I live with you and take care of you. I go to work and come home, go to work and come home. . . ."

More often, the principals bickered incessantly—particularly Mike and Archie. When, for example, Mike moaned, "Four years of school before I even begin to make a living! It feels like forever!" Archie wasn't the slightest bit sympathetic. "Lemme tell you somethin', sonny boy," he answered, "the same thought comes over me at least once a day. I tell ya, Gloria married the laziest white man I *ever* seen."

No one had ever talked like that on national television. Suddenly, *anything* was possible, and TV was a wide-open medium.

"All in the Family" owes a great deal to the talent and dedication of all its stars. Jean Stapleton, for example, was so involved with Edith that she inadvertantly began acting the part at home. But Carroll O'Connor deserves special credit for his carefully crafted portrait of an American bigot. He breathed extraordinary humanity into Archie Bunker, gave him the conflicts and concerns that a real "Archie" would feel, and thereby made him believable.

As a result, Archie is one of the greatest characters in television history. And "All in the Family" is a true American treasure.

When Edith thought she had a hereditary shoplifting problem, she consulted a clergyman. She was so pious that a book of her comments was issued by a Christian publisher.

FLASHBACK

ARCHIE: "If you're gonna have your change of life, have it right now! You got exactly thirty seconds.... Change!"
EDITH: "Can I finish my soup first?"

ARCHIE: "Suppose everyone ran off to one of the communes. Who'd run the machines? Who'd drive the subways? How would I get to work?"
MIKE: "Archie, not everybody's gonna run off to a commune. It's a question of each man doing his own thing. Your thing is grubbing for a living in this polluted, crime-ridden city."
ARCHIE: "And your thing is spongin' off my thing."

ARCHIE: "After twenty-four years of stifles, the dingbat turns on me!"

VITAL STATS

POLL RESULTS:
First
PROGRAM INFO:
- Half-hour show. CBS.
- First show: Jan. 12, 1971
- Last show: Sept. 21, 1983
- 325 episodes

TIME: The '70s through the early '80s.

PLACE: The home of Archie and Edith Bunker, at 704 Houser Street, Queens, New York. Most of the action takes place in the living room. Occasionally, Archie relaxes at the neighborhood bar, Kelsey's. Edith spends most of her time in the kitchen.

BACKGROUND: Archie Bunker, a lower-middle-class laborer, sees himself as the ruler of his small kingdom. His traditional wife Edith fawns all over him and is eager to serve him beers when he comes home to sit on his throne/easy chair. But when daughter Gloria and her new husband, Mike, a hotheaded liberal, move in, Archie's world turns upside down. Mike and Archie are bitter foes politically and ethically. Both are extremists, but both have to learn to live with each other. Luckily, the loving but not-too-bright Edith can usually smooth things over. Until the next barrage.

MAIN CAST:

- **Archie Bunker** (Carroll O'Connor): Dock foreman for the Prendergast Tool and Die Company. An ignorant bigot who blasts his outrageous opinions at the top of his lungs.
- **Edith Bunker** (Jean Stapleton): A.k.a. "Dingbat." Archie's loving, somewhat dim-witted wife; she's the real heart of the family.
- **Mike Stivic** (Rob Reiner): Archie's knee-jerk liberal son-in-law, a sociology student in college. Makes good points but is as intransigent and closed-minded as Archie. Redeemed by his devotion to Gloria.
- **Gloria Stivic** (Sally Struthers): The Bunkers' baby-voiced daughter, who gradually becomes more politically aware through Mike's influence and her own native intelligence.
- **George Jefferson** (Sherman Hemsley): The next-door neighbor, a black who's just as prejudiced as Archie.
- **Louise Jefferson** (Isabel Sanford): George's wife, Edith's friend.
- **Lionel Jefferson** (Mike Evans): George's son. Loves to bait Archie.
- **Stephanie Mills** (Danielle Brisebois): Archie's niece, abandoned by her father and adopted by the Bunkers in 1978.

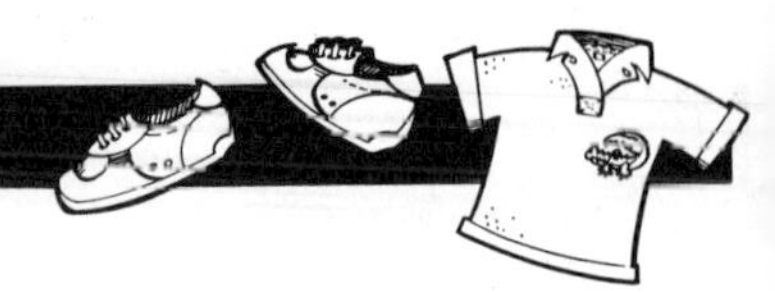

MISCELLANY

•Norman Lear's first choice for the role of Archie Bunker was Mickey Rooney. Rooney rejected the idea, telling Lear, "if you go on the air with that, they're gonna kill you dead in the streets!"

•Edith Bunker was so important to Americans that when she "died" of a stroke in 1980, *Newsweek* ran a half-page obituary, as they would have for a real world leader.

•Rob Reiner wore a toupee for his role as the long-haired Mike Stivic—he's actually as bald as his father, Carl Reiner. Even without hair, however, fans recognized him on the street wherever he went and yelled "Meathead" after him. He hated it.

•"All in the Family"'s twelve-and-a-half season run was second only to "Ozzie and Harriet" (which ran fourteen) among TV sitcoms. This seemed an unlikely possibility at first—the show initially scored low in the ratings (fifty-fourth). But word of mouth and a lot of press sparked viewers' interest. Six months after its premiere, "All in the Family" was ranked number one.

•When Gloria "gave birth" to Joey in 1975, the event inspired another first—the "Joey" doll, billed as " the first anatomically correct male doll."

THEMES OK

The original title of the show was "Those Were the Days"—hence the name of the theme song.

•The theme was performed with only a piano and two voices (Archie's and Edith's) because Norman Lear had only $800 left in his budget to record it and that was the cheapest way to go.

•The song was redone several times over the years because audiences couldn't quite understand the line "Gee our old LaSalle ran great."

•Stapleton, whose voice cracked memorably during "Those Were the Days," is really a fine singer. She can be heard singing on the Broadway soundtracks of *Bells Are Ringing* and *Damn Yankees*.

In 1976 Archie joined the ranks of the unemployed. By then Meathead and Gloria had moved out, so the Bunkers had to take in a boarder to make ends meet. Wouldn't you know it? She turned out to be one of "them ethnic types" Archie couldn't stand. She was Teresa Betancourt (Liz Torres), a Puerto Rican. It was an interesting gimmick that didn't work—so the next season Teresa moved out and Stephanie, Archie's abandoned niece, became part of the family. Archie's chair, by the way, is now in the Smithsonian Institution.

ALL IN THE FAMILY

In 1974, Carroll O'Connor went on strike for more money. At first it seemed that his demands couldn't be met—so, according to *TV Guide*, the show's writers came up with an emergency plan to have Archie attend a convention, where he would be mugged and murdered. That way the show could continue with the rest of the cast. O'Connor settled for $2 million per year.

•Jean Stapleton worried about keeping her identity separate from Edith's, both professionally and personally. She was an accomplished actress who didn't want the public to restrict her to "Edith" roles on the screen; plus she actually found herself "acting like a dingbat" at home.

•The cast was in love with the show. The final episode in which they all appeared together, in 1978, took 100 rehearsals. They were too upset to get through it. "It was like bidding good-bye to your real family," one writer said.

CRITICS' COMMENTS

Michael apolgizes to Gloria during her pregnancy after one of his insensitive remarks. Ultimately, the lovely couple found they were incompatible and got a divorce—which enabled Sally Struthers to have her own show for one season, "Gloria." Unlike "All in the Family," it bombed. Rob Reiner went on to become one of Hollywood's hottest directors.

ABOUT ITS MEANING:
"I'm sure that the world thinks that what it was about was controversy. They had transvestites, and rape, and blockbusting, and religious prejudice, the polarization of the country, asked, 'Is John Wayne crazy?', 'Is the press crazy?' But the writers and Norman Lear always asserted that they weren't looking for issues—they were looking for stories that would bring out and develop their characters; it's just that they weren't *afraid* of issues."

—Sandra Konte,
***L.A. Times* syndicate**

"People seem to forget that the title was 'All in the Family.' And the key word is 'family.' If you asked Norman Lear, he would probably say that it really was about a family sticking together through thick and thin, and when it came down to it, really caring about each other."

—Rick Mitz,
The Great Sitcom Book

"What was bad about it, even though Lear obviously had a liberal point of view, is that it did allow a racist to sit there and see Archie as some kind of hero. That would drive both Lear and O'Connor crazy whenever it was mentioned to them. But what I think they would have said is that even though bigots laughed at what Archie said, he was such a ridiculous character that subliminally maybe some kind of progress was made."

—Ed Siegel, *Boston Globe*

ABOUT O'CONNOR:
"Carroll O'Connor's performance was among the greatest ever on television, in any kind of a show....Even as Archie was being buffoonish and abusive to people, there was a poignance there. A lesser actor would have made him just a vicious caricature. But it was important to see that Archie was not a demon from hell—that he was a human being with many flaws. It was the deepest and most complex comedy ever, up to that time."

—Tom Shales,
Washington Post

ABOUT EDITH:
"Edith Bunker was probably the best example on TV of what most mothers and wives of her generation were. The evolution of her character probably did a lot to show many of her contemporaries, who were stifled all their lives, the options open to them. I wouldn't be surprised if housewives who'd never been out in the world went and got their first jobs after Edith came out of herself like that."

—Diane Albert,
TV Collector

THE MARY TYLER MOORE SHOW

Mary Tyler Moore didn't consider herself a feminist. "I was never a militant women's libber," she told a reporter in 1977. "There's a lot of Mary Richards in me—but there's also a lot of Laura Petrie, the housewife I played on 'The Dick Van Dyke Show.'" Yet her sitcom did more to establish the women's movement and bolster the spirits of people who were trying to live out its ideals than a lot of serious feminist efforts.

You might call "Mary" a sugar-coated revolution. Without shedding the veneer of sweetness or the relentless optimism that characterized traditional sitcoms, it managed to introduce the modern world—and specifically, the modern woman—to the small screen.

Mary Richards was a "nice girl." She was ultra-normal. (On a first encounter with Mary, her neighbor Rhoda asked incredulously, "Who'd you get that nightie from, Tricia Nixon?") She was friendly, perky, involved, good at her job (she even got promoted). She was attractive and had her share of dates.

But she was also an unmarried career woman in her thirties, single because she *chose* to be.

In a TV first, she demonstrated to her audience that life without a mate didn't have to be dull or depressing—and that women didn't have to be dependent on husbands. She had fun with her *girlfriends.* She entertained by *herself.* She hinted at having an *affair.*

"Don't forget to take your pill," Mary's mother once said to her father. "I won't," Mary responded absently.

That was different.

Yet it didn't make Mary threatening, as some TV executives predicted; it just made her realistic. Unlike Lucy, Mary didn't have to take pratfalls to be funny. She could get laughs by giving disastrous dinner parties (Johnny Carson once accepted her dinner invitation, and then the electricity went out—the episode was performed in the dark); she could take us along on bad dates (a frequent occurrence—she once estimated that 90 percent of her dates were bombs); and she could crack us up by acting mildly neurotic, not wacky (Mary couldn't go to her hairdresser unless she washed her hair first, and she once moved rather than fire a housekeeper).

But Mary didn't have to gather all the laughs herself. "The Mary Tyler Moore Show" was the first sitcom to feature an ensemble cast of multidimensional, really *funny*, supporting characters. There was Ted Baxter ("Hi, guys!"), the pompous, idiotic, but lovable anchorman; Rhoda Morgenstern, the fat girl who became a swan ("Why am I bothering to eat this chocolate? I might as well apply it directly to my thighs."); Sue Ann Nivens, the homemaker with hotpants ("Hello. You are the most gorgeous hunk of flesh I have ever seen."); Lou Grant, her boss, an overweight, bad-tempered boozer with a hidden sensitive streak ("Mary, Mary, Mary..."); Murray, the sarcastic writer ("You're Ted. Does it ever bother you that you're Ted?"); and Phyllis, her pretentious landlord.

These characters were so important that although most of them were single, their presence turned the program into a classic *family* sitcom.

In one of its most important legacies, "The Mary Tyler Moore Show" stated that in the modern era friends *are* family. Mary's immediate relatives didn't live in Minneapolis. But she found a substitute—as we all do—in her apartment building and at work. She set the stage for the many "work-place" sitcoms to come when she said to her newsroom friends, "What is a family? I think I know. A family is people who make you feel less alone and really loved. Thank you for being my family."

Mary Tyler Moore has left an indelible mark on television. Along with Lucy, she is probably the most important female ever to star in a sitcom.

In a 1974 episode, Murray and Marie Slaughter tried to adopt a child.

FLASHBACK

SUE ANN: "Mary, what do you think turns on a man?"
MARY [exasperated]: "Sue Ann, I haven't the slightest idea."
SUE ANN: "I know that, dear, I was just trying to make your day."

MARY [on being told she's an innocent]: "That's not true, Mr. Grant.... I've been around.... well, not around, but nearby."

TED [to a handsome man]: "Boy, I bet you have to beat 'em off with a stick."

[*Mary is being interviewed for a job.*]

LOU: "How old are you?"
MARY: Thirty."
LOU: "What religion are you?"
MARY [reluctantly]: "Mr. Grant, I don't know how to say this. You're not allowed to ask that when someone's applying for a job. It's against the law."
LOU: "Wanna call a cop? Are you married?"
MARY: "Presbyterian."

VITAL STATS

POLL RESULTS:
Second
PROGRAM INFO:
•Half-hour show. CBS
•First show: Sept. 19, 1970
•Last show: Sept. 8, 1977
•168 episodes

TIME: The early '70s.

PLACE: Minneapolis, Minnesota, home of Mary Richards, producer of Channel 12's "Six O'Clock News" program. Action takes place at the Snyder Building, in the offices of WJM-TV, and at 119 North Weatherly, Apartment D, in Mary's studio apartment.

BACKGROUND: Mary Richards moves to Minneapolis after breaking up with her longtime boyfriend. Although she's reached thirty without marrying, she isn't particularly concerned about it. She gets a job as associate producer at WJM-TV and instantly begins to form close familial ties with her coworkers. At home, she also develops tight bonds. These warm friendships sustain her as she tries to make it "after all."

MAIN CAST:
- **Mary Richards** (Mary Tyler Moore): Bright, friendly, but occasionally insecure, she's the first respectable single woman on TV to even hint at having slept with her boyfriend. Equally adept at her job and winning close, devoted friends.
- **Lou Grant** (Ed Asner): The newsroom boss, gruff, overweight, hard-drinking. But essentially goodhearted. Becomes Mary's surrogate father and close friend.
- **Ted Baxter** (Ted Knight): Egotistical, dumb anchorman. So inept as a newscaster that what little audience he has tunes in just to laugh at him.
- **Murray Slaughter** (Gavin MacLeod): Head newswriter. Warm and friendly, except for barbs at Ted. Has a secret crush on Mary but remains devoted to his wife, Marie.
- **Rhoda Morgenstern** (Valerie Harper): Mary's neighbor and best friend. A window dresser at Hempel's Department Store. Desperately wants to get married but is convinced her weight problem and negative self-image will prevent it.
- **Phyllis Lindstrom** (Cloris Leachman): Mary's pretentious landlady, struggling to be the perfect wife, mother, and citizen.
- **Georgette Franklin** (Georgia Engle): Ted's girlfriend, later his wife. Another Hempel's window dresser, endearingly dumb, loyal.
- **Sue Ann Nivens** (Betty White): The station's horny "Happy Homemaker." Nursing an unrequited crush on Lou.

Lou Grant got pretty emotional in the newsroom. Here he berates his nephew for slacking off.

Great moments in broadcast journalism: Ted Baxter, the best darned anchorman in America, gives CBS's Walter Cronkite a few pointers about how the pros do it.

UNLIKELY ROMANCE

As every "MTM" buff knows, Mary's relationship with Mr. Grant (she couldn't bring herself to call her boss by his first name) was borderline romantic but never quite got there. Not that the writers didn't think about it. One possible scenario had Mary and Lou getting married. They would turn off the lights, and Mary would murmur, "Oh, Mr. Gra-ant."

ORIGINS

In the original format of the show, Mary Richards was a divorcee trying to make it on her own. CBS balked, believing that divorcees were not sympathetic characters—and besides, they said, viewers would assume she had divorced Dick Van Dyke.

• So in the second version, Mary became a widow trying to make it on her own. That didn't work either. As one producer recalled, "We didn't want to kill off another man to get Mary on the air."

• So finally "MTM" made Mary Richards single (what else was left?)—and Mary Richards made Mary Tyler Moore very, very rich.

SCOREBOARD

The Mary Tyler Moore Show" was the most honored show in Emmy history. It received twenty-seven awards, including three for best comedy show, one for directing, and five for writing. Moore, Asner, and Harper received three Emmys each, Ted Knight and Betty White two, and Cloris Leachman one.

• The show spawned more successful spinoffs—three ("Rhoda," "Phyllis," and "Lou Grant")—than any other sitcom. In the 1975 season, two of the spinoffs placed in the annual top ten ("Phyllis" was six; "Rhoda" was eight), outstripping even "Mary," which was ranked nineteen.

HOME SWEET HOME

Remember that neat house at 119 North Weatherly where Mary supposedly had her apartment? It was owned by a University of Minnesota humanities professor. She was initially delighted to let MTM Productions shoot its exterior for use on the show (the interior scenes were done in the studio).

But when the program became popular, doorbell ringers began showing up regularly, asking for Mary, Rhoda, and Phyllis.

The professor's life was so disrupted that she refused to let MTM film the outside of her house anymore. When MTM ignored her wishes and showed up to film the house anyway, the professor hung banners reading, "Impeach Nixon" out of the window that was supposed to be Mary's. That stopped the film crews.

Soon after that, Mary Richards "moved" to a high-rise.

ON SPUNK

One of the most famous "MTM" scenes is the one where Lou Grant, interviewing Mary for a job, waves a finger at her and says, " You know what?... You got spunk ...I *hate* spunk."

Ed Asner on that moment, in *Playboy*:

"Ooohh...That 'I hate spunk' line was one of those moments when everything—the build-up, the physicality, the voice, the look, the timing—everything was absolutely perfect. Athletes have those moments sometimes. Actors have them less often. But that moment Mary and I had together was transcendent. I felt such an inordinate power; the megalomania it induces in a performer is almost frightening. You feel you have those three hundred people right there in your hand and you could squeeze them into a pulp if you so wished. I'm speaking about ultimate power."

And here we thought it was just funny.

Mary Richards is stuck on another one of her awful dates—this time with a mortician she met at a convention.

CRITICS' COMMENTS

ABOUT "MARY" AND REAL LIFE:

"A lot of fans handle real-life situations by referring to episodes of 'The Mary Tyler Moore Show.' In fact, I give advice from 'Mary Tyler Moore.' I can say, 'Well, it's just like in the "Mary Tyler Moore Show" when Mary was so worried about going to that wedding and then it turned out that she was gonna be un-invited anyway.... So why worry about it?'

"I think you *could* live your life by the 'Mary Tyler Moore' scripts, if you selected them carefully."

—Robert Bianco,
Pittsburgh Press

"It was a good time to tell viewers that people on television are pretty ordinary. And if they try to pretend otherwise, they do so at their own peril. That's what the Ted Baxter character was all about."

—John Marten,
Providence Journal-Bulletin

"This is *the* most important comedy show for women *ever*. Mary was single, she was trying very hard, she was successful, but she seemed very real.... She had *our* flaws—like her lack of confidence. But it didn't destroy her; she laughed about it."

—Douglas Durden,
Richmond Times Dispatch

ABOUT THE CHARACTERS:

"Sue Ann Nivens was the *last* thing you'd expect from Betty White. Remember, most of us knew her only from the game show 'Password.' To write that part for her, to put her in *that* role, was a stroke of brilliance. Nobody except the writers ever *dreamed* she'd play it was well as she did."

—Greg Bailey,
Nashville Banner

"Mary Richards...really *did* make it. She had a lovely apartment, a wonderful job, friends who loved and adored her. She didn't have kids, but she never really wanted them....And she never really wanted for a date; if she had one, it was great, but it didn't seem to matter much. Mary, in fact, never really wanted for anything. She was a single woman on her own, but had a totally safe life. In that respect 'Mary Tyler Moore' was a typical sitcom, because every sitcom woman— except Lucy— had a safe life."

—Monica Collins,
USA Today

"They were authentic characters that you developed a rapport with and felt some concern about. Like if Lou Grant got a divorce, or had a problem with booze, you actually worried a little about him."

—John Carman,
San Francisco Chronicle

"The characters in 'The MTM Show' were 'viewer friendly.' They didn't have a hard edge like the characters on a Norman Lear type show."

—Michael Duffy,
Detroit Free Press

M*A*S*H

Before "M*A*S*H, sitcoms treated the American military as a joke. In the '50s, there was Bilko's army, full of con men and incompetents. And in the '60s, "McHale's Navy" and "Hogan's Heroes" took us to wacky World War II , where Nazis and Japs were so inept that it was amazing they could even zip up their flies, let alone win a battle or two.

But in 1972, "M*A*S*H brought a different type of war to the sitcom. It had blood. And death. And sorrow. It was still funny, but the humor was derived from people's attempts to escape the horror around them, not from silliness. And if characters did act silly, it was because the rest of the time they had to be deadly serious.

Nominally, "M*A*S*H" was about the Korean War. But the conflict was really meant to be generic. Producers Larry Gelbart, Gene Reynolds, and Burt Metcalfe were trying to make a statement about Vietnam, about the horror of combat, and above all, about the resilience of men and women who manage to retain their humanity through the worst experiences. "We wanted our show to be about grace under pressure," Gelbart explained.

It was a tough assignment. But although there was no precedent for a sitcom that juxtaposed its humor with the constant presence of death, "M*A*S*H" still succeeded.

One reason was the quality of its writing. The dialogue *sounded* like wartime conversation. It was sharp and abrasive, thoughtful, touching, outrageous, clever. And there were more good one-liners in "M*A*S*H" than in any other TV series ever.

HAWKEYE [offering a bottle of homemade booze]: "Care for a snort?" WINCHESTER: "No, thank you. I make it a practice never to drink anything that's been in a radiator."

Another reason: "M*A*S*H" managed to clothe its serious message in wacky sitcom antics. A warmongering general who sent too many young men to needless deaths was, for example, put out of commission by a fake emergency appendectomy. And the chief surgeon often visited his wounded patients dressed as Groucho Marx or as a gorilla.

"Why does he do such things?" his sidekick, Trapper John, was asked.

"I guess he's just unstable," Trapper replied. "You see, he took this weird oath as a young man never to stand there and watch people die."

The most powerful reason for "M*A*S*H"'s success, however, was the way the characters changed and grew. During the eleven years that it was on the air, its characters developed a depth that no sitcom inhabitants had ever displayed. "Hot Lips" Houlihan gradually stopped being an army clown and became a sensitive part of the team; Klinger stopped wearing dresses and learned responsibility; B.J. had an affair or two; Winchester overcame his pomposity (sometimes) and showed a vulnerable side. And Hawkeye—well, he was all things to all people in the '70s: a wisecracking womanizer, a sensitive modern man, a brilliant surgeon, a drunk. He was America's hero.

As the characters developed complex personalities, they began to seem incredibly real to their audience; tuning in "M*A*S*H" became more like visiting old friends than watching a TV program. In fact, Corporal Max Klinger probably spoke for a huge segment of America when he said, "I may not have a family in Toledo, but I got one here."

"M*A*S*H" sometimes took itself a little too seriously, and sometimes its message was about as subtle as the meatball surgery it deplored. But it proved that sitcoms can have depth and humanity and characters we care about. And with its effective anti-war message, it proved that a sitcom can be a powerful weapon itself.

The happy couple, Larry Linville and Loretta Swit. The original movie parts of Maj. Burns and Hot Lips were played by Robert Duvall and Sally Kellerman.

FLASHBACK

KLINGER: "Lunchtime, folks. Grab your platter and watch it splatter....Have some stew, Colonel?"
POTTER: "What kind is it?"
KLINGER: "Could be beef, pork, or water buffalo. [Confidentially] We'll never know, and *it* won't tell."
POTTER: "Well, as long as it's dead. Spoon it on, son...no toast.
KLINGER [to co-server]: "One brown puddle, hold the shingle."

WINCHESTER: "I loathe you, Pierce."
HAWKEYE: "I call your loathe and raise you two despises."

RADAR: "How can I ever thank you?"
HAWKEYE: "Well, you can give us your firstborn."
B.J.: "And an order of fries."

VITAL STATS

POLL RESULTS:
Third
PROGRAM INFO:
- Half-hour show. CBS
- First show: Sept 17, 1972
- Last show: Sept. 19, 1983
- 251 episodes

TIME: 1950-53, during the United States' Korean "police action," when 142,091 Americans lost their lives in an effort to prevent "Communist agression."

PLACE: Three miles from the front lines, at the M*A*S*H 4077th. M*A*S*H stands for Mobile Army Surgical Hospital; it is a field hospital where "meatball surgery" is performed to save the lives of soldiers wounded in battle.

BACKGROUND: During the Korean conflict, 910 doctors were stationed at various M*A*S*H units. The action here focuses on one group of army doctors and nurses. Their shared peril causes them to develop tight bonds despite their disparate personalities, and they go to great lengths to avoid being driven insane by the pressure.

MAIN CAST:
- **Maj. Benjamin Franklin "Hawkeye" Pierce** (Alan Alda) : A brilliant surgeon from Crabapple Cove, Maine. An incorrigible practical joker, incurably randy. Our hero.
- **Capt. "Trapper" John McIntyre** (Wayne Rogers): Hawkeye's high-spirited bunkmate.
- **Capt. B. J. Hunnicut** (Mike Farrell): Trapper's replacement. Straight, serious family man who becomes the biggest practical joker in camp.
- **Maj. Margaret "Hot Lips" Houlihan** (Loretta Swit): By-the-book chief nurse. Eventually loosens up.
- **Maj. Frank Burns** (Larry Linville): Prissy, incompetent surgeon. Flips out when Hot Lips leaves him.
- **Lt. Col. Henry Blake** (MacLean Stevenson): Tolerant, wacky CO.
- **Col. Sherman T. Potter** (Harry Morgan): His replacement, a "regular army" officer who learns to put up with the staff's insanity.
- **Cpl. Maxwell Klinger** (Jamie Farr): The dress-wearing company clerk who's trying to get out of the Army on a "section eight," for mental incompetence.
- **Cpl. Walter "Radar" O'Reilly** (Gary Burghoff): The unit's pet, a shy, efficient company clerk. Called "Radar" because of his uncanny abilities to anticipate his CO's requests and the incoming wounded.
- **Father Francis Mulcahy** (William Christopher): The army chaplain who adds a necessary voice of conscience to the proceedings.
- **Maj. Charles Emerson Winchester III** (David Ogden Stiers): The pompous Boston blue blood who replaces Burns in 1977.

Radar O'Reilly and friend.

ANACHRONISMS

Every once in a while, even "M*A*S*H" slipped up in the accuracy department. For instance, if the M*A*S*H unit was only a couple of miles from the front, why were the wounded brought out in helicopters instead of ambulances?

• Real M*A*S*H doctors pointed out that there were no metal gurneys (hospital beds on wheels) at the front—patients were brought in on litters and placed on sawhorses for surgery.

• When Henry Blake was sent home, he was told he had enough "points" to go. Actually, the army gave up the point system after World War II.

• For real nitpickers, *My Darling Clementine*, the "first-run" movie that the unit saw in 1951, was actually made in 1946.

• Most ironic of all, the military-hating Klinger's serial number was once given as RA19571782. But RA was only given to volunteers; US was used for draftees.

AUTHOR-ITY

Dr. Richard Hornberger (a.k.a. Richard Hooker), who wrote the book on which the series was based, hated the show. Dr. Hornberger, a Republican and former M*A*S*H surgeon, believed in the Korean War and said, "I operated on a thousand or so wounded kids, and I know more about war than a bunch of undereducated actors who go around blathering sanctimonious, self-righteous noises."

GOING, GOING. . .

• Wayne Rogers departed the M*A*S*H unit in 1974 because he realized that Alda, not he, was becoming the focus of the show. He said he'd been promised when he signed on that Trapper John would be the star.

• Larry Linville left the show because there was nothing left to do with the character of Burns.

• Gary Burghoff, the only actor who went from the *M*A*S*H* film to the sitcom, left after seven years because he was suffering severe burnout and didn't like being recognized on the street.

IDLE STATS

• Alan Alda's initial salary was a paltry $10,000 per episode. By the last season, it had soared to $5 million a year.

• The last episode, "Goodbye, Farewell, Amen," was a 2 1/2 hour movie seen by more than 125 million people, making it one of the most-watched programs of all time.

Hawkeye and Hot Lips started out as enemies and ended up allies—a development that symbolized the growth and change of the characters.

CRITICS' COMMENTS

ABOUT THE TURNING POINT:
"'M*A*S*H' was one of the first shows to use characters' histories...the way dramatic shows like 'Hill Street Blues' would in the '80s. The relationship, say, between Hawkeye and Hot Lips started out as very crudely comic in the beginning. But through a series of encounters between them, it grew to one of respect, affection, and tenderness.

"That show really came of age, I think, when they killed Henry Blake. The reason for it, I've been told, was that McClean Stevenson was such a pain to work with that the writers wanted to make sure there would never, ever be pressure put on them to write him back into the script, for any reason.

But the result was spectacular; seeing that show was such a jolt. Kill a beloved character in a sitcom? I mean, genial old Henry Blake? With his cap full of fishing lures and everything? It sort of brought home some of the reality of the war, and it gave the rationale for the changes in the characters."

—Phil Kloer,
Atlanta Constitution

"'M*A*S*H' was terrific in the early years, when Hot Lips was still Hot Lips and Hawkeye was like the character in the movie....I always thought the turning point was when Trapper left and B.J. came. B.J. screwed the show up—you know, Mr. Sensitive, Mr. Phil Donahue in 1950.

"After the fourth or fifth year, they never called Hot Lips that again. She became Margaret. And they began putting mid-1980s social mores onto a 1950s setting. That was Alan Alda for you. It shows you how good the show was when it started, that they were able to overcome him.

"The early years of that show were terrific. The later years, when Hot Lips became Margaret and Hawkeye became Betty Friedan, aren't."

—Tom Jicha,
Miami News

ABOUT WAR COMEDY:
"People had shied away from portraying real war as a comedy on TV before. But there's always a lot of humor in war. For one thing, when you have all those people from all over the country together in one small group, you immediately have comedians. They're the ones who turn to humor to survive, to cover up the tragedy they're involved in. After all, a M*A*S*H unit was probably the worst aspect of that war ...when they brought the bodies in and there were guys blown half to pieces...and they had to try to cheer them up. This had never been shown before on TV in any entertainment genre."

—Bob Foster,
San Mateo Times

ABOUT ITS PROS AND CONS:
"'M*A*S*H,' although it was technically good, took itself far too seriously. In fact, it sort of hollowed itself out as a shrine.
"I don't mind that it wrestled with problems. What I minded was that it seemed to think it had solutions. And that's a real dangerous thing for a comedy to do."

Jim Gordon,
Gary Post-Tribune

BARNEY MILLER

At the time "Barney Miller" first went on the air in 1975, most Americans thought of cops as either avenging angels (like Kojak), or the real-life head-crunchers who brutally patrolled Mayor Daley's Chicago in 1968. The possibility that cops might just be regular working stiffs with normal problems was a radical concept—which might explain why, in its first season, "Barney" didn't do too well.

Fortunately, viewers warmed up to the notion. "You watched these guys deal with the daily insanity of their work," recalls one critic, "and you couldn't help thinking, 'So *that's* what it's like to be a cop.'"

"Barney Miller" probably didn't set out to change America's perception of policework. But for six years, tens of millions of Americans tuned in the show religiously every Thursday night; it had to have an effect.

At the very least, "Barney Miller" expanded the possibilities for cop shows. There were no speeding cars, no evil killers, no meetings with stoolies in back alleys. All the action took place on a single set—in a dilapidated squad room. There Barney, levelheaded and compassionate ("Look, I can appreciate your frustration, Mr. Osborne, but that is no reason for breaking and entering"), presided over a group that one critic called "the Keystone Cops under the ethnic quota system."

He had a point. The original cast included two Jews, an Asian, a Black, a Chicano, and a Pole. Without trying too hard, the series could have been as racially insulting as "Beulah" or "Life with Luigi." But in a TV first, the writers didn't make this ethnicity the focus of the show's humor; instead, they made it incidental to the personalities, concerns, and quirks of the characters.

Wojohowicz, the Polish detective, displayed a sincerity and sensitivity beneath his linebacker's physique and Dopey voice. The dapper black, Harris, was more concerned with his stockbroker and literary agent than with crooks. Yemana, the Japanese, made coffee (if you could call it that), read racing forms, and surveyed the chaos through world-weary eyes. Dietrich, the intellectual, spread his dry wit and cynicism. (Man: "I'm looking for Sergeant Wojohowicz." Dietrich [looking up from his desk]: "Yeah. We're all looking for something.")

And Fish, the ancient Jew, obviously on his last legs (which were usually headed for the bathroom), moaned about everything. In one episode the detectives were accidentally given hash brownies and Fish began leaping tall buildings with a single bound. When he found out the cause, he sighed, "The only time I feel good, it has to be illegal."

Where else could you see a cop get stoned...and enjoy it?

"Barney Miller" was almost entirely character-driven, so it relied heavily on its exceptional dialogue. This, in turn, established a patient, steady pace for each episode. The cops arrived; they chatted; the phone rang; Barney wandered in and out; a local looney was hauled in; a victim complained loudly while a prisoner made cracks about his or her situation. In the end, everything was resolved as well as it could be, which wasn't always to everyone's satisfaction. And then the guys went home.

It was unexciting, but once you got inside the characters' heads, it became absolutely fascinating. You could understand what it felt like to try to deal fairly with the steady stream of disoriented citizens who paraded through the squad room.

"Barney Miller" respected people. And it recognized that the law is a tool to make life better—not to punish and destroy. It was a quiet revolution...which is just what you'd expect from Barney.

Max Gail refused to play Wojo unless the producer agreed to make him him sensitive as well as dumb.

FLASHBACK

WOJO [to a hooker]: "Any previous convictions?"
HOOKER: "Yeah, I once thought cleanliness was next to godliness."

HARRIS [writing a report on a confiscated porn film]: "The second act tends to ramble, and the denouement seems lacking in force."

FISH: "Do you know what it's like to be chasing a guy on Forty-third Street while your partner is cornering him on Fifty-second?"

BARNEY: "Any coffee left?"
YEMANA: "You must be a glutton for punishment."

Jack Soo died in 1978, mid-season.

VITAL STATS

POLL RESULTS:
Fourth
PROGRAM INFO:
- Half-hour show. ABC.
- First show: Jan. 23, 1975
- Last show: Sept. 9, 1982
- 170 episodes

TIME: The mid-'70s.

PLACE: The 12th Police Precinct, a dilapidated, chaotic squad-room in the heart of New York's Greenwich Village, from which chief of detectives Barney Miller dispatches his staff to investigate an endless array of crimes, big and small.

BACKGROUND: It's not easy being a cop, which is evident in the day-to-day grind of Captain Barney Miller's staff. Their days are full of bureaucracy, mundane investigations, and the occasional major crime that requires still *more* paperwork. The detectives struggle to retain their sense of humor, humanity, and dreams amid the daily routine and in the face of the parade of loonies (criminals, victims, and their families) who march into the squad-room by the hour. Luckily, there is Captain Miller, an oasis of sanity in the anarchy. The detectives frequently retire to the couch in Barn's office and stretch out like psychiatric patients to ruminate about their lives.

MAIN CAST:
- **Barney Miller** (Hal Linden): Sane, gentle, compassionate. Never too busy to dispense advice or calm down one of his excitable staff members. Once talked a "human bomb" out of self-detonating.
- **Phil Fish** (Abe Vigoda): Jewish detective. Crochety complainer, the old man of the squad. Looks on his impending retirement with fear and dread.
- **Nick Yemana** (Jack Soo): Asian. Horse-racing fan, always quick with a sardonic comment. Maker of the squad's legendary bad coffee.
- **Stanley "Wojo" Wojohowicz** (Max Gail): Slow-witted Pole. A Vietnam vet, notoriously horny.
- **Ron Harris** (Ron Glass): Elegant black. Impeccably dressed. An aspiring writer, published a book called *Blood on the Badge.* Now dreams of a literary career.
- **Arthur Dietrich** (Steve Landesberg): Squad-room intellectual. Master of trivia. Was a doctor, lawyer, and a teacher prior to joining the force. A political activist.
- **Officer Carl Levitt** (Ron Carey): Abnormally short cop who wants to be promoted to detective.
- **Inspector Luger** (James Gregory): Old-time cop, windbag.
- **Chano Amengule** (Gregory Sierra): The Puerto Rican detective.

Fish plays Santa.

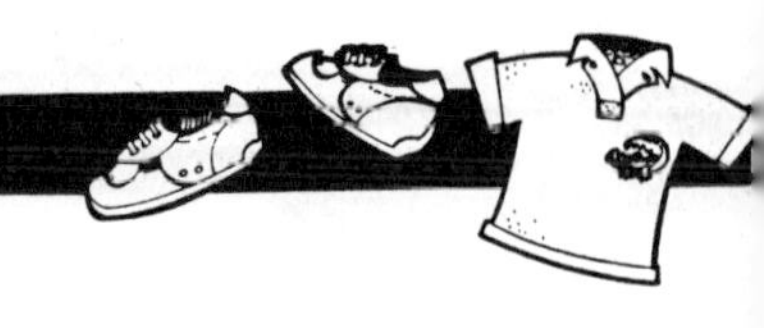

Inspector Luger, the aging crank who loves to reminisce about the good old days, when cops were still allowed to bash heads and intimidate prisoners, shakes hands with Harris, the foppish modern cop. Harris may be a snob, but he's still a humanist who'd rather handle people peacefully.

CHEERS

On the show's fifth anniversary, the NYPD made each of the show's stars honorary detectives. Moreover, Mayor Tom Bradley of Los Angeles declared it "Barney Miller " Week, and the show was praised on the floor of the U.S. House of Representatives. Pretty good for a sitcom.

MISCELLANY

•Hal Linden's real name is Harold Lipschitz. He got his stage name from a sign he saw in Linden, New Jersey.

•The station house was fashioned after a real one that producer Danny Arnold once visited to bail out his production crew after they were arrested for pitching pennies.

•Jack Soo was hired by Danny Arnold to fulfill a promise he'd made in the early '50s, when they were both on the burlesque circuit. Arnold had sworn that someday he'd be a TV producer and would give Soo a job.

TIMING

•Most half-hour sitcoms are taped within four hours. "Barney" sessions began at 8 A.M. Friday and often extended to 6 A.M. the following day.

•Scripts were sometimes rewritten only a few hours before the show was to be taped, which meant that the actors often barely had time to learn their lines. Said the producer: "The actors never knew how the show was gonna end, or even what the next scene would be. While this terrified them, to a certain extent it was stimulating as hell. It kept their interest alive to the last second."

•The job of producing the show was so demanding that Danny Arnold kept a cot in his office so he'd be able to work around the clock when necessary. "He tried to do everything," says Jim "Inspector Luger" Gregory. "You almost expected him to grab a broom and sweep up the floor, too." One result of Arnold's dedication was quadruple-bypass heart surgery in 1979, when he was only 54 years old.

SOMETHING FISHY

When "Barney Miller" first caught on, the most popular character was Fish. So Abe Vigoda, who played the character, suggested the show be renamed "Fish and Barney." The answer was an unequivocal no, but he eventually got his own spinoff series, "Fish"—which promptly flopped. He tried to return to his old friends at the 12th Precinct, but he'd already been replaced—and besides, he wanted too much money.

Vigoda, by the way, is totally unlike his wheezing character. He is an athlete who jogs and plays handball.

CRITICS' COMMENTS

ABOUT THE WRITING:
"Barney Miller was so intelligently written that it could have been done on radio and would have been just as entertaining."
—Ken Hoffman,
Houston Post

"Above all, there was an enormous sense of humanity in the show, an appreciation of life, and of offbeat characters, of people not in the mainstream. It understood people's egos, their desires, their dreams, their hopes. It was a poignant slice–of–life comedy, week after week."
—Rick Du Brow,
Los Angeles Herald Examiner

"Every episode of 'Barney Miller' was an exquisite one-act play. They juggled no less than three plots on every single episode of that show, which made it one of the most difficult shows to write. So it's a show that demonstrates the real craft of the situation-comedy writer.
"It's so well written that it's one of the few situation comedies where you can actually read the scripts and get a few belly laughs—and I speak from experience."
—Vince Waldron,
Classic Sitcoms

ABOUT THE ACTORS:
"They really made good use of talent in 'Barney Miller,' and not just with the regular cast. The regulars stood back and let the guest cast do their bit, too. I think there must a hundred and fifty actors in Hollywood who had their very best turn on network TV being dragged into that precinct....These are people who would probably normally only have a few lines in a much bigger production. But even though nobody ever heard of them, they were the real stars of this show. I can't think of any show *before* this that made such good use of character actors."
—Peter Farrell,
Oregonian

ABOUT THE CHARACTERS:
"The funniest character was Fish. He's the only guy on TV who's ever used impotence as a gag and made it work, so to speak."
—Joel Pisetzner,
Bergen Record

This jail cell is now on display in the Smithsonian Institution.

"Yemana always struck me as the kind of guy you'd work with for thirty years and then on the day he died, find out he was a hero in World War II. He's the guy you might sit with in a car pool all your life, and never even know what his job is."
—Sandra Konte,
***L.A. Times* Syndicate**

"My favorite is Wojo, who started out as the kind of obligatory right-wing reactionary musclehead jerk. And by the end of the series, you actually understood the guy. He grew; he became more mellow, and he opened up. It would probably never happen in real life, so Max Gail did a fantastic job in making Wojo so likable."
—Michael Dougan,
San Francisco Examiner

ABOUT THE CONTENT:
"It dealt with some fairly dark themes in a way that did not trivialize them but made you see the humor in them as well—in cases of homelessness, schizophrenia, jealousy, death. All these things were dealt with in jokes that never gave you the feeling they were cheap shots. Humor evolved *from* them."
—Peter Bieler,
Video Ticket

ABOUT THE SET:
"The set looked like a disaster area; people would actually throw their garbage on the floor and leave cigarette butts there.... If one of the actors brought a carton of milk or orange juice, it would just be left lying around— and it would become part of the show."
Eirik Knutzen,
Syndicated TV columnist

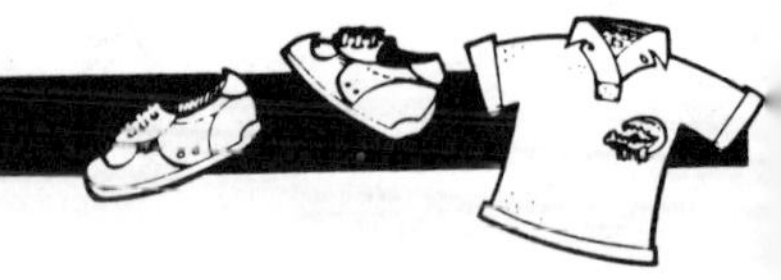

TAXI

When Dave Davis, Ed. Weinberger, Stan Daniels, and James Brooks—the nucleus of MTM Productions—formed their own production company in 1978, they had no new TV shows in mind. All they had was the notion that after seven years of writing and producing a woman's program ("The Mary Tyler Moore Show"), they were ready to try something different.

They wanted to create a men's comedy.

"Except for 'Barney Miller,'" Weinberger told a reporter at the time, "I don't know of one show about men, and 'Miller' is mainly about their work. We think we should show the side of contemporary man, of the blue-collar man."

The inspiration for their program came from an unlikely source. Brooks remembered having seen an article in *New York* magazine about cabbies who drive at night, and he suggested that it might make a good series. His partners agreed. So did Fred Silverman, head of ABC, who bought the idea without a pilot, script, or star.

By the time the quartet sat down to write the show—an ensemble comedy set in a Manhattan taxi garage—they 'd already chosen "the perfect actor" for their lead character, Judd Hirsch. The only thing was, Hirsch didn't want any part of television anymore; he'd been too disappointed by previous experiences with the medium.

Undaunted, the producers flew to New York to see him. "What they talked about," Hirsch says, "was acting....We hit it off right away. I was very impressed. Actors don't usually get that kind of consideration." Enthusiastic, he agreed to read the pilot script—and then signed on as Alex Reiger, the first driver in the Sunshine Taxi Company.

Reiger, explained Ed. Weinberger, "is the focus of the show, the only guy in the garage who says, 'I am a cab driver.'...[and] he is [the] father figure, the older one in the group." When the other cabbies need someone to turn to for advice or assistance, Reiger gets the call. And he rarely lets them down, even when he'd prefer to. In one episode, Tony, one of the drivers, is courted by a gay man. Freaked out, he asks Alex to explain to the guy that he's not "that way." Alex refuses. ALEX: "For once in my life, I am not going to let this thing get dumped in my lap." TONY: "Come on, Alex, please, please, please, please..." ALEX: "Ummm...All right."

So much for willpower.

In addition to his sincere concern for other human beings, Alex possesses modesty bordering on self-deprecation ("My shorts have more ambition than I do") and a healthy dose of cynicism. "Be it ever so humble," he muses, casting a glance around the garage, "there's no place like hell."

The character who does his best to keep it that way is the abusive little tarantula of a boss, taxi dispatcher Louie DePalma—the most unredeemably nasty character in sitcom history. "Don't pick up cripples," Louie screams at his drivers. "You can pick up four people who can walk in the time you pick up a cripple. Cabs are for people who can get in 'em." Louie will do almost anything for a dollar bill, and his only goal seems to be making life miserable for the people who work under him—a motley collection of dreamers who can't quite believe that the Yellow Brick Road might really end in a grimy underground taxi garage. There's Tony Banta, a slow-witted boxer; Bobby Wheeler, who's trying to make it as an actor; Elaine Nardo, who fantasizes about running an art gallery. And there are two "cartoon" characters— "Reverend" Jim Ignatowski, TV's first burned-out druggie, and Latka Gravas, an elfin mechanic from some Eastern European country (or maybe outer space).

These characters depend on each other for emotional survival—because all they've *got* is each other. But that's enough. Ultimately, the bond between them is so strong that the audience can feel it, too.

"We [were] trying to do character comedy as opposed to situation comedy," Ed. Weinberger said. "It is hard to define."

But it's easy to watch. "Taxi" is one of the most poignant comedies television has ever produced.

Danny DeVito married Rhea Perlman on the "Taxi" set, during a lunch break.

FLASHBACK

JIM [to a runaway little boy]: "School's very important. If I dropped out of grammar school, I'd never have been able to drop out of college."
BOY: "Teach me what you know, Jim."
JIM: "That would take hours, Terry. [Thinks about it for a moment.] Ah, what the heck! We've all got a little Obie Wan Kenobie in us."

[*Louie is troubled because his new girlfriend, Zena, is too nice for him.*]
LOUIE: "I like Zena...I really do...but I can't even bring myself to kiss her."
ALEX [sarcastically]: "Well, there's only one thing you can do, Louie—break up with this lovely, warm person who obviously feels a great deal for you and spend the rest of your life floating through meaningless affairs with cheap strangers who you'll have to pay to satisfy your [vehemently] disgusting physical lust!"
LOUIE [thoughtfully]: "Great advice!"

VITAL STATS

POLL RESULTS:
Fifth
PROGRAM INFO:
- Half-hour show. ABC/NBC
- First show: Sept. 12, 1978
- Last show: July 27, 1983
- 130 episodes

TIME: The late '70s.

PLACE: The Sunshine Taxi Company, New York City.

BACKGROUND: New York is a city of ambitous dreamers, but even dreamers have to eat. So while they're waiting for their big breaks, some work as cabbies. Because they spend so much time together at the garage, waiting for cabs to become vacant, they develop into an extended family. They love to discuss their dreams, but the group is constantly brought down to earth by the starkness of their surroundings, their respective failures, and their viperish little boss, Louie, who won't even give them their phone messages unless they pay him for them. Luckily, they have their pragmatic but ridiculously loyal friend Alex to lean on for support.

MAIN CAST:
- **Alex Reiger** (Judd Hirsch): Divorced, has one daughter. A man at peace with himself and his profession (although he once quit to become a waiter). Goes to preposterous lengths to aid his friends.
- **Louie DePalma** (Danny DeVito): The slime-ball dispatcher of the cab company. Takes sadistic interest in seeing the cabbies fail, yet a part of him wants to be liked and accepted by them. Lives with his mother.
- **Latka Gravis** (Andy Kaufman): English-garbling mechanic from Ork. Occasionally lapses into schizophrenia that transforms him into obnoxious lounge lizard Vic Ferrari.
- **Tony Banta** (Tony Danza): Cabbie who is *really* a boxer. Likable but dumb, the butt of some of Louie's best zingers. In real life, became a teen heartthrob.
- **Bobby Wheeler** (Jeff Conaway): The cabbie who's *really* an actor. Convinced that big break is just a phone call away. Very self-involved.
- **Elaine Nardo** (Marilu Henner): Divorced mother of two who dreams of running an art gallery. The token female. Sweet, warm, friendly.
- **Simka Gravis** (Carol Kane): Latka's wife, also from outer space.
- **"Reverend" Jim Ignatowski** (Christopher Lloyd): Ex-Harvard student, scion of a wealthy family. But an acid casualty who can barely remember his own name. Favorite food: Spaghetti-O's and herring.
- **John Burns** (Randall Carver): Naive romantic. One-season driver.

Andy Kaufman was known to fans as the world champion of inter-gender wrestling.

EMMY AWARDS

"Taxi" won three consecutive Emmys for best comedy series. Judd Hirsch, Christopher Lloyd, and Carol Kane won dual Emmys in the acting category. Danny DeVito won one.

Hirsch won his second Emmy after the series had been canceled, and caused considerable controversy during the awards ceremony when he pointed out this irony in a less-than-polite way. "If you can't get us out of your mind," he said to the audience, "if you have to keep giving laurels to us, then you should put it back on the air."

PEOPLE WATCHING

Familiar faces who made early appearances on Taxi:
•Tom Selleck, as a handsome passenger in Elaine's cab.
•Ted Danson, as an egotistical hairdresser.
•Martin Short, as a television executive.
•Louise Lasser, as Alex's ex-wife.
•Marcia Wallace (Carol Kester on "Bob Newhart") as...Marcia Wallace.
•John David Carson (Johnny's look-alike son), as a homosexual interested in Tony.

MISCELLANY

•Latka's phrase "*Ibi da*" translates into English as "That is right!" Actually, Latka's entire language was created by Andy Kaufman. When Carol Kane joined the cast as his girlfriend, Simka, he took her out to dinner and insisted she speak nothing but his gibberish.

•Andy Kaufman reportedly didn't want the full-time responsibility of a series. So his contract was for a limited number of appearances per season only.

•Reverend Jim's first appearance, on the eighth episode of "Taxi," was supposed to be a one-shot deal. In it, he presided over Latka's marriage to a call girl—and impressed everyone on the set. "From the first minute Christopher Lloyd hit the stage, he was destined to stay," recalls cocreator Ed. Weinberger. "That very night, we all agreed we had to get him on the show."

•They decided to make him a regular beginning the second season, and as a result, Randall Carver, who played John Burns, lost a job. At the end of the first season he was dropped because, as Weinberger said, "We just had too many people. We couldn't write for everybody."

NAME GAME

The last names of Tony Banta and Elaine Nardo are an inside joke by the former MTM employees who created them. Nardo is a reference to Pat Nardo, a scriptwriter for "The Mary Tyler Moore Show." Banta is named after Gloria Banta, Nardo's writing partner.

When he was approached by Weinberger and crew to star in "Taxi," Judd Hirsch had instructed his agent to say no to any TV deals. In fact, Hirsch didn't even feel like working on stage for a while—he had bought a cabin in the Northeast, and planned to spend his time there, incommunicado.

CRITICS' COMMENTS

ABOUT THE CHARACTERS:
"The nice thing about Louie is that they kept him bad. One of the producers said that people are always coming to him saying, 'Well, here's a script that shows that Louie has a good side.' Well, they would just reject it, out of hand, because they never wanted to do that story, and they never did. It was crucial to the show that they keep him a louse."

—Jim Gordon,
Gary Times-Register

"Taxi presented one of the two most outrageous characters in the history of television—Reverend Jim. (The other was Mr. Carlin, of 'The Bob Newhart Show.') Both of those characters were totally brain damaged, and they made no bones about it."

—Ken Hoffman,
Houston Post

"They were have-nots, but it didn't get me depressed the way 'The Honeymooners' did. These were not cartoon people. These were not people who yelled and screamed at each other. They were looney, but they were sensitive people with dreams. Their lives were hard, but they weren't bleak."

—Yardena Arar,
Los Angeles Daily News

"We don't have a lot of people on TV with extremes of emotion. There's Archie Bunker and Ralph Kramden and some of Sid Caesar's stuff. They're all great big characters who blow so hard and yell and carry on....People get a vicarious pleasure out of watching them, because it's behavior we can't get away with in what passes for real life.

"Louis DePalma belongs in that group. He yells and screams and stamps his little feet and acts like a crazy person. And in a way, he's even funnier than the rest, because he's not a big man, like Ralph was."

David Cuthbert,
New Orleans Times-Picayune

ABOUT THE SCRIPTS:
"The classic scene in 'Taxi' is the time that Marylu Henner invites Reverend Jim to an upscale, Upper East Side party. They're all kind of hanging around, and the pianist doesn't show. So Reverend Jim says, 'Oh, I'll play.' And he sits down and starts hammering something like 'Mary Had a Little Lamb.' And they're about ready to stop him when he suddenly breaks into this beautiful classical music. Everyone's amazed. After a while he stops and looks up and says, 'I must have taken lessons.' Wonderful writing."

—John Keiswetter,
Cincinnati Enquirer

ABOUT THE SET:
"I visited the 'Taxi' set several times and was always impressed....The actors tended to be very relaxed around each other. Instead of heading off for their dressing rooms when they were finished shooting—which happens on most sets—they would actually sit around afterward and chat, or they'd sit together over in a corner for a smoke while the next scene was being set up.

"A happy set usually means a good show. When a show is rotten, everybody knows it, and they tend to withdraw and go separate ways, not giving a damn about who they're working with. But these guys seemed to care about each other. Most of them weren't making a hell of a lot of money—they just enjoyed what they were doing."

—Eirik Knutzen,
Syndicated TV columnist

70s

Connie Booth played Polly and John Cleese played her boss, Basil Fawlty.

FAWLTY TOWERS (1976)
"This may be the funniest show ever seen on American television (although it's not an American show). John Cleese, of Monty Python fame, plays Basil Fawlty, who owns the worst-run hotel in England. Fawlty is a maniac who sees nothing wrong with hiding in a closet until everyone goes away. He's an unctuous bootlicker with wealthy guests and he's insultingly rude to others. And his hotel, like his personality, is a disorganized mess. John Cleese is a comic genius, and he was given the freedom in this show to create a sitcom in his own image, with wonderful physical humor and an overriding sense of absurdity. Unfortunately, he made only twelve episodes, but they're all worth watching over and over again."

—Michael Dougan,
San Francisco Examiner-

WHEN THINGS WERE ROTTEN (1975)
"TV satire has done so poorly overall that it's no surprise that even a comic genius like Mel Brooks can't get a show to last more than ten or twelve episodes. In 1975, he came up with this wonderful satire on Robin Hood, a little like 'Get Smart' in that everyone was a complete imbecile—Robin only managed to stay alive because Prince John was even dumber than he was. But the Brooks style was in full flower. It's a terrifically funny show. The lead role is played by Dick Gautier, who was Hymie on 'Get Smart.' I've been waiting to see this one in reruns for a long time."

—Peter Bieler,
Video Ticket

PAUL SAND IN FRIENDS AND LOVERS (1974)
"This is one of those MTM shows you never hear about. It did pretty well in the ratings, but it was still canceled after only about three months. I never figured out why. Paul Sand played—are you ready for this?—a bass violinist in a symphony orchestra who was always falling in love. The show was funny, but it also had a gentle sensibility and literate writing that made it a standout. Haven't seen it in almost fifteen years, but I'd love to."

—Ed Siegel,
Boston Globe.

Robin Hood gets set to screw up.

Worst of the '70s

Sex came out of the sitcom closet in the '70s. In shows like "Mary Tyler Moore," where it was suddenly permissible to admit that a 30-year-old woman might have an occasional affair, this represented real maturity. But in cases like "Three's Company" it was offensive lateral movement.

Sex had been implicit in '60s shows like "I Dream of Jeannie," with its scantily clad airhead pursuing her "master" in his own bedroom, and "My Living Doll," the comedy about the live-in bimbo robot. But with "Three's Company"—the critics' overwhelming choice for worst show of the decade—ABC dropped any pretense about premise or plot. They just bounced the female anatomy in front of the audience for thirty minutes every week. It worked, and naturally, the show's success opened the floodgates for more of the same.

The two grossest of the ensuing "jiggle" comedies wound up in a virtual tie as the third-worst show of the decade: "Sugar Time!" and "Rollergirls." They're actually a lot worse than "Three's Company," but they were less potent because practically nobody ever saw them.

Of the non-jiggle sitcoms, one show has emerged as the least favorite—"Me and the Chimp." The critics enshrined it here as the worst domestic/gimmick sitcom of the '70s, in the tradition of "My Mother, the Flying Nun."

THREE'S COMPANY

In 1976, "Charlie's Angels" introduced a new entertainment phenomenon—the "jiggle" show, named after a distinctive portion of the female anatomy. "Three's Company" was the first "jiggle" sitcom. It purported to be bold, daring—the first sitcom exponent of the sexual revolution. In fact, it was little more than a thirty-minute dirty joke. Based on a British TV series called "Man About the House," it concerms two airheaded females named Janet and Chrissy who need a roommate. They find a guy sleeping in their bathtub after a party, and since he can cook better than either of them, they ask him to fill the role. Jack Tripper convinces the suspicious landlord, Mr. Roper, that he's gay, and the household lives platonically ever after. Except sex remains in the air. Boy, does it. Jack leers at everything in skirts. Chrissy and Janet are pursued by everyone who sees them in their tight jeans and shorts. And Mrs. Roper tries to get in the swing of things by igniting her long-dormant spouse.

ABC touted "Three's Company" as a sitcom for the age of consent, but Doris Day and Rock Hudson were doing the same thing (or not doing it) twenty years earlier. Some people also compared the show to a French bedroom farce. That's only apt in that whatever comedy there was revolved around the physical attributes of its stars and the kind of innuendo that was popular in junior high school.

A clue to the superficiality of the plots and characterization was the interchangeability of its leading ladies. When Suzanne Somers left the show over a salary dispute, she was replaced with ease by two other vacuous blondes. John Ritter, who has since proven himself a talented actor, subsisted here on a pratfall and a leer. When he somehow managed to win an Emmy for best actor in a comedy in 1983, he looked as amazed as everyone else.

"Three's Company" lasted for seven seasons, a symbol of TV's sexual revolution, America's need for mindless escapism, or, maybe, just its audience's level of intelligence.

BACKGROUND

Janet Wood, a florist, and Chrissy Snow, a typist, take in Jack Tripper, a self-employed caterer, as their roommate in a Santa Monica apartment. Their relationship is strictly platonic, but who'd believe it? So Jack poses as a homosexual and satisfies the girls' parents and their landlord that everyone is safe. This arrangement lasts through Jack's years at chef school and Chrissy's departure for Fresno and her replacement by two other lobotomized female bodies.

Eventually, Jack becomes a chef at Angelino's Restaurant, then winds up opening his own, called Jack's Bistro. His old roommates move out and his real girlfriend moves in.

MAIN CAST

- **Jack Tripper** (John Ritter): The man of the house, when he isn't pretending to be one of the women. Klutzy, leering, cackling.
- **Janet Wood** (Joyce DeWitt): The brunette, slightly more intelligent than the brainless blondes.
- **Chrissy Snow** (Suzanne Somers): The original sexy blonde airhead in the apartment.
- **Cindy Snow** (Jenillee Harrison): Chrissy's first replacement, her clumsy cousin.
- **Terri Alden** (Priscilla Barnes): Chrissy's second replacement.

FLASHBACK

JACK: "I have a splitting headache."

JANET/CHRISSY [simultaneously]: "Oh, poor baby."

JACK: "Janet, would you do me a favor? Would you ru-ub my temples? It feels so-o goo-ood."

JANET [emotionally]: "Oh, my pleasure."

JACK [as he lays his head in Janet's lap]: "And Chrissy, would you mind massaging my to-o-oes? "

CHRISSY [as she runs to his feet and begins rubbing them]: "O-o-oh, sure."

JANET [emotionally, as she cradles Jack's head in her lap and strokes his head]: "Jack, can you ever forgive us for leaving you alone?"

John Ritter was the anchor of the show for seven years, from March 15, 1977, to September 18, 1984.

Were they laughing with us or at us? "Three's Company" was a mid-season replacement that did so well in its first six episodes that it wound up the #11 show for the entire season!

CRITICS' COMMENTS

"The reason 'Three's Company' turns up on lists like this is not because it wasn't funny, but because it was offensive—because of the sexual stereotyping. And that dumb girl set new lows. If TV is a limbo contest, this show is a winner."

—Phil Kloer,
Atlanta Constitution

"I found everything about that show detestable. It's like everything that's ever written on a boy's room wall in kindergarten. I mean, that's where they got their scripts."

—Tom Jicha,
Miami News

"Usually when a sitcom is really bad, it doesn't last long. But this stinker lasted forever. I don't understand why it was so popular. Well, large breasts are one factor—even though they weren't that big. If you look really close, you'll notice that she just stuck her chest out everywhere she walked. And they put her in flimsy shirts. That's what this show was. Even the laugh track was offensive."

—Mark Schwed,
UPI

"It's an airhead show. But there was one saving grace. John Ritter is one of TV's truly great farceurs. He's a wonderful performer, a wonderful comedian, and it's usually a pleasure to watch him. But in this, there was nothing to watch."

—Rick Du Brow,
Los Angeles Herald Examier

ME AND THE CHIMP

Ted Bessell and his friend Buttons monkey around. This Garry Marshall stinker vanished after only five months, airing from January 13 to May 18, 1972.

There's an old vaudeville saying: "When in doubt, bring on the animal act." That saying should be updated for sitcoms, to: "When in doubt, don't." With the exception of Mr. Ed, Arnold the pig, and a few others, animals haven't succeeded too well as sitcom stars. Maybe it's simply the sight of those sad little creatures laboring under the hot lights without a SAG card. Or maybe it's just that a thirty-minute animal act goes a long, long way.

Which brings us to "Me and the Chimp," a show that combined the worst elements of the usual dumb domestic sitcom with the boring type of act we hated to sit through on "The Ed Sullivan Show." Dentist Mike Reynolds is a successful man with a big problem. His children found a runaway chimp named Buttons and decided to bring him home. Buttons has a perverse fascination with automated appliances (hence his name) and is constantly getting Mike into hot water with all his side-splitting antics. The kids want to keep the chimp, Mike doesn't. The chimp just wants to go home.

The problem with this sitcom is that the audience was on the chimp's side. It would have backed up Mike, too, if he weren't such a weiner. For most of us in this situation, the solution would have been simple. Find a good home for the chimp at a zoo, a circus, or a theme park. But our friend Mike bowed to domestic pressure week after week. Maybe a good name for the show would have been "Me and the Wimp." What's more, it might be amusing to watch a wild animal out of its native environment destroy property for a little while, but it does tend to limit the plot line.

This show was created by the usually golden-fingered Garry Marshall, the man behind "The Odd Couple," "Happy Days," "Laverne and Shirley," and "Mork and Mindy." It lasted four months before someone sent it back to the Humane Society. Ted Bessell, the star, who gained some popularity on "That Girl," subsequently left sitcoms forever and is now a producer.

The damage to Buttons's career is not known.

BACKGROUND

Mike Reynolds is a laid-back dentist in a southern California town called San Pascal. One day he gets home from work and he discovers his kids have brought home a chimpanzee they found in a local park. It's Buttons, on the lam from an Air Force research center (and you know what that means).

The kids beg Mike to let Buttons become a member of the family. Despite the chimp's penchant for pushing any and all buttons he finds on appliances, radios, cars, dental equipment, etc., spineless Mike agrees. Buttons is officially adopted, and Mike continually spends his time getting the chimp and inevitably the entire household, out of difficult situations. At one point, Buttons becomes a habitual thief, even stealing Kitty's teddy bear. What a bad chimp!

MAIN CAST:

- **Mike Reynolds** (Ted Bessell): Dentist who becomes the adoptive father of a chimp.
- **Liz Reynolds** (Anita Gillette): The wife who thinks it's wonderful to have a chimp around the house.
- **Scott Reynolds** (Scott Kolden): The chimp's champion.
- **Kitty Reynolds** (Kami Colter): Little sister, big chimp lover.
- **Buttons** (Jackie): The banana-eating protagonist.

FLASHBACK

[*Buttons helps Mike break into his house after Mike locks the keys inside*]
MIKE: "Buttons, you're more fun than a barrel of people."

[*Mike is spending the day with Buttons. It's Saturday, so he's home balancing his checkbook with an adding machine. Buttons is staring at him.*]
MIKE: "Do you have to look at me like that?"
[*The doorbell rings. While Mike answers, the chimp hits all the keys on the machine. Mike returns and discovers his calculations are off by $23,000.*]
MIKE: "How could I push so many wrong buttons?"
[*Mike does a doubletake, suddenly realizing the source.*]
MIKE: "Buttons!"

He may be the missing link, but not in television. Only one chimp show, "Daktari," has ever done well on TV.

CRITICS' COMMENTS

"It's a typical television attempt to use gimmicks instead of good writing. And the chimp didn't have enough lines."

—Walt Belcher, *Tampa Tribune*

"It's like 'My Mother the Car.' How many people do you know who hang around with a chimp? That's what it really comes down to. 'ALF' is just a fantasy. This wasn't even a fantasy—they wanted you to take it seriously!"

—Tom Jicha, *Miami News*

"It was a toss-up between who was worse, Ted or the chimp. It wasn't a particularly good chimp, first of all—he wasn't anywhere in the J. Fred Muggs class, or Bingo in 'Abbott and Costello,' or even Beulah in 'Truth or Consequences.' Those were real chimps. This chimp performed at about Ted Bessell's level of comedy. They looked cross-eyed at each other, and the whole show fell apart."

—Joel Pisetzner, *Bergen Record*

"Ted Bessell was a very accomplished, very sought-after actor. He actually did tons of pilots after 'That Girl' went off. And then he winds up going onto the network—I mean, actually getting on the *air*—with this thing called 'Me and the Chimp.'

"Garry Marshall sold the show based on a ten-page outline. It's hard to believe, but because of his success with 'Happy Days' and 'The Odd Couple,' he was hot. So if he wanted to write about a chimpanzee at a dentist's house, well, it sounded good to Fred Silverman."

—Bart Andrews, *The Worst TV Shows Ever*

Ted Bessell

"I saw it once—which was about as often as the rest of the country watched it, too. It's a testimony to Ted Bessell that he wasn't out-acted too badly by the chimpanzee. It was the kind of show that you just walked away from, like a bad traffic accident. The only thing that remained to be seen was how quickly the ambulance was gonna get there. I might've been young then, but I knew when I was looking at a meltdown."

—Jeff Borden, *Charlotte Observer*

SUGAR TIME!/ ROLLER GIRLS

Guess who? It's that swingin' rock group, Sugar, featuring Hugh's own little Barbi doll.

If this were a horror film, it might be called *The Singing Killer Bimbos on Wheels*, or *The Attack of the Rock-and-Roll Jiggling Bombers*. Whatever the case, this is our only dual entry. Although two separate sitcoms, they were basically the same show, and critics seem evenly divided on which one was worse.

Which plot would you like first? Oh, what the hell—how about "Rollergirls," the story of a group of braless, spandex-clad roller skaters called the Pittsburgh Pitts, who dream of roller-derby stardom, despite their precarious financial condition. You don't like sports? Okay, how about "Sugar Time!", the story of a group of braless, spandex-clad rock-and-roll singers who dream of stardom, despite their precarious financial condition.

Whatever way you slice it, the shows served a dual purpose. Literally. The late '70s were the era of the jigglers, and producers were looking for any excuse to put both of the jiggling actresses' talents on display. If they could sing or roller skate, so much the better. Unfortunately, in these cases, they couldn't.

Oh, they tried to jazz these shows up. Paul Williams was hired to write a complete original score for "Sugar Time!" every week. "Rollergirls" tried to inject off-the-wall humor (the show wins the ethnic stereotyping prize—one of the bimbo skaters was, get this, an Eskimo). But let's face it, stars like *Playboy* centerfold Barbi Benton were no threat to "I Love Lucy."

Both these shows were created by James Komack, who actually has produced some decent stuff ("Chico and the Man," "The Courtship of Eddie's Father"). We can only suspect that he was temporarily blinded by the allure of Barbi Benton in a spandex jumpsuit, singing off-key. Whatever the case, the shows lasted four weeks and four weeks, respectively.

BACKGROUND

ROLLERGIRLS

The Pittsburgh Pitts are a sexy all-girl roller-derby team who dream of making it in the big leagues, despite a lack of talent and money.

MAIN CAST

- **Don Mitchell** (Terry Kiser): The Pitts' conniving owner.
- **Mongo Sue Lampert** (Ronda Bates): The tall lead skater.
- **J. B. Johnson** (Candy Ann Brown): The token black skater.
- **Selma "Books" Cassidy** (Joanna Cassidy): The sophisticated one.
- **Honey Bee Novak** (Marcy Hanson): The token dizzy blonde.
- **Shana Akira** (Marilyn Tokuda): The wild and crazy Eskimo.

SUGAR TIME!:

"Sugar" is the name of a trio of "talented," gorgeous aspiring rock singers who live in the same apartment building. They're trying to launch their career by playing for free at Al Mark's Tryout Room, but to eat, they have to get day jobs. They're convinced they'll make it, though.

MAIN CAST

- **Maxx** (Barbi Benton): Beautiful hatcheck girl.
- **Diane** (Didi Carr): Fun-loving dental hygenist.
- **Maggie** (Marianne Black): Teacher at a children's dancing school.

FLASHBACK

[*The Rollergirls finish a practice session.*]

HONEY BEE: "Boy, we sure are getting the old teamwork down, huh?"

SUE [with heavy southern accent]: "Shoot, yeah. We're faster than a team of mules taking some manure to market."

[*One of the Rollergirls has been traded to another team.*]

SELMA: "That's just the way it is in sports. Heck, I've been passed around so much I feel like a tray of hors d'oeuvres."

SUE: "Well, it should have been you, Books. It sure would've lowered the crime rate around here, cause your face is a felony."

Here they are again—those wacky, busty rockers who jiggled the airwaves for four weeks in 1977. "Sugar Time!" ran from August 13 to September 15, 1977. "Rollergirls" made its debut on April 24, 1978, and had its fatal crash a month later, on May 10.

CRITICS' COMMENTS

"You can't make any argument for 'Sugar Time!' or 'Rollergirls.' You not only have the jiggle aspect, but they were triple threats: badly acted, badly directed, badly written."

—Mark Dawidziak, *Akron Beacon Journal*

"Barbi Benton figures into one of my rules for watching television. She's not in them much any more, but a few years ago, she was in a lot of specials. ...And one of my rules was: 'If they were desperate enough to use Barbi Benton in it, it can't be any good.' There was no need to review it. Just say, 'Barbie Benton was in it.' "
[Interviewer: "They did a whole series with her in it."]
"Not for long."

—Peter Farrell, *Oregonian*

"In the opening title shot of 'Sugar Time!' they had the girls all out in tee-shirts, playing volley ball, with no bras....They showed 'em a pair at a time; just watch 'em bounce up and down. And I don't think they ever quite figured out what to do beyond those opening titles....It was like looking at your first issue of *Playboy*. And it was offensive because, number one, it was a stupid show—the scripts were perfectly awful. And number two, you could see where the minds of the people behind it were. They were playing Barbies with these girls. In fact, Barbi was actually *in* it."

—R. K. Shull, *Indianapolis News*

Joanna Cassidy is the only one of the eight ladies who actually made it big. She's a movie star now.

"Both shows are pretty worthless, other than the T and A value, but they are good reflections of the Fred Silverman era. I'd call them illegitimate children of 'Charlie's Angels.'"

—Gary Gerani, *Fantastic Television*

"'Sugar Time!' and 'Rollergirls' were the kind of shows that made you ask, 'Why is there television?' Why bother watching these shows? Why not just put a pinup on your screen for thirty minutes?"

—R. D. Heldenfels, *Schenectady Gazette*

THE GIRL WITH SOMETHING EXTRA (1973-74)
Sally Field gave up her nun's habit and stopped flying. Now she's got ESP. And she's married to John Davidson. She says she can read his mind, but how can she be sure there's really something in it? The premise sounds like a *National Enquirer* story.

DIANA (1972-73)
This is just a regular bad show. The horror is that when Hollywood finally got Diana Rigg to make an American TV show, this is what they did to her.

The plot: Diana Smythe moved to New York to be "fashion coordinator" for a major department store. She was also housesitting for her brother, and he neglected to tell her that he'd given his apartment key to dozens of his pals. So sexy Diana found men popping into her apartment at all hours. After the show was canceled, the real Diana never ventured into our networks again.

TURNABOUT (1978)
This mid-season replacement featured a husband and wife who, in an idle moment, wished they could switch places. They probably didn't mean it, but they spoke in the presence of a magical Buddha statue—and Buddha doesn't kid around. Wish granted. Overnight, their spirits switched bodies. Now the guy, who was a tough sports writer, is a cosmetics exec in a woman's body. And the woman has to report on sports as a man. They only had to suffer through it for three months, though, until NBC mercifully yanked them both off the air. The woman, by the way, was Sharon Gless, who later won two Emmys for "Cagney and Lacey."

An odd couple: "The Girl With Something Extra" put two perky young actors on the screen together for the first—and last—time. Sally Field went on to win acclaim and two Oscars. John Davidson developed into a piece of plastic and went on to host "The New Hollywood Squares," a syndicated TV game show.

APPLE PIE (1978)
This is the ultimate absurdity in family sitcoms. It broke all sitcom records for brevity too, lasting exactly two weeks. The plot: In 1933, a hairdresser decided she wanted a family. So she advertised for one in the local paper. The result: a collection of weirdos that rivals *King of Hearts*—a con-man "husband," a "son" who thinks he's a bird, a "grandpa" who's barely still moving, and a "daughter" who likes to tap dance around the house .

THE WAVERLY WONDERS (1978)
Among television critics, this show is already a legend. Who thought it up? Is he still allowed into Hollywood? Joe Namath was the star, playing a basketball coach/history teacher at a small Wisconsin high school. Joe didn't know anything about history, as you might imagine. And his players didn't know anything about basketball. So what's the joke? The inept teacher? The inept basketball team? How about the inept TV network?

MAKIN' IT (1979)
A working-class Italian-American kid faces a major career decision: Should he go to college and become a teacher? Or should he hang around the neighborhood and disco dance? Tough choice. The show died before he made his selection; disco died shortly after.

CARTER COUNTRY (1977-79)
Jimmy Carter didn't get no respect. When JFK inspired a TV series, for example, it was a documentary called "Profiles in Courage." But poor old Jimmy had a *sitcom* named after him—while he was still in office. And it wasn't even a good one.

Carter country was Georgia, of course. The setting was the police station, where the sheriff was a dumb redneck and his deputy was an educated black. Do we have a conflict here? Yeah, but it's ok—they "respect" each other.

You're laughing already, aren't you?

COUNTRY CORN

Well gaw-lee! Look what the programmers brung in—hayseeds who jabber about vittles and see-ment ponds.

THE BEVERLY HILLBILLIES (1962— 71).

THE REAL MCCOYS (1957-63).

GREEN ACRES (1965-72).

PETTICOAT JUNCTION (1963-72).

ODD COUPLES

CATHY AND PATTY LANE (Patty Duke), "The Patty Duke Show" (1963-66).
Identical cousins. It's a genetic impossibility, but there they were, Patty (the American who loses control over hot dogs) and Cathy (the prim and proper Brit) Lane.

HENRY "HILDEGARDE" DESMOND (Peter Scolari) and KIP "BUFFY" WILSON (Tom Hanks), "Bosom Buddies" (1980-82).
Two guys dress in drag so they can live in an all-girls' hotel.

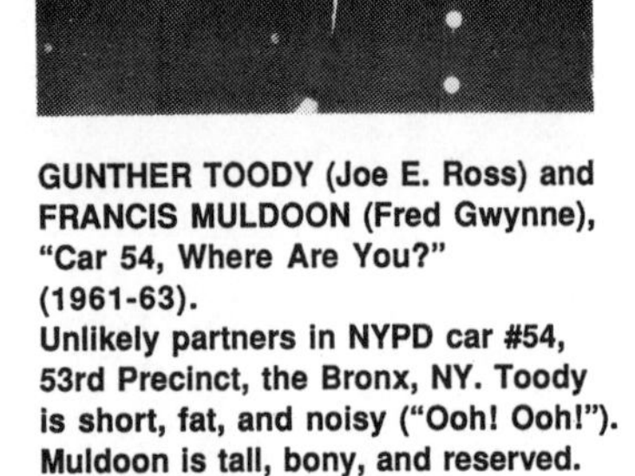

GUNTHER TOODY (Joe E. Ross) and FRANCIS MULDOON (Fred Gwynne), "Car 54, Where Are You?" (1961-63).
Unlikely partners in NYPD car #54, 53rd Precinct, the Bronx, NY. Toody is short, fat, and noisy ("Ooh! Ooh!"). Muldoon is tall, bony, and reserved.

CHICO RODRIGUEZ (Freddie Prinze) and ED BROWN (Jack Albertson), "Chico and the Man" (1974-77).
A slick, fast-talking young Chicano from the L.A. barrio goes into business with a cranky old fart who runs a tiny auto-repair shop.

OSCAR MADISON (Jack Klugman) and FELIX UNGER (Tony Randall), "The Odd Couple" (1970-75).
The original and still the greatest. A pair of divorcees—boyhood friends and reluctant roommates in Oscar's Manhattan apartment. Felix is compulsively clean; Oscar is a world-class slob. And so on.

Best of the '80s

For the most part, the best sitcoms of the '80s' first eight seasons weren't as innovative as the previous decade's. In fact, several have been called throwbacks because they so closely resembled domestic sitcoms of the '50s.

But the resemblance is superficial. While many stress entertainment over controversy and feature the '80s equivalent of suburban nuclear families, they aren't propagating the irresponsible mythology that father knows best, that kids should be seen and not heard, or that life is a silly plot with a happy ending. In fact, they take pains to stress the opposite.

Most quality comedies of the '80s have an underlying social conscience and a message of understanding. "The Golden Girls," for example, sandwiches an awareness of the concerns of the elderly between laughs. And "Family Ties" demonstrates that a family can overcome philosophical differences with love and tolerance. "All in the Family" was about confrontation; "Family Ties" is about coexistence. In a significant way, that represents maturity.

The closest any one program comes to "Ozzie and Harriet" is "The Cosby Show." But again, the unspoken message is radically different because—quite simply—the family is black. You get an idea of how important this is when you realize that the Nelson family first appeared in 1952, two years before the Supreme Court had even issued its landmark decision banning segregation. Now, thirty years later, a black man can represent the all-American father.

Only "Cheers" and "Newhart" seem to be direct descendants of the sitcom revolution of the '70s—"Newhart" because it's essentially a rehash of "The Bob Newhart Show" (although it can also be argued that it's a classic rural sitcom), and "Cheers" because it has plucked elements of style as well as substance from the major shows of the previous decade.

Most of all, however, the writing in all these shows is what makes them good. The characters are well drawn, the dialogue is believable and sophisticated, and the level of intelligence is consistently high. This was the kiss of death for TV shows in the medium's early days, but the fact that all of them have been popular in the '80s is proof (hopefully) that quality sitcoms and their audiences have developed a meaningful, mutually supportive relationship.

CHEERS

"Cheers" is heir to the legacy of '70s sitcoms like "Taxi" and "M*A*S*H." It's a workplace ensemble comedy that boasts superior writing and draws its humor from *characters* rather than situations. It can be poignant, romantic, and hilarious.And it has received almost unanimous critical acclaim.

But it has a new hook as well. It's the first modern sitcom to address that large (and growing) group searching desperately for love and companionship in the cold '80s.

Cheers, the Boston bar "where everyone knows your name," is a warm place where alienated patrons—and viewers—can hang out at night.

It's a refuge for a lonely, uptight psychologist named Frasier Crane; an opportunity of last resort for the dim-witted bartenders Woody and Nick ("I'll be back before you know it, Sam. In fact, I'll probably be back before *I* know it"); a home away from home for an overweight, unhappily married accountant named Norm; a place where people listen to a frustrated know-it-all mailman named Cliff.

These folks need and support each other. When Cliff gets a raise, for example, he offers to loan Norm some money—sort of. Cliff: "I know you're a proud guy, Norm, but you've been out of work a long time and I feel I've got to at least *try* to share my good fortune with you. So, uh...I know what your answer's gonna be to this...but would you please allow me to loan you five hundred dollars?" Norm: "Sure." Cliff [stunned]: "Uh-h...beg your pardon?" Norm: "Sure, I'd love it. Can I get it in cash?"

The high llama and owner of Cheers, ex-ballplayer Sam Malone, is as mixed up and unhappy as everyone else. On the surface, he has it all. He's good-looking, popular, and an indefatiguable ladies' man. When a friend asks him to coach a Little League team, he declines, saying, "I'd love to, but I don't have any time around here. I spend half my time trying to keep this bar on its feet, and the other half trying to keep Diane off hers."

But he has a darker side. We hear of an ex-wife and an alcoholism problem. Most of the women he dates, as one character says, "have elevated gum-snapping to an art form." And when he does meet an educated woman—Diane Chambers, a pedantic ingenue who doesn't seem to realize that college is over—it's clear that despite his bursts of sensitivity, he isn't exactly bright. "Let's go to the back room," Diane tells him. "It's empty and quiet and dimly lit, like your mind."

Diane is the other half of a couple inspired by Spencer Tracy/Katherine Hepburn films. For five years, the plot was based on their stormy relationship. (Sam: "This is between men. Women just don't understand....Sweetheart, this is part of me that's private...so it's hands off, no trespassing. End of discussion." Diane [thoughtfully]: "Very well. And from now on, there's a part of me that's hands off to you.") The two ultimately developed trust, understanding and communication (but only after Sam went back to the bottle and Diane had a nervous breakdown). Nonetheless, they were still too different to stay together.

Welcome to the '80s, where our search for romance and commitment often causes us pain. Where love *doesn't* necessarily conquer all.

Of course, Shelley Long was planning to leave the show anyway when the duo split up. But "Cheers" fans are quick to point out that it never would have worked out. Why? Diane: "Last night I was up until two in the morning finishing Kierkegaard." Sam: "I hope he thanked you."

It's too soon to tell how Sam's relationship with Cheers' new manager will work out. But audiences will doubtlessly continue dropping by to find out all about it.

Ted Danson applauded Shelley Long's departure from "Cheers," stating that in real life she was as unpleasant as Diane Chambers.

FLASHBACK

DIANE: "Sam, that's the stupidest thing I ever heard."
SAM: "I thought you weren't going to call me stupid now that we're being intimate."
DIANE: "No, I said I wasn't going to call you stupid *while* we were being intimate."

SAM [to Rebecca]: "Come on, smile. I bet you're the kind of person who lights up a whole room when you smile."
[She tries to ignore him, but he keeps making faces to get her to laugh. Finally, she does.]
SAM: "Nope. I was wrong."

SAM: "Hey, Norm. Whattya say?"
NORM: "It's a dog-eat-dog world out there, and I'm wearing Milkbone shorts."

VITAL STATS

POLL RESULTS:
First
PROGRAM INFO:
- Half-hour show. NBC
- First show: Sept. 30, 1982
- Still in production.

TIME: The 1980s.

PLACE: Cheers, the Boston bar owned and managed by Sam Malone, an ex-relief pitcher for the Boston Red Sox.

BACKGROUND: Sam Malone, once a popular athlete nicknamed "Mayday," had to leave baseball because he was an alcoholic. He conquered his problem. Then, ironically, he became the nondrinking proprietor of his own saloon. Cheers never seems to be teeming with people, the way a trendy singles bar might be, but it's a successful business with a group of regulars who show up every night. Eventually, Sam sells Cheers to a major corporation and departs for a new life. But he returns, content to be a mere bartender, needing to be with the friends and patrons who've become an important part of his life.

MAIN CAST:
- **Sam Malone** (Ted Danson): "Sammy," the Cheers guru. Overconfident, if not overbright. Lives for his romantic conquests, usually with nonthreatening bimbos. Main relationships, however, are with bright, liberated women.
- **Diane Chambers** (Shelley Long): Cheers barmaid and Sam's romantic interest. An intellectual snob, she eventually leaves Cheers and Sam to find success as a writer.
- **Rebecca Howe** (Kirstie Alley): Cheers' businesslike new manager. Cold, formal, but sexy. Sam is determined to conquer her.
- **Carla Tortelli** (Rhea Perlman): The sarcastic barmaid. Mother of six (or is it seven?) children; she seems perpetually pregnant. Downright nasty personality, but friends keep looking for the good person.

Woody Harrelson is waiting for a chance to do dramatic roles.

- **Ernie "Coach" Pantusso** (Nicholas Colasanto): Sam's ex-baseball coach, a dim-witted but sensitive bartender.
- **Norm Peterson** (George Wendt): An overweight accountant, constantly complaining about his wife, Vera. Popular at Cheers.
- **Cliff Clavin** (John Ratzenberger): A mailman and know-it-all. Despite bravado about his sexual prowess, he is lonely and insecure.
- **Woody Boyd** (Woody Harrelson): Dumb bartender, Iowa farmboy.
- **Dr. Frasier Crane** (Kelsey Grammar): A pedantic psychologist. Once engaged to Diane, he became a Cheers regular while she worked there. Now frequents the place, desperate to be "one of the gang."

After tricking her friend Marshall into believing he's the father of her unborn child, Carla decides to tell him the truth in the episode "Father Knows Best."

IDEA MAN

John Ratzenberger (Cliff) was originally cast in a bit part as a barfly. The producers were looking for typical "bar characters," and Ratzenberger suggested the inevitable know-it-all. They were so enchanted with the idea that they expanded the part. And Ratzenberger became a regular.

REAL LIFE

The exterior of the "Cheers" bar belongs to a real Boston bar called the Bull and Finch, on Beacon Street, right across from the Boston Common. But take it from first-hand experience—the dimly lit, crowded interior is nothing like America's beloved "Cheers."

HANGING OUT

Shelley Long was pregnant during most of "Cheers"'s third season. It was covered up by strategically placed trays and by having her stand behind the bar a lot. But, says Long, "I'm sure there were times when the audience said, 'My god, she's going to have a baby!'"

ORIGINS

Because of their success with "Taxi," producers Glen and Les Charles, and producer/director James Burrows (son of funnyman Abe) were offered a deal with NBC that guaranteed that the network would put at least one of their series on the air.

They wanted to do an ensemble comedy set in a hotel, so they'd be able to bring in new characters at will. But when they sketched out plots, they found that most of the action would take place in the hotel bar. So they dumped the hotel and kept the bar.

Despite critical acclaim, the show debuted in sixtieth place out of sixty-three shows.

But a publicity blitz, great word of mouth, and the network's surprise decision to renew the show despite lousy ratings helped "Cheers" find its audience. By the following season, the show was in the top twenty. Now it's in the top ten and is a simultaneous syndication success.

PRE-CHEERS

Ted Danson is proud of his most memorable pre-"Cheers" role, as an obnoxious beautician who gives Elaine Nardo a dreadful new-wave hairdo on "Taxi." He should be—he was so impressive in it that producers Glen and Les Charles took him aside and convinced him to audition for the lead role in a new series they were working on—"Cheers."

THOUGHTS

- "Cheers" was rejected by one network executive because "people don't go to bars anymore."
- The name Norm was intentionally picked by "Cheers"'s creators because he's supposed to represent the norm. No coincidence there.

CRITICS' COMMENTS

ABOUT ITS APPEAL:

"It is one of the first really *intelligent* sitcoms. I remember, for example, a bit they did back toward the beginning, where an old college friend of Diane comes into the bar. They start talking about Russian death poets, and she recites this made-up poem that one of the Charles brothers [the co-creators] wrote. It was like something out of *Love and Death* by Woody Allen. 'Cheers' is literate on that kind of a level.... That's what drew me into the series and has kept me coming back."

Phil Kloer,
Atlanta Constitution

"I like that bar; I would drink in that bar. I'd like to talk to Norm, sit next to him—in fact, I'd like to buy him a beer.

"And as for Diane...I'd like to *strangle* her. I'd probably like to play a little baseball with Sam. I'd probably slap him on the back. I figure, every few rounds he would buy me a damn drink. I just like that place."

—Mark Schwed,
UPI

ABOUT THE ULTIMATE SITCOM OF THE '80S:

"'Cheers' is the first sitcom to present characters that are flawed. Not flawed like Lucy Ricardo, where they...tripped over chairs and fell out of windows and all of that. They just had human, deeply felt, emotional frailties. 'Mary Tyler Moore' did it in a way, 'Barney Miller' did it in a way, but 'Cheers' was *totally* built on that premise. They're a bunch of losers.

"The most flawed is Sam, the owner of the bar and chief bartender....He's a walking contradiction. He looks and acts one way, and yet the audience is allowed to see that other side of him.

"To the guys in the bar, he's the big guy—macho, cool, a real man. And yet he has no idea what it means to be a man. With the women in his life he cares for, he can't express his feelings; it all comes out as great big stutters.

"He's a great comic character who symbolizes what people our age are going through in the '80s. He's groping, as is everyone else in that bar, and an awful lot of the audience."

—Monica Collins,
USA Today

ABOUT THE CHARACTERS:

"People have misjudged what 'Cheers' is about from the beginning. They seemed to think that Sam and Diane were some kind of perfect couple. But the relationship was a nightmare. They were two ill-suited people with absolutely nothing in common except under the sheets.

"In fact, I once did an interview with the Charles brothers [the show's co-creators] in which they confided to me that their perfect resolution—what they'd love to do to end the series but couldn't, of course—would be to have Sam and Diane kill each other in a double suicide. They would realize that they couldn't live with each other and couldn't live without each other and kill themselves."

—Steve Sonsky,
Miami Herald

"The writers really care about the characters. And they develop the characters as the season goes on. They do not come up with a year's worth of story lines in July. They don't know what's going to go on with Kirstie Alley five weeks from now. And I love that sort of spontaneity in putting a show together."

—Bart Andrews,
The Cheers Book

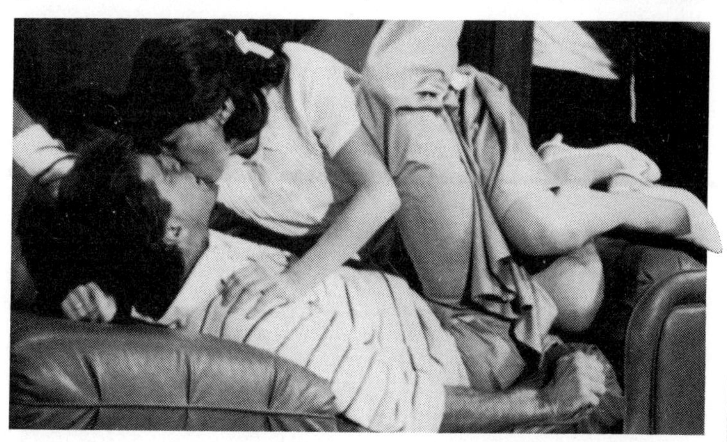

Sam's sex appeal is demonstrated when he's attacked by Carla's sister.

(MTM enterprises)

NEWHART

In 1977 Bob Newhart announced he was leaving his successful sitcom, "The Bob Newhart Show." "The next thing I knew," the comedian reminisced later, "we were having a wrap party and it was all over. I'm not sure I meant them to take me that seriously."

Newhart spent the next few years making films and performing in nightclubs, but he always wondered how to get back onto TV. Then in 1981 he stumbled onto the perfect situation for a new show. "It [happened] one day in Seattle," he told *TV Guide*. "We were staying at a little inn and I had some time to kill, and I couldn't help noticing how many characters come and go in a place like that."

He wandered into the coffee shop and was sitting there "listening to employees griping," when inspiration struck. "I suddenly thought, 'Here's a way to do the old show without doing the old show.'"

So Bob Newhart, master of the doubletake and the blank stare, the best straight man in America, became Dick Loudon, a writer of do-it-yourself books who buys a little Vermont country inn to get away from it all—then finds out that innkeeping and rural life aren't as idyllic as he imagined. It's sort of a sophisticated version of "Green Acres."Among other challenges, he has to cope with the eccentricities of the stubborn, simple townfolk, who refer to him as "that writer guy," and don't cotton much to books like *How to Grout Your Bathtub.*

As he predicted, the dynamics of "Newhart" are essentially the same as "The Bob Newhart Show". The lead character is again a reactor instead of an initiator. And he's a bastion of sanity in a loony world (which considers *him* crazy), with a loving, clever wife who's nearly as levelheaded as he is.

Once Dick is established in the community, he becomes the host of a local talk show, "Vermont Today," which serves as the equivalent of Bob Hartley's psychology practice. Instead of weird patients, we're introduced to bizarre guests like the Norwich woman with the biggest ball of string in town and the one-time cohost named Muffy who announces that "Dick and I are very, very, very, very, very, very glad to be here."

Once the man with "the smallest horse in the world" ended up on the show. Viewers began calling, each claiming to have an even smaller horse, and a swarm of them laid seige to the station. Newhart unflappably tried to weed out the ringers—like the dachshund with a saddle on his back—regarding each with his thoughtful stare, which, as always, spoke volumes.

In the best MTM tradition, "Newhart" is an ensemble comedy. Dick is surrounded by a company of strong supporting characters: Joanna, his wife; Michael, the quintessential yuppie; the shallow Stephanie; George, the bumbling handyman; and that yokel trio (who are arguably Zen masters in disguise), Larry, Darryl, and Darryl.

But this show is basically a star vehicle. The costars were selected as much for their ability to inspire Newhart's quizzical looks and doubletakes as their own acting talents—which is fine, because the strength of this program, as with the previous one, is that it lets Bob Newhart play his character. That's what audiences tune in to see. As Newhart himself remarks, "I've been doing the same thing for twenty-five years, and I'm still getting away with it.

Lucky for us.

Bob Newhart in the early days.

FLASHBACK

MICHAEL: "Hey, cardigan guy, pullover gals, seen my cashmere cutie?"
STEPHANIE: "Oh, Michael, you're here. My favorite fashion magazine came today, and it's awful. The winter look's been unveiled, and it's all wrong."
MICHAEL: "Oh, my God!"
STEPHANIE: "It's like all the fashion has suddenly turned against me. This is the worst-thing that's ever happened."
JOANNA: "Stephanie, a lot of worse things have happened in the world."
STEPHANIE: "Like what?"
JOANNA: " I don't know, floods, famines, fires."
STEPHANIE: "Where? I didn't read anything about that, and I get this every month."
MICHAEL: "Come on, my pretty and pink-cheeked gal. We'll take this page by page. There must be something we can salvage from this fashion freeze."
STEPHANIE: "Maybe you're right, Michael. After all, we survived khaki."
DICK [after a long look]: "Dammit, haven't they suffered enough?"

VITAL STATS

POLL RESULTS:
Second
PROGRAM INFO:
•Half-hour show. CBS
•First show: Oct. 25, 1982
•Still in production.

TIME: The 1980s.

PLACE: The Stratford Inn, Stratford, Vermont. Built in 1774 and newly restored. Now open for business.

BACKGROUND: Dick Loudon, a successful writer of do-it-yourself books, is weary of the Manhattan rat race. So he and his wife Joanna purchase the Stratford Inn in rural Vermont. It needs a lot of renovation, but the Loudons, both history buffs, are fascinated by the building and the notion of country life. However, living in the country isn't exactly what they fantasized it would be. For one thing, the people are pretty weird. Along with the inn, for example, Dick and Joanna inherit the live-in handyman, George Utley, whose family has worked in the place for 200 years. And then there's Larry, Darryl, and Darryl, who operate the Minuteman Cafe next door and show up at all hours, reintroducing themselves each time. Plus, the Vermonters are suspicious of the Loudons' big-city ways. After a while, though, the natives begin to accept the down-country folks. Bob is offered a job hosting a local TV show, and Joanna opens an aerobics studio.

MAIN CAST:
•**Dick Loudon** (Bob Newhart): Former ad exec. Serious, dignified. All he wants is peace and quiet, so he can write. But he never finds it.
•**Joanna Loudon** (Mary Frann): Sensible, efficient. Her interests in literature and the arts make her a little lonely among her practical rural neighbors.
•**Stephanie Vanderkellen** (Julia Duffy): Rich, self-centered snob who works at the inn as a maid because of a dispute with her father. Totally inept at her job.
•**George Utley** (Tom Poston): Colorful and crusty handyman, childlike in his pride about his work. Finds Dick and Joanna just as odd as they find him.
•**Michael Harris** (Peter Scolari): Producer of "Vermont Today," an obnoxious yuppie. Stephanie's boyfriend; calls her "cupcake" and considers the pair of them "the cutest couple in Vermont."
•**Larry** (William Sanderson), **Darryl** (Tony Papenfuss), and **Darryl** (John Volstad): Three weird brothers who run a business called "Anything for a Buck." Later they take over the Minuteman Cafe. Neither Darryl says anything; Larry is the family spokesman.

Tom Poston has been a familiar face on TV for thirty years.

LOCATION

• The exteriors of the show are really filmed in Vermont. They're shots of a little inn four miles fom Middlebury, called the Waybury Inn.
• There are no ethnic types on the show, because frankly, there are few "ethnic types" in Vermont, and the show is trying to be true to the character of the state.
• The characters don't affect accents, because most Vermonters don't have traditional New England accents like those heard in Maine and Massachusetts.

THREE'S COMPANY

• Larry, Darryl, and Darryl were originally one-shot characters. However, the studio audience's reaction to their appearance was so strong that the producers decided to make them regulars.
• William Sanderson (Larry) always wears a quarter in his ear (look closely for it). He's done it ever since his supporting performance in *Coal Miner's Daughter.* It's for luck.

NO KIDDING

Dick and Joanna don't have children. You might remember that Bob and Emily didn't, either. Says Newhart: "I don't want to be another stupid sitcom father. We debated doing kids on this show,

Julia Duffy.

and then we realized we were going to be doing what every other show was doing."

AND FORGOTTEN

The original supporting cast of "Newhart" included pathologial liar Kirk Devane (Steven Kampmann), who'd owned the Minuteman Cafe, and a different maid—rich yuppie Leslie Vanderkellen (Jennifer Holmes). However, the producers didn't feel that either character worked, so they simply eliminated them. In 1983, Kirk was "married off" to a professional clown named Cindy and left to tour Europe. Leslie "left to continue her education in England," and was replaced by her more entertaining cousin Stephanie.

VETERAN

For newcomers who think that Bob Newhart appeared out of nowhere with "The Bob Newhart Show" in 1972, here's a surprise: Newhart hosted a comedy/variety show in the 1961-62 season. It was called "The Bob Newhart Show." What's more, although the ratings weren't so hot, it won the 1962 Emmy for best comedy program.

Larry, Darryl, Darryl.

(MTM Enterprises)

CRITICS' COMMENTS

ABOUT BOB NEWHART:

"Newhart I compare to Jack Benny for timing and reaction. If you analyze the show, you see that Newhart seldom says any more than 'Oh' and 'Mmm' and 'Oh, yeah?' And yet it's consistently funny. Newhart's what Charlie Brown would be if he was real and grown up. He's not too flashy, he's not too attractive. He's intelligent, and the world around him is insane."

—Walt Belcher,
Tampa Tribune

"The hallmark of 'Newhart' is that it's not the yuk, yuk, slap your thigh kind of humor that people get sick of seeing. It's much more gentle. Bob Newhart is a different kind of sitcom star. He's not an incredibly handsome hunk. He's not in an occupation that brings up a lot of laughs. He's just a normal guy trying to keep up with an insane world."

—Mark Schwed, UPI

"I think the great thing about Newhart is that when he's not handling dialogue, he still commands the screen, because he lets you get inside of his head. Newhart reacting to situations is like *you* reacting to situations. There's something in his timing and the use of facial expressions that makes him about as good as anybody at doing that."

—John Carman,
San Francisco Chronicle

Bob Newhart and Tom Poston worked together a few years before "Newhart" debuted, in "The Bob Newhart Show."

"He gives a little look, and you know exactly what he's thinking. He's the one who makes that show work. He's so good, he makes everybody else sparkle."

—Gordon Javna,
Tough TV

"He's still a master at being a traffic cop. But I think the suporitng cast is weaker than in the original show—which means his doubletakes are less effective. He has no one to work off of."

—Tom Walter,
Memphis Appeal

ABOUT TOM POSTON:

"Tom Poston is one of those guys, like Newhart, who has been around so long, and is so talented, that you tend to take him for granted. And then he'll do something like he did the other night, where he's walking around with a ghetto blaster, singing along. It's an inspired sort of whimsey—the kind of stuff that's really off the wall. It's a much hipper show than anyone really imagines it is."

—Michael Duffy,
Detoit Free Press

THE GOLDEN GIRLS

There *have* been elderly characters in sitcoms during the last forty years. But they've usually been stereotyped as wacky grandparents. And they've generally been relegated to the kitchen or the living room, where they've made pickles or dispensed advice. When older folks have turned up zesty and youthful, their pep has been either an embarrassment ("Oh, Pop, act your age!" My Little Margie wailed every week), or, as in the case of "Mama's Family," a source of mean-spirited humor.

But now we have "The Golden Girls," the first sitcom to depict senior citizens as normal, whole people. In fact, "The Golden Girls" is the first *family* sitcom for the elderly.

The four main characters of "The Golden Girls" are well over fifty; one of them, Sophia, is even over eighty. But three of them hold down jobs, and although none are married (three are widowed, one divorced), they continue to enjoy romance, hobbies, travel, and most of all, each other. So much for the myth that people are doomed to grow old alone.

Moreover, although they all have humorous personality traits (e.g., Rose is a little dim-witted, Blanche is incorrigibly randy), these characteristics are never ridiculed. The golden girls are portrayed as people who, give or take a decade or three, are not much different from you and me. As Sophia declares, "We can have carpeting and cars and jewelry and condos and clothing, just like everybody else."

"The Golden Girls"'s credibility stems largely from its cast of veteran actresses, who can enhance a program merely by showing up. Beatrice Arthur, like Bob Newhart, is a great reactor. One sideways glance from her is worth several lines of dialogue. Betty White's timing with a comic line has been impeccable for thirty years. Rue McClanahan need only walk down a hallway, in an attempt to attract anyone from the mailman to a passing jogger, to get a laugh. And 60-year-old Estelle Getty is amazing as 80-year-old Sophia. Unlike Vicki Lawrence of "Mama's Family," she portrays a far older woman without turning her into a cartoon character, and despite her celebrated salty tongue, she makes her sympathetic and lovable .

"The Golden Girls" was created when changing demographics caught NBC chief Brandon Tartikoff's eye. He noticed that almost 37 percent of Americans were at least 45 years old in 1984, and there are now approximately 10 million more people over fifty than there were ten years ago. It was, he decided, about time for a positive program about aging. So he enlisted Susan Harris, veteran of "Maude," "Soap," and "Fay," to create one.

These roots are apparent from the sharp writing: Rose: "Those burglars were probably looking for drugs." Dorothy: "We have Maalox and estrogen. How many thieves do you know who have gas and hot flashes?"

Dorothy: "Did you know Jean is a lesbian?" Blanche: "What's wrong with that? Isn't Danny Thomas one?"

"The Golden Girls" is also not afraid to deal with the sensitive issues of aging. Alzheimer's disease, menopause, fear of death, and death itself have all been handled with care. But, as on "Maude," they've also been given a certain amount of shock value. (Blanche: "What if I die now? I'm too young...and I'm wearing the wrong underwear.")

"The Golden Girls" hasn't solved the long-lived stereotyping of the elderly in the media. But it has reassured its aging audience that one can grow old gracefully. And its four stars are proof that some people *do* get better as they get older.

Bea Arthur plays a no-nonsense school teacher in "The Golden Girls."

FLASHBACK

[*The Golden Girls are contemplating adopting a baby.*]
BLANCHE: "Girls, we have a big problem. We're all women."
DOROTHY: [*sarcastically*] : "No."
ROSE: "Sure we are."
DOROTHY: "Oh, shut up, Rose."
BLANCHE: "No, it says here in this Spock book that it's important to have male role models during your formative years."
DOROTHY: "Okay, we'll all wear our Yankees caps and scratch our behinds over beer."
ROSE: "We have nothing to worry about. If we give the baby love and attention and understanding, it'll be fine."
DOROTHY: "Why, Rose, that's beautiful."
ROSE: "Besides, what does Spock know about raising babies? On Vulcan they're all in pods."
BLANCHE: "Rose, did you take much acid during the '60s?"

VITAL STATS

POLL RESULTS:
Third
PROGRAM INFO:
- Half-hour show. NBC.
- First show: Sept. 15, 1985
- Still in production.

TIME: The 1980s.

PLACE: Miami, Florida, mecca of senior citizens.

BACKGROUND: Blanche, a recent widow, suddenly realizes that she's got all this empty space in her large suburban home. So she invites her friends Dorothy and Rose to move in and share it with her. It's good timing. Dorothy's 38-year-old marriage has just broken up (her husband left her for a stewardess). And Rose is still grieving after her own husband's passing. With the addition of Dorothy's sharp-tongued mother, Sophia, the quartet establishes a family and a loving, warm environment. Although they must deal with the challenges of aging, as well as the difficulties of facing the world as single women their closeness and mutual understanding help make the adaptation much easier and their new lives pretty enjoyable.

MAIN CAST:
- **Dorothy** (Bea Arthur): A teacher and recent divorcee. The most vulnerable of the four, she hides the pain of her failed marriage behind caustic comments and an aggressive demeanor. Nonetheless, she's warmhearted and sensitive.
- **Rose** (Betty White): A grief counselor. Sweet, spacey, a little dim-witted. Likes teddy bears, chocolate sundaes, old movies.
- **Blanche** (Rue McLanahan): An art-gallery assistant and a hot-to-trot southern belle. A hopeless flirt but also a devoted mother and friend.
- **Sophia** (Estelle Getty): Dorothy's mother; cantankerous and salty, due partly to a stroke that left her unaccountable for her mouth and partly to her marriage to Salvatore, a Sicilian she says had mob connections.

Sophia is Estelle Getty's first regular TV role. Here's what she really looks like.

In 1977, Betty White had her own sitcom, "The Betty White Show." It flopped.

Rue McClanahan has starred in three series prior to "The Golden Girls": "Maude," "Mama's Family," and "Apple Pie" (See the 1970s Chamber of Horrors). Above, she and Conrad Bain in a scene from "Maude."

BEA QUIET

In contrast to her bombastic character, Beatrice Arthur is actually quiet and shy. She seldom talks or mixes with her fellow cast members on the set.

THREE'S A CROWD

Betty White claims that her work situation would never play in real life. "The last thing I could imagine is moving in with three other friends, no matter how much I liked them," she says.

MISCELLANY

- "The Golden Girls" is coproduced by Tony Thomas, brother of Marlo and son of Danny.
- "The Golden Girls"'s theme song, "Thank You for Being a Friend," was a hit record for Andrew Gold over a decade ago.
- The role that all three of the actresses coveted at the outset was the one that Estelle Getty got. "Let's say we'd all like to be playing Sophia," Rue McClanahan admitted to a reporter.
- Getty's delivery is so good that even the show's camera crew breaks up laughing at her lines, even if they've already heard them a few times.

THE SWITCHER-RUE

The role of Blanche was originally designed for Betty White, based on Sue Ann Nivens, the man-chasing character she'd played in "The Mary Tyler Moore Show." But the writers decided to switch Rue and Betty's roles, giving them a chance to play new characters. They were both thrilled.

CRITICS' COMMENTS

ABOUT THE SUBJECT:

"For a while, they leaned too heavily on old people talking about sex. Every time they needed a joke, they'd go to that convention, and it kind of got on my nerves. But they've gotten out of that and become more of a character-driven show."

—Michael Hill,
Baltimore Evening Sun

"'The Golden Girls' is a great show because of the subject matter. Isn't it wonderful to take elderly women, who have traditionally been the butt of society's jokes—LOLs (little old ladies)—and make them into the heroines?

"Yeah, they're still perpetuating some of the TV stereotypes—the flirt, the dingy female, etc.—but the important thing is that the stereotypes aren't necessarily identified with older women. That's a breakthrough."

—Yardena Arar,
Los Angeles Daily News

ABOUT ITS APPEAL:

"It's not enough to have older women there. It's funny because each of the characters takes on a slightly exaggerated personality—bigger than real life, but not blown so out of proportion that they're caricatures. They've balanced it just right, and that makes the show work."

—Barry Garron,
Kansas City Star

"One of the reasons 'The Golden Girls' works is that three of the ladies knew each other very well before they got their parts in the series. Bea Arthur, Rue McClanahan, and Betty White have all worked together at one time or another and have known each other for many years. The result: they already respect each other as actresses, and don't feel they have anything to prove. So they work together comfortably, even happily, and it shows in their product."

—Eirik Knutzen,
Syndicated TV Columnist

ABOUT THE MESSAGE:

"I think they are right on target. Good lord, you look around at the dilemma of the older people in this country.... We probably do the poorest job of any industrialized society in taking care of our senior citizens. And this show manages to make some very telling points about that, even as it entertains.

"I certainly think they get their message across a *hell* of a lot better than, say, a documentary or a public broadcasting show with talking heads could—and to a larger audience. Fat lot of good if you're going to preach and no one's listening."

—R.K. Shull,
Indianapolis News

THE COSBY SHOW

Cliff and Clair invited Denise's new boyfriend over for dinner in a 1985 episode called "How Ugly Is He?"

With the debut of "The Cosby Show" in 1984, America's sitcoms went full cycle. The genre had begun with slow-moving, warmhearted family comedies like "The Goldbergs" and "I Remember Mama." Now, 35 years later, they were back.

But because "Cosby" appeared in the wake of a stream of gimmicks, idiot plots, and unsympathetic characters, its brand of gentle comedy was hailed as a breath of fresh air, a breakthrough. Viewers (and a number of critics) forgot that kindly, sagacious sitcom fathers had been wandering around the house in their sweaters since the days of Ozzie Nelson.

Still, "The Cosby Show" *is* revolutionary, in its own quiet way.

For one thing, the family is black. Although there have been upwardly mobile blacks in sitcoms before (the Jeffersons, Julia), Cosby's family isn't just "movin' on up." They've arrived—they're already living the American dream of the '80s and feeling quite comfortable with it. All five of the children are yuppie fashionplates. Mom and Dad have fulfilling, lucrative careers (he's an obstetrician, she's an attorney). The children go to college. And though they're all busy with their own lives, everybody still has time for the type of quality family life they tell you about in *Working Parents* magazine.

For another thing, the kids on "Cosby" aren't jive-talking hipsters (like Jimmie Walker) or cute ragamuffins. They're just regular American kids, and their problems are based on the sort of everyday angst a middle-class audience can relate to. Whole episodes are written around a daughter's misery about the death of a goldfish. (The entire family dresses in mourning togs and conducts a funeral next to the toilet.) Or an adolescent daughter wants to wear heavy makeup like her friends do. (Parents say no; she disobeys and applies it at school. All is resolved in a heart-to-heart talk with Cos.)

And then there's Cos himself, the first sitcom dad since Ozzie Nelson to be an integral part of his own show's production. Cosby serves as lead player, cocreator, coproducer, executive consultant, and cowriter of the theme song. If he doesn't like something, out it goes. (He once threatened to walk off the show when NBC wanted to remove an anti-apartheid sticker from Theo's door.) He's been known to change scripts at the last minute, to spend sleepless nights searching for the "right" solution to a fictitious family situation. He even utilizes the services of a bona fide psychiatrist, Harvard's Dr. Alvin F. Poussaint, to oversee the scripts and make sure the action is as realistic as possible—something the producers of "The Donna Reed Show" and "Father Knows Best" would never have dreamed of doing.

But in the end, the chief appeal of the show is really Bill Cosby's comic delivery. For years, he's been entertaining us with hilarious monologues about raising his own children, and it's a short step to a family sitcom and dialogue like this: "My boy, play football. My son, carry the ball for me. I sit in the stands. 'Is that your son?' 'Yes, my boy. See him running the touchdown with the name Huxtable on his back. I would have done it myself, but I'm too old now. So I gave him the business. Huxtable and Son. The circle will not be broken.'"

The sitcom breakthroughs pioneered by Norman Lear aren't apparent here; overall, it's still a throwback. But if most Americans want to spend thirty minutes a week tuned to a show that emphasizes love, family, and responsible parents—and showcases a great comedian like Cosby—so what? Maybe the traditional values of "Father Knows Best" really need to be updated every once in a while, just to keep us from losing touch with them.

With "The Cosby Show," Bill Cosby is the first black actor ever to play the lead in a #1 TV series.

FLASHBACK

CLIFF: "I am your father. I brought you into this world, and I can take you out."

CLIFF [gazing at his son's messed-up bedroom]: "Hard to get good help, isn't it?"

CLAIRE [exasperated]: "Why do we have five children?"
CLIFF: "Because we did not want to have six."

CLIFF: "Did you tell Denise she could go out tonight?"
CLAIRE: "Yes, I did."
CLIFF: "Have you seen him?"
CLAIRE: "Yes."
CLIFF: "Well, how ugly is he?"

CLAIRE: "If I died, would you marry again?"
CLIFF: "We'll talk about it when it happens."

CLIFF: "He's coming!"
DENISE'S DATE: "Who?"
CLIFF: "Elvin!"
DATE: "Who's Elvin?"
CLIFF: "He's the fellow Denise likes!"
DATE: "Then why am I here?"
CLIFF: "Because you're the fellow that *I* like!"

VITAL STATS

POLL RESULTS:
Fourth
PROGRAM INFO:
- Half-hour show. NBC
- First show: Sept. 20, 1987
- Still in production.

TIME: The 1980s.

PLACE: New York City, home of Dr. Heathcliff Huxtable, wealthy obstetrician, his attorney wife, Claire, and their five children. The action takes place chiefly in the Huxtable home, an attractive, impeccably furnished brownstone which is—despite the fact that it's constantly full of kids—never untidy.

BACKGROUND: Cliff and Claire Huxtable were high school sweethearts. Now they're busy professionals; but they're still family folks. First, they took the time to *have* the kids. Now they're taking the time to raise them right. Cliff's office is on the ground floor of their house, so he's home a lot, chatting with the kids about the problems of growing up. Cliff and Claire have plenty of time for each other, too. There's romance, and cash, and equality, and yes, wacky antics. Each week we drool as they lead their perfect lives on our TV sets.

MAIN CAST:
- **Heathcliff "Cliff" Huxtable** (Bill Cosby): An outgoing, charming obstetrician. Adored by his patients and his family. Solves both professional and personal dilemmas with laughter; even labor contractions can be put on hold while Huxtable performs one of his monologues.
- **Claire Huxtable** (Phylicia Rashad): Cool and self-assured. Doesn't take any guff from anyone. But underneath her businesslike exterior, is a loving mom and devoted wife.
- **Sondra Huxtable** (Sabrina Le Beauf): College-age daughter, a premed student, dreamily in love with semi-chauvinistic husband, Elvin.

Malcolm Jamal Wilkes

- **Denise Huxtable** (Lisa Bonet): Teenage daughter. Beautiful Denise is having trouble adjusting to her first year of college (and a spinoff series).
- **Theodore "Theo" Huxtable** (Malcolm Jamal Warner): Teenage son. Good-looking, popular, generally responsible. Occasionally convinced by his pal Cockroach to do something weird, like shaving his head for a rock video.
- **Vanessa Huxtable** (Tempestt Bledsoe): Adolescent, incurable gossip, and most trouble-prone of the kids. But she still tries to be good.
- **Rudy Huxtable** (Keshia Knight Pulliam): Five-year-old daughter. Cute, mischievous and definitely Daddy's girl.

AUNT EMMY

Bill Cosby hates the Emmys, believing actors should not compete with each other (even though he did win two for "I Spy.") It seems certain that he would have won at least one since the show's debut, but he removes his name from consideration each year. He lets others compete, though. "The Cosby Show" has won an award for best comedy series and has won numerous writing and directing awards. Keshia Knight Pulliam, age six, was nominated for an Emmy in 1986, making her the youngest performer ever to be so honored.

CALLING DR. COSBY

Cosby has an Ed.D. from Amherst College in Massachusetts. The subject of his dissertation: "An Integration of the Visual Media Via 'Fat Albert and the Cosby Kids' into the Elementary School Curriculum as a Teaching Aid and Vehicle to Achieve Increased Learning."

ORIGINS

NBC president Brandon Tartikoff awoke one night to the wails of his infant daughter. While soothing her, he turned on "The Tonight Show," where Bill Cosby was performing one of his monologues about being a parent. Tartikoff thought a sitcom built on this theme—and Cosby's talents—would be a surefire success. NBC wasn't so sure. Cosby: "They thought it was the wrong time, the wrong humor, and the wrong color." But Tartikoff persisted. "The Cosby Show" made its debut at number one.

MISCELLANY

- "The Cosby Show" is taped on the East Coast so its star can commute to his home in Connecticut.

- Phylicia Rashad is the sister of dancer/actress Debbie Allen ("Fame"). She's also the wife of NBC sportscaster Ahmad Rashad, who proposed to her on the air during halftime at a Thanksgiving Day football game.

- Lisa Bonet was named one of the ten most beautiful women in America by *Harper's Bazaar* magazine.

Left: Cliff and Theo work things out. "If Cliff yelled, screamed, and hollered like my father," says Cosby, "the show never would have made it....'The Cosby Show' hints that it's okay to *like* your kids."

On "The Bill Cosby Show," which ran from 1969-70, Cosby played gym teacher Chet Kincaid. The show was not a success.

CRITICS' COMMENTS

ABOUT THE SITCOM REVIVAL:

"'Cosby' is a throwback, more like 'The Andy Griffith Show,' than 'All in the Family.' It reminds me of 'Leave It to Beaver,' because you have a very normal family unit that doesn't seem to be going through any crises; everything gets resolved; everyone's very attractive; and there don't seem to be any outside threats."

—Douglas Durden,
Richmond Times Dispatch

"If the family sitcom was dead, he certainly revived it. It's a phenomenon I can't explain. It's very much like 'Newhart.' Each of them has taken control of his show, and doesn't let it get away from what he originally intended it to be.

"'Cosby' *is* a revival, but ironically, the show could never have happened in the '50s, when the genre was originally popular. Nor could it have happened in the '60s. You have to get into the '70s before you see black American families in situation comedies. I guess the Jeffersons were the first. But they were really ethnic. They were out of place. And that was part of the conflict in the series—they drew their jokes from being out of place.

"No, I really think 'Cosby' could happen only in the 80s. The Huxtables are a real symbol of this decade."

—Greg Bailey,
Nashville Banner

ABOUT ITS VALUE:

"Sure, it is glossy and very upscale and very idealized. But in some ways, that's better than something more downbeat or realistic. It fulfills one of TV's roles, which is to give us something to aspire to. They're upscale and materialistic, but they have something to go along with it—this strong sense of family, a strong sense of caring for one another and trying to make sure that everyone is the best he or she can be. It's really encouraging to see them place an emphasis on education and on bettering yourself."

—David Cuthbert,
New Orleans Times-Picayune

ABOUT ITS POPULARITY:

"It's widely thought in the TV industry that kids control the TV set from 8:00 to 9:00, and kids get the same basic sense of security from Cosby that they do from Mr. Rogers. He's gentle and fun-loving, but within strict parameters. That's why it's still popular.

"Originally, its popularity came from other sources. It was refreshing; Cosby had been quoted as saying this is the show where the parents win. After generation after generation of sitcoms where the father was a wimp, it was refreshing to see someone who was in control."

—Ed Siegel,
Boston Globe

FAMILY TIES

As Alex Keaton, Michael J. Fox visits London in a made-for-TV movie version of the NBC series which aired in September, 1985.

"Family Ties" started out to explore the comic possibilities of a clash between a pair of aging '60s flower children and their pragmatic '80s offspring. But producer/creator Gary Goldberg hadn't reckoned with a smash movie called *Back to the Future* and the sudden megastar status of a supporting player named Michael J. Fox. In a very short time, "Family Ties" was transformed from a modern domestic comedy to a star vehicle.

"Family Ties" focuses on the lives of a midwestern family known as the Keatons. Dad (Steven) is a liberal public-television station manager, Mom (Elyse) is an architect. They once dreamed their children would be similarly concerned with love, peace, and liberal causes. But things haven't exactly worked out that way.

Their son Alex is the consummate budding capitalist. As a child, he had a Richard Nixon lunch box and read the *Wall Street Journal* instead of comic books. Their daughter Mallory loves shopping and boys, and her lack of intellect is almost embarrassing. Jennifer wants to be a punk-rock star. And the baby, Andrew, is an Alex clone who listens to economic summit conferences on his Junior Walkman.

But despite this cavernous generation gap, the Keatons accept and love each other. They might make jokes about the William F. Buckley picture that Alex keeps over his bed, or Dad's down jackets and Birkenstock sandals. They might all look askance at Mallory's boyfriend, Nick, a dimwit who makes sculptures with titles like "Interstate Pileup," but no one in the Keaton family would think of trying to make the others change.

Neither, for that matter, would the show's talented writers—because the characters are too full of comic potential. There's still a lot of humor to be drawn from Steven and Elyse's struggle to learn, and adapt to, the attitudes of the '80s.

Elyse [baking cookies]: "Now, don't roll the dough too thin or the cookies will burn in the oven." Andrew [whining]: "Why can't we get 'em at the store, like everybody else does?" Elyse: "It's more fun this way. It's a special time between a mommy and her little boy. You know, just the two of us here together, working, sharing, creating." Andrew [patronizingly]: "Mom, we're just cooking."

Or Mallory's struggle to learn anything at all. Mallory [desperately]: "Okay, the light bulb burned out in my bedroom. What are we going to do now?"

Most of all, the show has Michael J. Fox, who has moved with ease from nameless sitcom kid to teen idol. Alex P. Keaton could have been as obnoxious as Eddie Haskell, with his pretentious, know-it-all attitude. But Fox makes the kid funny and likable.

It's a comment on a more tolerant society that the Keatons can coexist, and even thrive, in a house divided. Despite its satire of aging liberals, "Family Ties"'s message of acceptance is very much a product of Steven and Elyse's generation. Maybe Alex will always wince at Steven's Bob Dylan records. Maybe Steven will never understand why Alex wears a tie to gym class. The point is, they love each other. The phrase "Do your own thing" may be as out-of-date as underground newspapers. But in this case, it works. As Alex himseff once said in a rare burst of insight, "We're all good people, and that's the real message."

A bearded Steven Keaton.

FLASHBACK

ALEX: "I don't know why you're fighting me on this, Jennifer."
JENNIFER: "It just doesn't sound right, that's all."
ALEX: "Okay, lemme try and explain it to you again. You are what's called a 'consumer.' You buy gum, candy, a pair of wax lips every now and then...."
JENNIFER: "Right...."
ALEX: "Right. Okay. Now you need money for all this, right?"
JENNIFER: "But I get an allowance."
ALEX: "That's true, but don't you remember...?"
JENNIFER: "Oh, yeah....I've been hard hit by inflationary pressures.
ALEX: "Right. Now I am willing to supplement your income by 25 cents a week in exchange for a service. What could be more reasonable?"
JENNIFER: "Alex, I don't *want* to clean your room."
MALLORY: "Why don't you clean your own room?"
ALEX: "I could do that, Mallory, but that'd be the easy way out. By paying Jennifer to do it, I'm allowing her to participate in the American free-enterprise system. Don't do it for me, Jennifer, do it for America."
JENNIFER: "You have no shame at all."

VITAL STATS

POLL RESULTS:
Fifth
PROGRAM INFO:
- Half-hour show. NBC
- First show: Sept. 22, 1982
- Still in production.

TIME: The 1980s.

PLACE: Columbus, Ohio, home of Steven and Elyse Keaton and their children, Alex, Mallory, Jennifer, and Andrew.

BACKGROUND: Steven and Elyse Keaton meet at a peace rally. They fall in love while working on an underground newspaper together and marry as soon as they finish college. Steven goes out and gets a politically correct job at a public television station while Elyse works as a freelance architect in between pregnancies. While they still try to stay true to their liberal '60s values (Steven even toys with the idea of resurrecting the newspaper), their children are definitely products of the Me generation—even little Andrew, born (appropriately enough) while Elyse was singing folk songs during a public TV fund-raising event. However, "Family Ties" are strong enough to hold the family together in the '80s, as they were twenty years ago when Steven and Elyse were worrying *their* parents.

Tina Yothers in a 1983 episode, "The Fifth Wheel."

MAIN CAST:
- **Elyse Keaton** (Meredith Baxter Birney): Beautiful, sensitive mother. Manages to balance her career and family with ease—without losing her gentleness or levelheadedness. Has a tendency to break into "Blowin' in the Wind" at weird moments.
- **Steven Keaton** (Michael Gross): Gentle, idealistic dad. Occasionally can't stand his kids' values anymore but still loves them.
- **Alex P. Keaton** (Michael J. Fox): The ultimate capitalist. Carries monogrammed briefcases to school (the P doesn't stand for anything—he just likes the sound of it). Cocky and arrogant, snide. Politically to the right of just about everyone. But fundamentally a decent kid.
- **Mallory Keaton** (Justine Bateman): Airheaded daughter. Reluctantly attends junior college; would rather work in a mall boutique.
- **Jennifer Keaton** (Tina Yothers): Thirteen-year-old tomboy. Smart but hides it from boys. Good singer, longs for a rock career.
- **Andrew Keaton** (Brian Bonsall): The four-year-old son, perilously close to becoming an Alex clone, up to the tie and fascination with shows like "Wall Street Week."

EAT IT

The show's producers had trouble selling Michael J. Fox to NBC chief Brandon Tartikoff. Tartikoff: "The kid's good, but can you see his face on a lunchbox?" After "Family Ties" became a hit, the show's producers had a Michael J. Fox lunchbox made for Tartikoff and added a note: "Dear Brandon, this is for you to put your crow in."

FILM ROLE

Needless to say, the success of *Back to the Future* resulted in a larger role for Michael J. Fox in the show. How much larger? In 1984, pre-*Future*, he was nominated for an Emmy Award for outstanding supporting actor in a sitcom. In 1985 and 1986, he won for outstanding actor.

THIS IS YOUR LIFE

"Family Ties" was created by Gary David Goldberg, who was inspired to become a TV writer by one of the worst shows of the '70s. "I was watching 'Get Christie Love,'" he says, "and I turned to [my wife] and said, 'I can definitely do that.'" And he did. Though the father of two children, he still considers himself a holdover from the '60s—which is how "Family Ties" came into being in the first place. A TV executive suggested, "Let's do your life as a series."

Grown-up children of the '60s—Elyse and Steve Keaton pose for NBC during "Family Ties"' first season.

WHO-BU?

Fans of "Family Ties" have probably seen in the credits that the company responsible for the show is called Ubu Productions. Why Ubu? The "Family Ties" production company is named after Goldberg's late, lamented Labrador retriever. The dog pictured at the end of each episode is the actual Ubu, who used to play Frisbee with Goldberg during his college days.

REAL TIES

Meredith Baxter Birney has five children of her own. She was pregnant with two of them, twins Peter and Mollie, during "Family Ties"'s third season—which is why Andrew was created. Inspired by "I Love Lucy," the producers decided to work her condition into the script.

CRITICS' COMMENTS

ABOUT ALEX:
"Everybody wants to make money and get rich, but you don't go around talking about it, because you'll sound greedy. Well Alex is the opposite. He's the personification of the Me generation; money is all he thinks and talks about.

"It's the emotional stuff—love and affection—that are hard for him. He has that in him, but he has a hard time expressing it. He so often says the opposite, tries to come on like money and achievement are much more important than relationships. He's got a different kind of struggle than most sitcom characters. It's a nice change."

—Yardena Arar,
Los Angeles Daily News

ABOUT ITS APPEAL:
"What I like about 'Family Ties' is the family relationship. It strikes me as being very real, with people who tease each other and joke with each other and sometimes really get on each other's nerves—who don't always like each other, but *do* always love each other. As the show has drifted away from the family and focused on Alex, I've liked it less. But still the nature of the relationships really appeals to me."

—Joseph Walker,
Salt Lake City Deseret News

ON THE MICHAEL J. FOX PHENOMENON:
"In the original 'Happy Days,' Fonzie was envisioned as a minor character; it wasn't until producer Garry Marshall saw that something was really happening with Fonzie that he began to bill him as a major character. There's a parallel here to 'Family Ties,' where they started out thinking of it as a family show—the parents were supposed to be the leads and the kids their foils—and gradually, we've watched it become the 'Michael J. Fox Show.'

"In a more general sense, this illustrates something common to modern sitcom writing. Once a show gets established enough with its audience to preclude cancellation, the writers begin to follow where their characters are going and allow them to grow more. That seems to happen more on a situation comedy than it does on a private-eye show or a cop show. There's more evolution of character here."

—Alex McNeil,
Total Television

"Michael Fox is a very enjoyable person to watch. People say it was unfair that they pushed the parents back. The fact is, there was no interesting show about them; the interesting show was Alex Keaton.

"'Family Ties' has reached various generations for various reasons.... Younger viewers like it because the kid is so successful, even though he was successful in a way that's increasingly put down by his parents....And older viewers think of him as an ideal son—he's clean-cut, nice, and all that."

—Peter Farrell,
Oregonian

Even Alex can't escape his feelings. In 1985, in a two-part episode called "The Real Thing," he actually fell in love.

80s

Wilfred Hyde-White, a distinguished British actor, starred as Emerson Marshall in "The Associates."

SQUARE PEGS (1982-83)
"To begin with, 'Square Pegs' took place at Weemawee High School. If *you* went to Weemawee High School, you'd be pretty weird, too. What I liked about this show is that it didn't offer the audience impossible role models—impossibly cute, impossibly talented,impossibly successful—it was just a couple of normal kids, not popular or special, just trying to do what we all tried to do—survive high school.If there were more shows that portrayed the experience the way it really is, you'd have a lot less anxiety among teenagers. Great show. Naturally, it didn't do well."

—Yardena Arar,
Los Angeles Daily News

OPEN ALL NIGHT (1982)
"This was a lovely slice-of-life, set in an all-night grocery store. But what happens in an all-night grocery store that could attract 20 million viewers? Viewers didn't expect to have much fun watching clerks ring up the milk, ice cream, and assorted junk food that people go in to convenience stores to buy, so they stayed away from the program. But surprisingly, the characters were hilarious, and the writing was superb. This was one of those offbeat gems that's almost too good for the tube. If you ever get a chance to see an episode, take the time—you won't be disappointed."

—Gene Sculatti,
The Catalog of Cool

THE ASSOCIATES (1979-80)
"This was a sophisticated comedy that just went over the mass audience's head, I think. It was a sitcom about a law firm, which you don't see particularly often. But the main thing was that the characters were great. Wilfred Hyde-White, who was in 'Buck Rogers,' of all things, was the perfect image of an old but cagey Englishman, and the rest of the cast—a guy who was trying to make it with everything in skirts, a Boston blue blood, a liberal, a greedy sonuvabitch—were all wonderful. In a way, it was a comedy version of 'L.A. Law.' But it never even got out of the box. It lasted about one season."

—Gordon Javna,
Calling All Monomaniacs

POLICE SQUAD (1982)
"There were only six episodes, but I've got them all on tape. I still think it was the funniest show of its time. I laughed—and continue to laugh—at every episode. There were a lot of sight gags, which you'd expect from the guys who made the film *Airplane*. And it was a comedy without a laugh track; in fact, it couldn't take a laugh track, because the laugh track would have had to run all the way through, nonstop. There were so many things going on that you could watch an episode four or five times and pick up new little things in the background every time. In one scene, Leslie Neilsen, who was Detective Frank Drebin, is driving down the street and you see the Leaning Tower of Pisa in the background for no reason. And once they also gunned down Florence Henderson in the opening credits, which I found gratifying. It was a great satire on detective shows."

—Ed Bark,
Dallas Morning News

Worst of the '80s

Given the breakthroughs in characterization, subject matter, plot construction, etc., over the last two decades, TV audiences in the '80s have a right to expect more from situation comedies than previous generations have—especially since networks have finally begun to acknowledge that quality programs are worthwhile investments.

This, however, doesn't mean that we'll get what we deserve. "Bad sitcoms," commented a southern TV critic, "like the poor in the Bible, will always be with us." Amen.

There doesn't seem to be any pattern to the shows that critics selected as the worst three of the '80s—except that they all celebrate the worst side of human existence. Nobody could be as dumb as Mickey in "We Got It Made," or as mean-spirited as "Mama's Family," or as self-consciously cute as Punky Brewster (yes, cuteness is a vice).

And perhaps that offers an insight into what makes a sitcom bad. At their best, situation comedies are little celebrations of day-to-day life, bursting with humanity. They're not always happy, but they always treat their subject with respect.

But the shows that denigrate human beings by stripping their characters of dignity are intrinsically bad—even destructive. Critics are appalled at the way these three programs portray human beings, and they named all three to the list by a wide margin.

WE GOT IT MADE

Teri and the boys first showed up on NBC on September 8, 1983. The last episode was seen on March 30, 1984. It was resurrected on September 27, 1987.

During the '60s, there was a popular soap opera called "Dark Shadows" whose hero, Barnabas Collins, was secretly a vampire. Whenever anyone threatened him with a weapon, he'd smirk: "You can't kill me. I'm already dead."

That pretty much describes "We Got It Made." The critics hated it. Nobody watched it. And yet it's back again in 1987, in first-run syndication. Consider the implications: Hollywood has finally created a show so bad that *nothing* can affect it—not bad ratings, not protests, not even network apathy.

This show is so unoriginal that it actually performs an unheard-of triple ripoff: Besides the obvious imitation of *Dracula*, it copies "Three's Company," right down to the last jiggle; and its basic concept, the gorgeous—albeit harmless—blonde who innocently threatens every female in sight, is virtually identical to a show called "My Friend Irma," which aired in 1952.

"We Got It Made" concerns two Manhattan bachelors who hire a blonde bimbo to be their live-in housekeeper. It's an innocent situation (except for the usual double entendres and rib-jabbing humor). But their two girlfriends seethe. That's the plot. Period.

"We Got It Made" (maid-made, get it?) breaks no new ground, features generally forgettable performances, and, after the sophisticated scripts and high standards maintained by shows like "Cheers," seems to belong to another decade. Of course, it was the brainchild of Fred Silverman, the man behind such shows as "Petticoat Junction," and "Thicke of the Night." But he defends "We Got It Made," equating its humor and broad comedy style with the works of Moliere. But he probably never watched it; its stars plainly think that Moliere is what a dentist takes out.

Silverman may eventually find an audience for Teri Copley's inane jiggling, but that's still no excuse. With this show, television takes a giant step backward.

BACKGROUND

Two upwardly mobile New York bachelors decide their demanding careers leave them no time for housework . (Dave is a lawyer, Jay is a "new-wave" importer and "idea man," whatever that means.) They scour New York for the perfect maid and end up with Mickey, a bubbly and totally stupid blonde bimbo who just so happens to be a terrific housekeeper. She moves in and starts cleaning. The duo's girlfriends are extremely suspicious and are constantly devising ways to catch one or the other in the act...and to convince Mickey to go on to greener apartments. It doesn't work. Micky stays, and the whole situation is quite harmless. Really.

MAIN CAST

- **Mickey Mackenzie** (Teri Copley): The gorgeous, dumb housekeeper.
- **Jay Bostwick** (Tom Villiard): The new-wave importer of marginally useful merchandise.
- **David Tucker** (Matt McCoy): The straight-laced lawyer.
- **Beth** (Bonnie Urseth): Jay's girlfriend, a kindergarten teacher.
- **Claudia** (Stepfanie Kramer): David's girlfriend.

FLASHBACK

[*Mickey is in the living room vacuuming. But the vacuum cleaner isn't plugged in.*]
DAVE [strolling through the room]: "I hear they work better if you plug them in."
MICKEY: "Can't talk now. Gotta vacuum. [To herself, giggling] Mickey, you goofball."

DAVE: "Let me guess. You have a date with Barry tonight."
MICKEY: "Oh, Barry [sighs]. Did you know there's a city in Vermont called Barre, and Barry comes from New Hampshire, which is the state next to Vermont?"
DAVE: "Talk about your small worlds."

Tom Villiard and Matt McCoy were the males in the NBC version of the show. In the syndicated program, McCoy was replaced.

CRITICS' COMMENTS

"This was a program about a pair of breasts. It was one of the ogling, leering comedies. There was no attempt to be clever. It was like peeping through a keyhole for half an hour a week."

—Tom Jicha, *Miami News*

"Puerile, utter trash, mind candy. And it isn't funny. I can forgive anything if it's funny. But this show is just not funny."

—David Cuthbert, *New Orleans Times-Picayune*

"This was sort of Fred Silverman's last gasp—his last attempt to create a jiggle show. He found Teri Copley in the 1970s or '80s equivalent of Schwab's drugstore and put her on the air. He thought she had... perfect sex appeal. She certainly is adorable, but it was a terrible, boring, trite jiggle show that was years *after* its time."

—Steve Sonsky, *Miami Herald*

"It was Fred Silverman's first show after leaving as chairman of NBC; it's almost as though the network agreed to take the first thing he produced, whatever it was. He got a nice time slot for it, and they promoted it heavily. But it was just so transparently Fred; it spells out his entire career in a nutshell. It was such a simpering, dumb comedy...and the fact that they're bringing it back now is just beyond belief.."

—Ed Bark, *Dallas Morning News*

"It was a real Cro Magnon approach to humor in the '80s; the level of humor was so low that someone was using crayons to write the script."

—MikeDuffy, *Detroit Free Press*

In 1984, after this show bit the dust, Teri Copley starred in the TV movie, "I Married a Centerfold."

"In 7 1/2 years as a TV critic, I think it might be the most God-awful sitcom pilot I ever saw. It was...an ugly, horrible, U-turn to the past, featuring two of the most unattractive...jerk guy leads in television history, and...I don't know how you would describe the Mickey character except to say that she was just senseless. I don't see how she could feel, think, see, or do anything, she was so stupid."

—Jeff Borden, *Charlotte Observer*

MAMA'S FAMILY

"Mama's Family" burst onto NBC on January 22, 1983. It was chased off on September 15, 1984.

On the old "Carol Burnett Show," writers Dick Clair and Jenna McMahon developed an ongoing skit about the unpleasant Higgins family, comprised of shrewish Eunice (Burnett), dumb Ed (Harvey Korman), and Eunice's snappish, beer-chugging mama, played by the show's resident ingenue, Vicki Lawrence. The skit was pretty popular, so when CBS canceled "Carol Burnett" in 1979, it seemed like a natural for a spinoff.

Unfortunately, the Harper/Higgins clan is best taken in small doses. TV has had its share of unpleasant families (the Bunkers certainly had their moments). But "Mama's Family" is more than unpleasant. It's *intolerable*, unredeemed by heart, character likability, basic intelligence, or the underlying love that made the Bunker disagreements work so well. Here, Mama snarls, Vint whimpers, Naomi pouts—and that about does it in the plot department. Thirty minutes of watching this family snap at, insult, and demean each other are enough to make you apply for a handgun permit so you can put them out of their misery.

Moreover, the show takes the inroads in the portrayal of aging exemplified by "The Golden Girls" and moves them back about ten walker steps. It is studded with scenes of Mama attempting to jog and collapsing in agony as though having a heart attack, or Mama trying to eat a chewy piece of candy and losing her dentures. and it features waiters who say, "May I suggest the senior citizens' plate? All the meat is pulled off the bones."

Well hardy-har-har. May we suggest a writer transplant? Anyone who'd take credit for lines like "I must be going scenic" and "In a hen's heinie" obviously needs a long rest.

And maybe they'd take Mama with them. The show originally ran for a year and a half, but cancelation didn't save us. For some reason, the show received a new life in syndication in 1985. Is anybody out there really watching? A scary thought.

BACKGROUND

The lovable Harper family live in a midwestern blue collar suburb known as Raytown. Despite Mama's bullying ways and nasty personality, her overaged offspring obviously can't live without her. Her son Vint moves in with his annoying teenage children, Buzz and Sonja, after his wife leaves him to become a Las Vegas showgirl. He remarries, to Mama's next-door neighbor Naomi, but all four cling to Mama's apron strings. The family, along with visitors like Mama's two married daughters, Eunice and Ellen, spend all their time squabbling and insulting each other.

MAIN CAST

- **Mama (Thelma) Harper** (Vicki Lawrence): A gray-haired widow with an acid tongue.
- **Vinton Harper** (Ken Berry): Her lazy son, a locksmith by trade.
- **Naomi Oates Harper** (Dorothy Lyman): Vint's wife, whom Mama calls "that floozy."
- **Vinton "Buzz" Harper, Jr.** (Eric Brown): Vint's mischievous teenage son.
- **Sonja Harper** (Karin Argoud): Vint's pretty, self-centered teenage daughter.

FLASHBACK

MAMA: "Maybe that wife of yours could learn to use an iron. Tell her the flat side goes down."

MAMA [folding Vint's clothes]: "There's got to be more to life than sittin' here watchin' 'Days of Our Lives' and holdin' your Fruit of the Loom."

[*Vint and Mama are eating lunch. Mama is decked out in costume jewelry.*]

MAMA: "I feel like a million bucks."

VINT: "And you look like it, Mama. Just like eating baloney with Joan Collins."

MAMA [ordering merchandise over the phone]: "Oh yes, Travis, my living room is just crying out for that portrait of Elvis that lights up."

Sonja, Vint, and Buzz.

CRITICS' COMMENTS

"Vicki Lawrence was the most obnoxious character ever in the history of American television comedy. For sheer obnoxiousness, on a scale of ten, this was a twelve. The aim was that this was a charming, knowing type of folksy old lady. But it was a transparently bad character."

—David Jones, *Columbus Dispatch*

"It was nice that Vicki Lawrence got work, but they just simply did not bring any of the Burnett-Korman humor to it. It was quite sad, really"

—Peter Farrell, *Oregonain*

"It's people with curlers in their hair shouting at each other. And one minute of *that* is enough to last a lifetime."

—John Carman,
San Francisco Chronicle

"When people complain about sitcoms being nothing but people yelling at each other, this is the show they're talking about. It's just four brain-damaged people screaming at the top of their lungs."

—Ken Hoffman,
Houston Post

"There's nothing terribly funny about just how dumb people can be. I don't think the audience is laughing *with* 'Mama's Family'—I think the audience laughs *at* 'Mama's Family'—if they laugh at all. I don't think that's a very good comedy device, putting pathetic characters on TV. It might do something for the audience's ego to realize that even when they feel their worst, there's always someone stupider on television. But I wouldn't put money into a project based on that premise."

—John Marten,
Providence Journal

Mama soaks her feet in the episode, "The Flaming Forties."

PUNKY BREWSTER

"Punky Brewster" was first broadcast on September 16, 1984, in an episode entitled "Punky Finds a Home." She was evicted on September 3, 1986.

Once upon a time, when he was just a boy, NBC chief Brandon Tartikoff had a girlfriend named Punky Brewster. He always thought that would be a good name for a TV series, but it wasn't until he was named head of programming at NBC that he could do anything about it. Lucky us. Punky Brewster became an adorable little girl who brought sunshine into all the lives around her. How inspiring! How endearing! How cute!

Punky was a seven-year-old who'd been abandoned by her parents. She ended up in an abandoned apartment in New York, setting up housekeeping with her loyal dog, Brandon (gee, where did they get that name?) She was soon discovered by the building manager, Henry Warnimont, who immediately stopped being a cold-hearted son-of-a-gun and took Punky in.

Punky promptly took the fun out of Henry's life, teaching him to say his prayers, wipe his mouth with a napkin, and so forth. But heck, he didn't mind. Not with Punky spreading all that sunshine.

The problem is, this concept has been done to death. Shirley Temple did it in the movies. *Annie* did it on stage. In an age where kids are sophisticated and streetwise, Punky's unremittting philanthropy comes off as unbelievable. She spends all her time reuniting estranged parents, helping lonely children, and saving abandoned animals. After a while, you start longing for her to get into a good fistfight. Moreover, the ubiquitous Soleil Moon Frye tends to say most of her lines while gazing straight into the camera. She has obviously been told one too many times how cute she is. She may be self-sacrificing, lovable, and a great role model, but she's also extremely obnoxious.

The real Punky, by the way, was tracked down on the East Coast, where she is married to a lawyer, and was asked for permission to use her name on the show. Now Punky probably remembers Brandon as fondly as he remembers her; she gets a royalty every time the show airs.

BACKGROUND

Penelope "Punky" Brewster is an abandoned waif who is spunky enough to set herself up as a squatter in an abandoned New York apartment. However, she is smoked out by Henry Warnimont, an old, mean bachelor. He's all set to give her up to the authorities when Punky turns on the old charm. He persuades the child welfare people to let her stay with him awhile, and she soon lights up Henry's life. They do have problems adjusting to each other, but all conflicts are usually resolved by a heartwarming hug at the end of the show.

MAIN CAST

- **Penelope "Punky" Brewster** (Soleil Moon Frye): The adorable, seven-year-old heroine.
- **Henry Warnimont** (George Gaynes): The crusty bachelor who takes Punky in.
- **Eddie Malvin** (Eddie Deezen): The goofy building maintenance man.
- **Cherie Johnson** (Cherie Johnson): Punky's playmate.
- **Mrs. Johnson** (Susie Garrett): Cherie's mom and Henry's buddy.
- **Margaux Kramer** (Ami Foster): Punky's stuck-up, rich friend.

The regular cast of "Punky" posed in 1984, as the NBC show debuted on Sunday nights at 7:30.

FLASHBACK

HENRY: "My life was empty, Punky, until you came into it. You brought the sunshine to me."

HENRY: "Punky, what have I told you about responsiblity?"
PUNKY: "I have to have it."
HENRY: "That's right. You see, Brandon can't take care of himself. He's not a human being. Put yourself in his place. It's not easy being a dog, you know." [Punky falls asleep and dreams she's a dog.]
PUNKY: "Holy mackanoly! I'm a dog. Please God, undog me."

[*Punky can't go out shopping with Margaux and Cherie.*]
MARGAUX: "Gee, Punky, I feel terrible that you can't go shopping with us...[gives Cherie a look, laughs]...but I'll get over it."

CRITICS' COMMENTS

"'Punky Brewster' is one of those shows that make you want to shower after you've seen it once....And I don't think anything could make me see it twice. Soleil Moon Frye is one of the best cases you could make about why minors should never be allowed to perform in television."

—David Bianculli, *New York Post*

"If my kids knew that I put this down, they'd probably leave me. They love that show, and I guess that says something for it—it spoke to its audience. But I'm sorry— Soleil Moon Frye just drove me nuts. The character was just so studied in her ragamuffinishness—I think I just made that word up—that it grated on me....And the star herself was grating....The writing was grating....The whole *show* was grating."

—Joseph Walker, *Salt Lake City Deseret News*

"Gives a new meaning to the word *juvenile.* It's cute beyond words. Everything about the show is cute. It's so boring I can't imagine why anybody would watch it."

—Rick Du Brow, *Los Angeles Herald Examiner*

"I don't believe they should make shows for children. Most shows are for children anyway, but to design them *specifically* for children is just diabetes time."

—Bart Andrews, *The Worst TV Shows Ever*

George Gaynes went from the opera to NBC's "Punky Brewster."

"Punky Brewster suffered from terminal cuteness. It got to be so syrupy that you were almost afraid to change the dial for fear that your fingers would stick to the set."

—Barry Garron, *Kansas City Star*

"It reminded me of something I read in J.D. Salinger, in *Raise High the Roof-beams, Carpenter.* Seymour Glass quotes somebody who said, 'Sentimentality is giving to a thing more tenderness than God gave it.'...There's something wrong with turning a kid into a forty-year-old know-it-all. I really resented the hell out of that show."

—Jim Gordon, *Gary Times Register*

80s

"Love, Sidney" was revolutionary, but it was still a lousy program.

THE CHARMINGS (1986)
Prince Charming and Snow White are awakened after an extended sleep and become a sitcom family in the '80s.

THE LUCY SHOW (1986)
The sitcom zombies return. Lucille Ball staggers back onto the small screen as Lucy, and the audience cringes. It is not funny watching a seventy-something-year-old woman act like she's still forty, trying to get a laugh with slapstick antics—especially when she was the best in the business thirty-five years ago. You really notice the difference. It's like rubbing the audience's nose in the fact we're all a lot older and not particularly better.

STILL THE BEAVER (1984-85)
No he's not. He's a dopey overweight guy who ought to be selling insurance. How can they do this to America? We *loved* the Beaver until we saw this.

MR. MERLIN (1981-82)
What hath "My Mother the Car" wrought? Another sitcom about resurrection, every bit as bizarre. And inane. Merlin the Magician shows up in the 1980s. No, he's not a car, or a tractor, or a sixteen-wheeler. But he does work on them; he's a garage mechanic. Merlin the Mechanic. Next time you tell a repairman he's a real wizard, think twice. You might be responsible for a sitcom.

GIMME A BREAK (1981-85)
As Rick Mitz put it in *The Great Sitcom Book*, "That's what the critics said about this show when they got a look at it." Nell Carter played a housekeeper for the police chief of Glen Lawn, USA. He was a tubby white widower; she was a gargantuan black wisecracker. Lots of fat jokes, lots of put-downs, no heart at all. Gets a "why-is-there-television?" award.

LOVE, SIDNEY (1981)
Tony Randall played "your typical middle-aged Jewish homosexual who lives in a huge apartment in New York City." That made it a TV first, and also made it rather difficult to get good ratings in the Midwest. Or the Bible Belt.

Well, maybe it was the principle of the thing....no, this is TV. Anyway, television has come a long way since NBC censors wouldn't expose Barbara Eden's naval in "I Dream of Jeannie." Unfortunately, it's debatable which direction they've gone.

WEBSTER (1983)
How much of a ripoff is this show? "If you ever needed an example of plagiarism on TV," said one critic, "then this is it. This thing is so close to 'Diff'rent Strokes' it's like a Siamese twin." Well, then, maybe they're *both* unwatchable. Webster, a little black kid, joined Alex Karras's white family when his parents were killed in a car accident, and he brought love and joy into their lives. And sweetness. And cuteness-lots of cuteness. And good feelings and heart. And warmth. And cuteness. Pass the Pepto Bismol and insulin, please.

DOMESTIC HELP

HAZEL (Shirley Booth), "Hazel" (1961-66).
The Ted Key comic character come to life. Crusty, unconventional, unbelievably capable, and of course, beloved. The unchallenged boss of the Baxter household. "Comin' right up, Mr. B."

FLORENCE (Marla Gibbs),"The Jeffersons" (1974-84).
A TV first —a black maid working for a black family. Acid-tongued, sarcastic, irreverent. George Jefferson's household nemesis. Told to get the doorbell, she retorts: "You get it; you're closer." "I don't take any guff."

PETER (Sammee Tong), "Bachelor Father" (1957-62).
Sitcoms' only Oriental "houseboy." A Chinese caricature. Intense, orderly, inscrutable. Despite fits of temper, is devoted to Bentley Gregg and his niece. "Tell Mis-sah Gregg din-nah ready, niece Kelly."

FLORIDA (Esther Rolle), "Maude" (1972-74). Intelligent, funny. She's not trying to join the family she works for. Housework is a job—a hard one—and she wants to do it in peace. "I don't have time to join you for a drink, Mrs. Findlay."

GILES FRENCH (Sebastian Cabot), "Family Affair" (1966-71).
The portly gentleman's gentleman of the Davis household. Has to learn to take care of the kids.

SITCOM JOBS

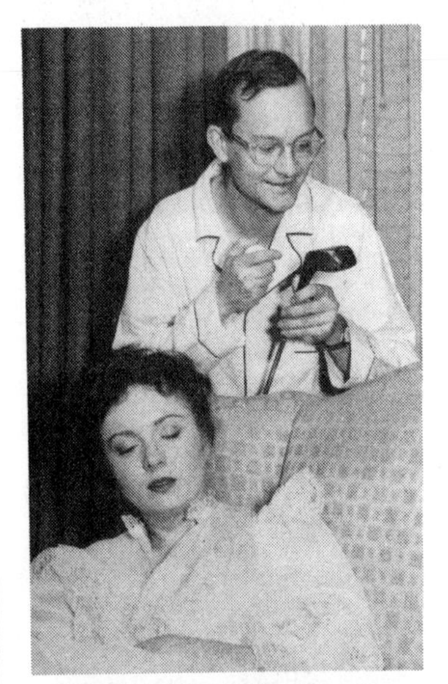

Robinson J. Peepers (Wally Cox), junior high school biology teacher. "Mr. Peepers" (1952-55).

Robert Hartley (Bob Newhart), psychologist. "The Bob Newhart Show" (1972-78).

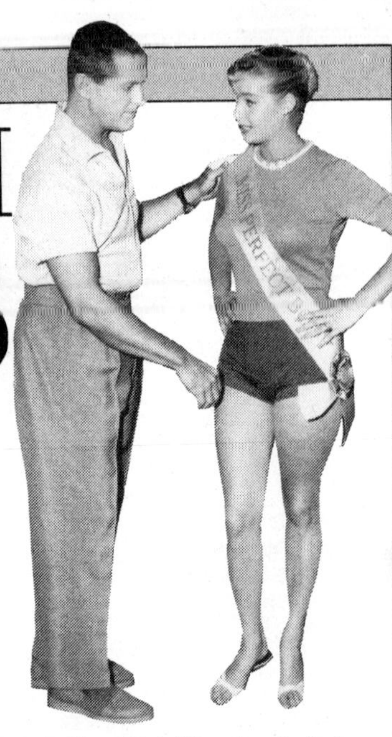

Bob Collins (Bob Cummings), fashion photographer. "The Bob Cummings Show" (1955-59).

Wilbur Post (Alan Young), architect. "Mr. Ed" (1960-65).

Gabe Kotter (Gabriel Kaplan), inner-city high school teacher. "Welcome Back, Kotter" (1975-79).

Mickley Dolenz, Peter Tork, Davey Jones, Mike Nesmith, rock group. "The Monkees" (1966-68).

Taro Takahashi (Pat Morita), inventor. "Mr. T and Tina" (1976).

Joe Calucci (James Coco), supervisor at a branch of the New York State Unemployment Office. "Claucci's Department" (1973).

Tom Smothers (Tom Smothers), apprentice angel. "The Smothers Brothers Show" (1965-66).

Otto Sharkey (Don Rickles), career Navy man, chief petty officer at the Navy Training Center, San Diego, CA. "CPO Sharkey" (1976-78).

George Jefferson (Sherman Hemsley), dry-cleaning mogul. "The Jeffersons" (1975-85).

Jose Jimenez (Bill Dana), bellhop. "The Bill Dana Show" (1963-65).

Fred Sanford (Redd Foxx), junk dealer. "Sanford and Son" (1972-77).

FANTASY FOLK

THE MUNSTERS (1964-66).
A family sitcom with a twist: the entire family, except niece Marilyn (who looks like a cute-as-pie Midwesterner), is a refugee from a horror film. Herman, the Dad, is a goofy Frankenstein monster who works ina funeral home. Lily, the Mom, is a vampire. Eddie, whose middle name is Wolfgang, is a ten-year-old wolfman. And Grandpa is a ghoulish mad scientist who's been experimenting with God-knows-what for over three hundred years. The thing is, although they seem creepy to normal humans, they're jes' plain folks to each other. They're sweet and kind and actually, quite naive. When Herman clumsily crashes through walls, he can't understand why onlookers suddenly shriek and flee. He's obviously a little slow on the uptake, since it's been happening his whole life. The show was created by Connelly and Mosher, originators of "Leave it to Beaver."

I DREAM OF JEANNIE (1965-70).
The American male's secret fantasy come to life. A beautiful blonde who wears slave-girl clothes and calls the man she loves "Master" moves in with him. She lives to fulfill his every desire. And—hot stuff—she's got magical powers, too, because she's a genie. Only on TV would anyone try to pass this off as innocent family fare. Guess again.

TOPPER (1953-55)
George and Marion Kirby were skiing in Switzerland when an avalanche buried them. Now they're dead...but they're not buried—they're ghosts. And there's a third ghost: Neil the St. Bernard, an innocent bystander who happened along with some brandy just as the avalanche hit.

The Kirbys return to New York City, where henpecked Cosmo Topper, a VP of the National Security Bank, has just purchased their old home. George ("that most sporting spirit") and Marion ("the ghostess with the mostess") decide that Topper needs a little loosening up. So they haunt him. Only Cosmo can see and hear them as they wreak havoc on his personal and business life.

SOURCES

RECOMMENDED READING

I LOVE LUCY
The I Love Lucy Book. Bart Andrews (Dolphin-Doubleday).

THE HONEYMOONERS
The Honeymooners' Companion: The Kramdens and the Nortons Revisited. Donna McCrohan (Workman Press).

The Official Honeymooners Treasury. Peter Crescenti and Bob Columbe (Perigee Books).

The Honeymooners Lost Episodes. Donna McCrohan and Peter Crescenti (Workman Press).

LEAVE IT TO BEAVER
The World According to Beaver. Irwin Applebaum (Bantam Books).

BURNS AND ALLEN
Say Goodnight, Gracie. Cheryl Blythe and Susan Sackett (E.P. Dutton).

THE DICK VAN DYKE SHOW
The Dick Van Dyke Show. Ginny Weissman and Coyne Steven Sanders (St. Martin's Press).

THE ANDY GRIFFITH SHOW
The Andy Griffith Show Book. Ken Beck and Jim Clark (St. Martin's Press).

The Andy Griffith Show. Richard Kelly (John F. Blair).

GET SMART
The Life and Times of Maxwell Smart. Donna McCrohan (St. Martin's Press).

ALL IN THE FAMILY
Archie, Edith, Mike and Gloria. Donna McCrohan (Workman Press).

The Wit and Wisdom of Archie Bunker. Tandem Productions (Popular Library).

M*A*S*H
*The Complete Book of M*A*S*H.* Suzy Kalter (Harry N. Abrams).

*M*A*S*H (The Exclusive Inside Story of TV's Most Popular Show).* David Reiss (Bobbs-Merrill Co.).

CHEERS
The Official "Cheers" Scrapbook. Bart Andrews (Fireside).

TAXI
The Taxi Book. Jeff Sorenson (St. Martin's Press).

GENERAL TV
Cult TV. John Javna (St. Martin's Press). Informal viewer's guide to 45 shows, including "I Love Lucy," "The Honeymooners," "The Dick Van Dyke Show," etc.

Total Television. Alex McNeil (Penguin Books). Definitive listing of every show that's been on the air.

Complete Directory to Prime Time Network TV Shows. Tim Brooks and Earle Marsh. Definitive listing, limited to prime time shows.

The Complete Encyclopedia of Television Programs, 1947-1985. Vincent Terrace (A. S. Barnes). Definitive listing, with the most obscure shows.

The Great TV Sitcom Book. Rick Mitz (Perigee). The definitive sitcom encyclopedia.

Watching TV. Walter Podrazik and Harry Castleman (McGraw Hill). Well-written history of TV, including sitcoms.

Sitcoms in Syndication. Joel Eisner (Scarecrow Press). Complete episode guide to syndicated sitcoms.

Classic Sitcoms. Vince Waldron (Collier Books).The Top Ten sitcoms of all time, with amazingly complete credits.

GENERAL TV MAGAZINES
You never know what you'll find in these publications, but they're always interesting, and they're all TV.

TV Collector. P.O. Box 188, Needham, MA 02192.

Reruns. P.O. Box 1057, Safford, AZ 85548.

SOURCES

PHOTOS AND COLLECTIBLES

The following list includes stores and mail order houses with which I've worked at one time or another. I've always found them reputable, but of course I can't guarantee anything about them—this list is only for your reference. If you write for information, be sure to send a self-addressed, stamped envelope with the letter.

Comic Relief
2138 University Ave.
Berkeley, CA 94704
(New and old comic books, including, of course, "I Love Lucy," "Get Smart," etc.)

The Cinema Shop
604 Geary St.
San Francisco, CA 94102
(Original photos, including many of the most obscure sitcoms—my favorite photo place.)

Jerry Ohlinger's Movie Material Store
242 West 14th St.
New York, NY 10011
(Huge selection of photos)

Larry Edmunds Book Store
6658 Hollywood Blvd.
Hollywood, CA 90028
(Photos, books—the best TV book store I know of.)

Still Things
13622 Henny Ave.
Sylmar, CA 91342
(Photos, scripts, collectibles.)

Scooby's Toys and Collectibles
2750 Adeline St.
Berkeley, CA 94703
(You never know what they'll find.)

Chic-A-Boom
6905 Melrose Ave.
Los Angeles, CA
(America's best pop collectibles store.)

Artie Rickun
7153 W. Burleigh St.
Milwaukee, WI 53210
(Nice guy who keeps a warehouse full of collectibles. You never know exactly what he'll have.)

Hollywood Movie Posters
6727 5/8 Hollywood Blvd.
Hollywood , CA 90028
(Photos.)

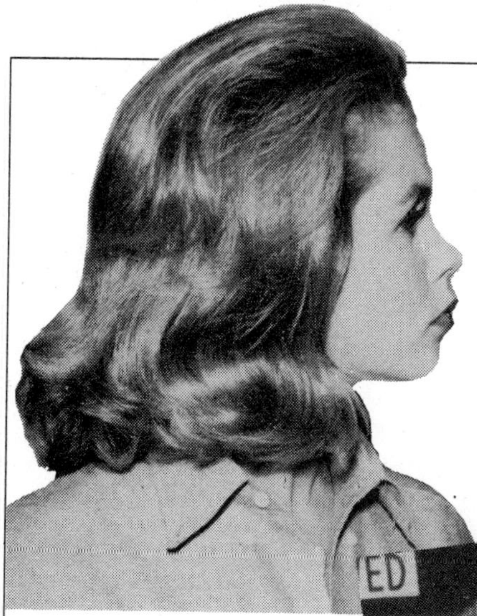

FAN CLUBS

The Andy Griffith Rerun
Watchers' Club
27 Music Square East
Suite 146
Nashville, TN 37203

I Put a Spell on You
The Bewitched Fan Club
1551 Eaton Avenue
San Carlos, CA 94070

The Mr. Ed Fan Club
PO Box 1009
Cedar Hill, TX 75104

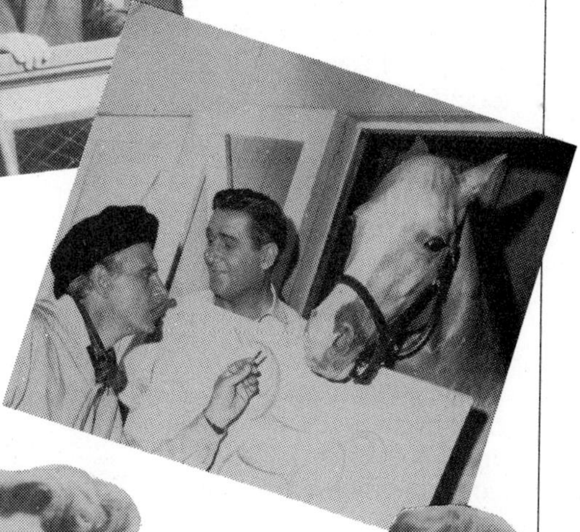

We Love Lucy
Box 480216
Los Angeles, CA 90048

The Honeymooners Fan Club
RALPH
C/O C.W. Post Center
Greenvale, NY 11543

ACKNOWLEDGMENTS

First, I'd like to express my gratitude to the experts who took the time to speak with or write to me about sitcoms. Many of you went way out of your way to help, despite the fact we've never actually met in person. And those of you whom I *did* finally meet were kind enough to assist me a second time. You're all listed in the introduction, so I won't name each of you here. But I want you to know how much I appreciate your good will and clever comments. Thanks.

AND MANY THANKS TO

Melissa Schwarz, my editor at Harmony, a pleasure to work with, and one of the toughest people I've met in the book world.

Andrea Sohn, who designed the book, stuck with the project, and managed to keep me organized in the process.

Lonnie Graham, who designed the heads and icons, and who'd better keep on doing them for me...or else.

Steve at the Cinema Shop, who has become one of my most valuable resources. Not only did he help me find great photos at the store, he lent me some from his own collection.

Sandra Konte, a wordsmith who provided essential assistance with the text.

Peter Johnson, for his proofreading help—even though he was about to move at the time.

Ron McCutchan, Harmony's Art Director, who helped pull it all together—particularly the cover, which he ultimately designed.

Elania, Jay, and Doug at Co-op Type, who provided constant advice, the VT-600, and did all the photos.

Mary Mahaney, whose fine and timely assistance kept us from flipping out under pressure.

Peter McCracken, for his advice on the last book.

Rachel, for her valuable help whenever she had the time.

Allison Towle, for proofreading.

Lynn Schneider and **Bob Migdal**, of Virginia Street.

Sandy Ferguson at "Legwork," my stalwart researcher.

Kevin McGarvey, for helping put *Behind the Hits* together in Mexico.

Hank Aaron, my favorite baseball player when I was a kid.

The Easybeats, for "Friday on My Mind."

The entire town of **Montpelier, Vermont**, particularly the Horn of the Moon cafe, and the Novogrodsky family.

And **Sharon**.